columbia 33CX
label discography
by john hunt

Acknowledgement

These publications have been made possible by contributions or advance subscriptions from

Richard Ames	Stefano Angeloni
Yoshihiro Asada	J.M. Blyth*
Marc Bridle	J. Camps-Ros
Brian Capon	Edward Chibas*
Robert Dandois	Dennis Davis
John Derry	Hans-Peter Ebner*
Henry Fogel*	Nobuo Fukumoto
Peter Fülop	Philip Goodman
Jean-Pierre Goossens	Johann Gratz
Alan Haine	Michael Harris*
Tadashi Hasegawa*	Naoya Hirabayashi
Bodo Igesz	Andrew Keener
Rodney Kempster	Koji Kinoshita
Detlef Kissmann	Elisabeth Legge-Schwarzkopf*
Douglas MacIntosh	John Mallinson*
Carlo Marinelli	Philip Moores
Bruce Morrison	W. Moyle
Alan Newcombe	Hugh Palmer*
Jim Parsons*	Laurence Pateman
David Patmore*	J.A. Payne
James Pearson	Tully Potter
Ingo Schwarz	Tom Scragg*
John Shackleton	Yoshihiko Suzuki*
Michael Tanner	Urs Weber*
Nigel Wood*	Graeme Wright*

*indicates life subscriber

Columbia 33CX Label
Published by John Hunt.
© 2004 John Hunt
reprinted 2009
ISBN 978-1-901395-17-4

Sole distributors:
Travis & Emery,
17 Cecil Court,
London, WC2N 4EZ,
United Kingdom.
(+44) 20 7 459 2129.
sales@travis-and-emery.com

Columbia 33CX: an introduction
If one had asked any collector of classical gramophone recordings around the middle of the last century what were the most prominent labels offering a guarantee of technical and artistic quality, he would doubtless have cited names like His Master's Voice, Decca – and Columbia.

Founded in the USA as early as 1894 as the Columbia Phonograph Company and named after the district in which it was based, Columbia began its British activities in 1907, soon adopting the familiar Magic Notes trademark. Columbia Phonograph Inc. New York continued to use the Columbia name, modifying it later to Columbia Broadcasting Systems, precursor of CBS and now Sony. A split with the original American father company in 1925 gave English Columbia an independence of only seven years before it was assimilated in 1931 into the Gramophone Company (later Electric and Musical Industries or EMI) alongside the His Master's Voice and Parlophone labels. This was a significant acquisition for the EMI conglomerate, for Columbia boasted a roster of artists which included Henry Wood, Felix Weingartner, Thomas Beecham, Bruno Walter and Hamilton Harty, just to mention the conductors. And it was Beecham himself who in the 1930s had been impressed by the capabilities of a young Gramophone Company employee named Walter Legge, who was to become Columbia's chief recording producer for the entire period which concerns us in this discography. It was the end of Legge's supremacy in that position which coincided in the mid 1960s with CBS claiming back sole use of the Columbia logo and trademark.

The Columbia 33CX series was launched in October 1952 to be a showcase for the newly-developed long-playing vinyl record (already pioneered by CBS and Victor in the USA). For a period of thirteen years it came to represent, under the aegis of Legge and his team of associates and assistant producers, the closest which Britain ever came to achieving a continental standard of excellence in the serious recording field. For the first few years certain American Columbia titles were included on the Columbia LP schedule, and Columbia even produced recordings on behalf of American Columbia, like the series of Pablo Casals recordings from the Prades and Perpignan Festivals. However, it was the recordings with Walter Legge's own orchestra, the Philharmonia, and its first main recording conductor Herbert von Karajan, that constituted the backbone of the early catalogue. Some lesser conductors complained about Karajan getting the lion's share of recording work, but in fact no less care was lavished on the work of men like Alceo Galliera, Igor Markevitch, Malcolm Sargent, Issay Dobrowen, Lovro von Matacic and Walter Susskind. Carlo Maria Giulini and Otto Klemperer came into their own as Karajan's participation lessened with his move to the Berlin Philharmonic Orchestra and rival recording companies Decca and Deutsche Grammophon.

By the late 1950s stereophonic recordings were beginning to take over from the standard mono, but mono versions not only continued to be produced alongside stereo but also demonstrated a clearly perceptible excellence which can be best described as a mellow blending without undue highlighting of the orchestral strands (Walter Legge used to query the wisdom of stereo separating out these strands which he and his engineers had taken such pains to integrate into the mono sound picture). As examples of the stunning refinement achieved I would cite Galliera's LP of Respighi tone poems (33CX 1339) and Karajan's Hänsel und Gretel (33CX 1096-1097) or Philharmonia Promenade Concert (33CX 1335). To this day the latter has not seen a CD transfer, although re-issue companies like Testament have done much good work in putting out many other fine early Columbia LPs.

It is because of my personal predilection for monophonic sound that I have built this discography around the mono numberings, even into the period when stereophonic versions became the norm: stereo numbers are shown on the first line of catalogue details along with all the other Columbia numbers from the various European territories (a guide to catalogue prefixes is given at the end of this introduction).

It could be said that Walter Legge was basically a conservative who made use of technical advances for the promotion of his and his musicians' artistic credos. He was less happy towards the latter part of his reign at EMI when purely technical and commercial developments in the classical record industry began to dictate the way forward. Compromise was not Legge's forte, and I endorse his contention that it has little place in the achieving of the sort of artistic excellence demonstrated on so many of these Columbia records (he was even prepared to jettison a stereophonic version of the Strauss opera *Capriccio* (33CX 1600-1602) when questions of balance could not be agreed among some of the participating singers).

From 1960 until 1963 I was a member of a team based at EMI's production plant in Hayes (West London) to oversee the scheduling and production of the long-playing records. Once a master tape for a recording had been assembled and approved, lacquers were eventually cut corresponding to the LP sides, and from these were made test pressings which had to be submitted to the artists' department for approval. In the case of HMV classical recordings (at that time supervised by Victor Olof and Peter Andry) as well as in the case of the entire popular repertoire (including the first LPs by the Beatles), the process was relatively straightforward. But when it came to Columbia classical, it was a different matter: tracking down Walter Legge or one of his assistants Walter Jellinek or Suvi Raj Grubb was no easy matter, let alone getting them to approve the test pressing, which was more often than not rejected and a new transfer requested with amended instructions as to how it should be carried out. One could understand the frustration of EMI's marketing people when the announced LPs did not reach the shops on time, but for the Columbia team artistic standards were not to be compromised!

Walter Legge's pride and joy had been the creation of an Angel label specifically for marketing his Columbia recordings in the USA. It was launched with the series of operetta recordings starring his wife Elisabeth Schwarzkopf, and with the first Italian operas with the new partnership of Maria Meneghini Callas and Giuseppe di Stefano. A decade later an Angel label was launched in Britain, but may have been viewed as a ploy to lessen Legge's influence by pooling the resources of the Columbia and HMV labels so that their respective artists could star together in a series of de-luxe opera recordings. Such developments sadly coincided with Legge's decision to disband his Philharmonia Orchestra and his leaving EMI, in future acting as free-lance producer for a number of significant LP recitals still to be made by his wife.

With the co-operation of Malcolm Walker I have been able to include in the heading for each LP not only the recording dates but also names of producers where known (interesting to note that Legge sometimes entrusted work to musical scholars Alec Robertson, William Mann or Geraint Jones), publication date (that is publication date of the 33CX edition but not necessarily that of any earlier edition, for example 78rpm or American Columbia) and the mono (not stereo) LP matrix numbers which were used to identify the LP sides during the production process. As many LP issues and re-issues as I could trace have been included. American Angel equivalents are listed only with their 5-digit catalogue number (4-digits for LP sets), excluding the prefix "S" which was used to denote stereophonic versions (with the same number). Certain short-lived formats such as stereosonic tapes and quadrophonic LPs, as well as almost all Japanese Toshiba LPs, are omitted (excerpting Toshiba's 1980s LP re-issue sets of all Karajan's mono orchestral recordings with the Philharmonia Orchestra in their EAC series).

By 1965 and Walter Legge's departure certain Columbia hallmarks were beginning to lose their character. Catalogue numbering was aligned so that the same series was used for mono and stereo (CX 5250/SAX 5250), and the distinctive LP cover designs produced in France for use in all EMI territories began to be disfigured in the UK with a crudely designed version of the Columbia logo, before even this disappeared and all classical issues appeared on the HMV "ASD" imprint. Typically, or ironically, depending on which way you view the modern trend towards half measures, EMI UK declined to adopt the newly devised uniform numbering system for all its territories, sticking doggedly (excuse the pun!) with the ASD prefix and 4-digit number throughout the 1970s.

My discography therefore covers the 945 blue-and-gold label 12-inch (30cm) LPs from 33CX 1001 to 33CX 1945, together with the 10-inch (25cm) LPs from 33C 1001 to 33C 1065 as well as any classical material included on 33SX (12-inch) and 33S (10-inch) LPs, a green-and-gold label series shared with non-classical material and in essence the equivalent of HMV's plum label. Artists on the 33SX and 33S labels like conductors Henry Krips and George Weldon may have been of marginally lesser calibre, but they were served by the same production teams as those on the premium 33CX and 33C series. They certainly constituted part of the Columbia catalogue as envisaged by Walter Legge, to whom this book is after all a modest tribute for his all-pervading influence on classical recordings in the twentieth century.

In addition to thanking Malcolm Walker, I have to acknowledge helpful comments from Michael Dutton, John Hancock, Roderick Krüsemann and Arthur Ridgewell, and assistance on American Columbia and Epic recording dates from Mike Gray. Much help was obtained from lists prepared by Phil Rees and from the Walter Legge discography by Alan Sanders (Greenwood Press), although I have traced certain sessions supervised by Legge which were not included in that volume.

The Columbia prefixes
33CX	12-inch LP (later stereo equivalent SAX)
33C	10-inch LP (later stereo equivalent SBO)
33SX	12-inch LP (later stereo equivalent SCX)
33S	10-inch LP
SEL	7-inch EP (later stereo equivalent ESL)
SEB	7-inch EP
SED	7-inch EP
SEG	7-inch EP
SCB	7-inch standard (playing time equivalent to 78)
SCD	7-inch standard (playing time equivalent to 78)
L	12-inch 78rpm
LX	12-inch 78rpm
LCX	12-inch 78rpm
DX	12-inch 78rpm
ROX	12-inch 78rpm
LC	10-inch 78rpm
DB	10-inch 78rpm
DC	10-inch 78rpm

LCX, LC and DC were an international series

France
FCX	12-inch LP (later stereo equivalent SAXF)
FC	10-inch LP (later stereo equivalent SBOF)
ESBF	7-inch EP
SCBF	7-inch standard
LFX	12-inch 78rpm
LF	10-inch 78rpm

Re-numberings of LPs occurred during the life of the FCX series; prior to the introduction of international numbering system around 1970, issues of Columbia material also appeared on LPs in France with prefixes CCA, CVA, CVB, CVC, CVD, CVL, CVPM, CVT and re-issues on TRI

Italy

QCX	12-inch LP (later stereo equivalent SAXQ)
QC	10-inch LP
SEBQ	7-inch EP
SEDQ	7-inch EP
ESLQ	7-inch EP (stereo)
SCBQ	7-inch standard
SCDQ	7-inch standard
GQX	12-inch 78rpm
GQ	10-inch 78rpm

Prior to introduction of the international numbering system re-issues of Columbia material also appeared on LPs in Italy with prefixes QIMX (mono) and SQIMX (stereo)

Austria

VCX	12-inch LP
VC	10-inch LP
VSX	12-inch LP
VS	10-inch LP
SCV	7-inch standard
LVX	12-inch 78rpm
LV	10-inch 78rpm
SVX	12-inch 78rpm
DV	10-inch 78rpm

Austrian Columbia later adopted UK and German Columbia numberings

Switzerland

LZX	12-inch 78rpm
LZ	10-inch 78rpm
DZ	10-inch 78rpm

Swiss Columbia appears to have adopted UK and German Columbia numberings for its LP issues

Norway

LNX	12-inch 78rpm
LN	10-inch 78rpm

Germany

C 90000	12-inch LP (later stereo equivalents STC 90000/SMC 90000)
C 80000	12-inch LP (later stereo equivalents STC 80000/SMC 80000)
C 70000	10-inch LP (later stereo equivalent STC 70000)
C 60000	10-inch LP
C 50000	7-inch EP (later stereo equivalent STC 50000)
C 40000	7-inch EP (later stereo equivalent STC 40000)
LWX	12-inch 78rpm
LW	10-inch 78rpm
DWX	12-inch 78rpm
DW	10-inch 78rpm

Until around 1960 all German Columbia LPs and EPs carried an additional so-called export catalogue number which was usually, but not always, based on the UK numbering in the series WCX/SAXW (C90000/STC 90000), WSX/SCXW (C80000/STC 80000), WC/SBOW (C70000/STC 70000), WS (C60000), SELW/ESLW (C50000/STC50000) and SEGW/ESGW (C40000/STC40000); re-issues of Columbia material also appeared on LPs in Germany with prefixes SMVP (Volksplatte series) and HZE/SHZE (Hör Zu series)

Spain
Columbia LP classical material was issued in Spain on the HMV label with the prefix LALP

Australia

OCX	12-inch LP
OSX	12-inch LP
LOX	12-inch 78rpm
LO	10-inch 78rpm
DOX	12-inch 78rpm
DO	10-inch 78rpm
ED	12-inch 78rpm
EA	10-inch 78rpm
EC	10-inch 78rpm

Much Columbia LP classical material was issued or re-issued in Australia by World Record Club

The above summary of Columbia numbering categories in various territories does not claim to be comprehensive, referring only to record prefixes which occur in this discography

Columbia 33CX: label discography
Published and copyright 2004 by John Hunt
ISBN 1 901395 17 0
Printed by Short Run Press Exeter

33CX 1027

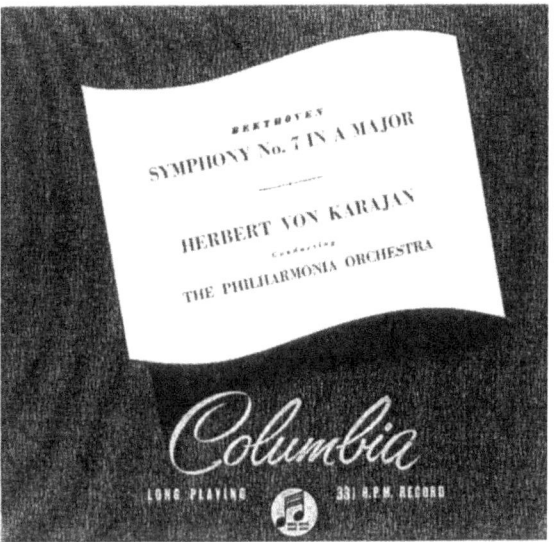

33CX 1035

33CX 1168

33CX 1404

33CX 1419

 *Pictures at an Exhibition*
HERBERT VON KARAJAN
PHILHARMONIA ORCHESTRA

33CX 1421

33CX 1001/orchestral works by richard strauss
recorded in kingsway hall london on 3-4 december 1951/producer walter legge/published in october 1952/lp matrix numbers XAX 165-166

karajan	**don juan**
philharmonia	78: LX 8920-8921/GQX 8039-8040
	lp: FCX 159/QCX 159/VCX 532/WC 528/WCX 1001/ C 70425/C 90290
	other lp issues: toshiba EAC 37020-37038/ emi RLS 7715/1C137 54364-54367M
	cd: emi CMS 763 3162
	till eulenspiegels lustige streiche
	78: LX 8908-8909/GQX 8037-8038/LVX 173-174
	lp: FCX 159/QCX 159/VCX 532/WC 528/WCX 1001/ C 70425/C 90290
	other lp issues: toshiba EAC 37020-37038/ emi RLS 7715/1C137 54364-54367M/2M 055 43228
	cd: emi CMS 763 3162

selected by walter legge as one of the first group of columbia lps showcasing his orchestra and its first principal recording conductor

33CX 1002/balakirev symphony in c
recorded in kingsway hall london on 18 november 1949/producer walter legge/published in october 1952/lp matrix numbers XAX 78-79

karajan	78: LX 1323-1328/LX 8746-8751 auto
philharmonia	lp: FCX 170/QCX 170
	other lp issues: toshiba EAC 37020-37038/ emi XLP 60001/RLS 7715/1C137 54364-54367M
	cd: emi CMS 763 3162/CDM 566 5952

one of several columbia/philharmonia recordings from this period which was made under the auspices of the maharaja of mysore's musical foundation

14

33CX 1003/overtures by berlioz
recorded in kingsway hall london on 5-7 september 1951/producer walter legge/published in october 1952/lp matrix numbers XAX 159-160

kletzki   **béatrice et bénédict**
philharmonia   78: LX 1529/GQX 11524/LOX 818
                 45: SEL 1502/SEBQ 103/EW 29
                 lp: FCX 173/QCX 10027
                 other lp issues: american columbia RL 3071/emi XLP 30014
                 benvenuto cellini
                 78: LX 8935-8936
                 45: SEL 1502
                 lp: FCX 173/QCX 10027
                 other lp issues: american columbia RL 3071/emi XLP 30014
                 cd: emi CZS 575 4682
                 les francs juges
                 78: LX 8926-8927
                 lp: FCX 173/QCX 10027
                 other lp issues: american columbia RL 3071/emi XLP 30014
                 le corsair
                 78: LX 1533/GQX 16654
                 45: hmv 7P 354
                 lp: FCX 173/QCX 10027
                 other lp issues: american columbia RL 3071/emi XLP 30014

33CX 1004/beethoven symphony no 5
recorded in musikvereinssaal vienna on 11-17 november 1948/producer walter legge/published in october 1952/lp matrix numbers XHAX 4-5

karajan   78: LX 1330-1333/LX 8752-8755 auto/LCX 140-143/
vienna   LVX 79-82
philharmonic   lp: FCX 107/QCX 107/VCX 506/WCX 1004/C 90291
                 other lp issues: american columbia RL 3063/toshiba EAC 30111
                 cd: emi CDM 566 3912/CMS 566 4832/javelin HADCD 134/
                     grammofono AB 78792

33CX 1005-1006/wagner die walküre, act three
recorded in the festspielhaus bayreuth at rehearsals and at a performance on 12 august 1951/ producer walter legge/published in october 1952/lp matrix numbers XRX 1-4

karajan	78: LX 1447-1454/LX 8835-8842 auto
bayreuth	lp: FCX 111-112/QCX 111-112/VCX 501-502/
festival	WCX 1005-1006/C 90280-90281
orchestra	*other lp issues:* emi 1C181 03035-03036
varnay	cd: emi CDH 764 7042
rysanek	*excerpts*
s.björling	lp: emi 1C047 01373

acts 1 and 2 of this performance also recorded but remain unpublished

33CX 1007-1009/mozart le nozze di figaro
recorded in musikvereinssaal vienna between 17-21 june and 23-31 october 1950/ producer walter legge/published in october 1952/lp matrix numbers XHAX 45-50

karajan	78: LWX 410-425
vienna	lp: FCX 174-176/QCX 10002-10004/VCX 503-505/
philharmonic	WCX 1007-1009/C 90292-90294
vienna opera	*other lp issues:* american columbia SL 114/emi 1C147 01751-
chorus	01753M/2C165 01751-01753M/1C197 54200-54208M
schwarzkopf	cd: emi CMS 769 6392/CMS 567 0682/membran 222157
seefried	*excerpts*
jurinac	78: LX 1575
felbermayer	lp: 33CX 1558/FCX 30170/WC 518/WSX 548/C 70373/
höngen	C 80531
kunz	*other lp issues of excerpts:* american columbia RL 3050/angel 35326/
london	emi RLS 684/1C137 43187-43189M/1C047 01444M/
	1C063 00839/1C187 29225-29226M/EX 29 10563
	cd: emi CDH 763 5572/CDM 763 6572/CMS 763 7902

excerpts also issued on preiser lps and cds
first lp recording of a complete opera in the columbia catalogue: although much criticised for lack of recitatives, it represented the immediate postwar vienna mozart style more consistently than rival mozart opera lp recordings which were soon to appear on the decca and philips labels

33CX 1010/beethoven piano concerto no 5 "emperor"
recorded in kingsway hall london on 8-9 june 1951/producer walter legge/published in october 1952/lp matrix numbers XAX 131-132

karajan	78: LCX 5008-5012
philharmonia	lp: FCX 135/QCX 135/VCX 507/WCX 1010/C 90295
gieseking,	*other lp issues:* american columbia ML 4623/3216 0029/
piano	toshiba EAC 37001-37019/emi 3C153 52425-52431M
	cd: emi CDM 566 6042
	cd: philips 456 8112

33CX 1011/beethoven violin concerto/american columbia
recorded in philadelphia on 5 november 1950/lp matrix numbees XLP 4004-4005

ormandy	lp: FCX 126/QCX 126/WCX 1011/C 90296
philadelphia	*american columbia issues*
orchestra	45: A 1086
francescatti,	lp: ML 4371
violin	cd: biddulph 802 052

33CX 1012/brahms piano quartet no 1
recorded in abbey road studios london on 25-26 may 1949/lp matrix numbers XAX 1-2

serkin, piano	78: LX 1217-1221
a.busch, violin	lp: FCX 106
gottesmann,	*american columbia issues*
viola	78: M 909
h.busch, cello	lp: ML 4296/Y-34638
	other lp issues: world records SHB 61/emi EX 29 08061/
	1C147 01555-01556M
	cd: emi CDH 565 1902

33CX 1013-1015/mozart die zauberflöte
recorded in musikvereinssaal vienna between 2 and 21 november 1950/producer walter legge/ published in december 1952/lp matrix numbers XHAX 51-56

karajan	78: LWX 426-444
vienna	lp: FCX 150-152/QCX 150-152/VCX 508-510/
philharmonic	WCX 1013-1015/C 90296-90298
wiener	*other lp issues:* american columbia SL 115/emi SLS 5052/
singverein	1C147 01663-01665M/1C197 54200-54208M/
seefried	2C163 01663-01665/3C153 01663-01665
lipp	cd: emi CHS 769 6312/CMS 567 0712/membran 222157
loose	*excerpts*
jurinac	lp: 33CX 1572/FCX 30172/WSX 549/C 80532
riegler	*other lp issues of excerpts:* emi RLS 764/1C137 43187-43189M/
schürhoff	EX 29 10563/1C147 03580-03581M/1C187 29225-29226M/
dermota	toshiba EAC 30112
kunz	cd: emi CDM 763 5572/CDEMX 2220
weber	*excerpts also issued on preiser lps and cds*
london	

33CX 1016-1018/bizet carmen
recorded in théatre des champs-élysées paris on 6-8 october 1950/producer francois agostini/ published in december 1952/lp matrix numbers XLX 14-19

cluytens	lp: FCX 101-103/WCX 1016-1018/C 90299-90301
opéra-comique	*78 rpm issue:* american columbia MOP 33
orchestra	*other lp issues:* american columbia SL 109/emi TRI 33308-33310
and chorus	cd: emi CMS 565 3182
michel	*excerpts*
angelici	45: SEL 1553/SEL 1558
jobin	
dens	

33CX 1019/berlioz harold en italie
recorded in abbey road studios london on 12-15 november 1951/producer lawrance collingwood/ lp matrix numbers XAX 176-177

beecham	lp: FCX 178/QCX 10005
royal	*american columbia issues*
philharmonic	45: A 1074
primrose,	lp: ML 4542/Y-33286/77395
viola	*other lp issues:* philips classical favourites GL 5715/G03627L/ philips fontana KFR 4002/676 002KR
	cd: sony MPK 47679/SMK 91167

33CX 1020/guitar music
recorded in abbey road studios london in 1949/producer lawrance collingwood/published in december 1952/lp matrix numbers XAX 60-61

sherman	**castelnuovo-tedesco guitar concerto**
new london	78: LX 1404-1406/LFX 914-916/LVX 104-106/
orchestra	QCX 11505-11507
segovia, guitar	lp: FCX 127/QCX 127
	american columbia issue
	78: 15137-15139
	cd: testament SBT 1043
segovia, guitar	**ponce sonatina meridional; torroba arda and fandanguillo, arranged by segovia from suite castellana; turina fandanguillo**
	lp: FCX 127/QCX 127
	cd: testament SBT 1043

33CX 1021-1025/wagner die meistersinger von nürnberg
recorded in the festspielhaus bayreuth during rehearsals and at performances between 27 july and 21 august 1951/producer walter legge/published in december 1952/lp matrix numbers XRX 19-28

karajan	78: LX 1465-1498/LX 8851-8884 auto
bayreuth	lp: FCX 128-133/VCX 523-527/WCX 501-505/
festival	C 90275-90279
orchestra	*other lp issues:* angel seraphim 6030/emi RLS 7708/
and chorus	RLS 143 3903/1C151 43390-43394M
schwarzkopf	cd: emi CHS 763 5002
malaniuk	*excerpts*
hopf	78: LVX 190-191
unger	lp: emi 1C147 03580-03581M
edelmann	
dalberg	
kunz	

33CX 1026/tchaikovsky symphony no 6 "pathétique"
recorded in musikvereinssaal vienna on 4-8 november 1948/producer walter legge/published in december 1952/lp matrix numbers XHAX 38-39

karajan	78: LX 1234-1239/LX 8699-8704 auto/LVX 87-92
vienna	GQX 11367-11372
philharmonic	lp: FCX 105/WCX 1026/C 90302
	other lp issues: american columbia ML 4299/toshiba EAC 30105/ emi 2C153 03200-03205M
	cd: emi CDM 566 3922/CMS 566 4832/grammofono AB 78792
	recording completed on 15 january 1949

33CX 1027/brahms piano concerto no 2/american columbia
recorded in philadelphia on 15 march 1945

ormandy	78: LX 1276-1281/LZX 250-255
philadelphia	lp: QCX 10010/WCX 1027/C 90303
orchestra	*american and canadian columbia issues*
serkin, piano	78: M 584/D 142
	lp: ML 4014
	other lp issue: philips fontana 699 022CL

33CX 1028/symphonies by haydn/american columbia
recorded in cleveland on 27 april 1949 and in philadelphia on 10 may 1949 respectively/ lp matrix numbers XLP 1842-1843

szell	**symphony no 92 "oxford"**
cleveland	lp: QCX 10006/VCX 518
orchestra	*american columbia issues*
	78: M 880
	lp: ML 4268
	other lp issues: philips classical favourites GBL 5521/ G03526L
ormandy	**symphony no 101 "clock"**
philadelphia	lp: QCX 10006/VCX 518
orchestra	*american columbia issues*
	78: M 894
	lp: ML 4268
	other lp issues: philips classical favourites GBL 5521/ G03526L

33CX 1029/song cycles by ravel and mussorgsky/american columbia
recorded in new york on 21-25 january 1950

bernstein	**shéhérazade**
columbia	*american columbia issues*
symphony	78: M 337
tourel	lp: ML 4289
	cd: sony SMK 60695
tourel	**songs and dances of death**
bernstein,	*american columbia issues*
piano	lp: ML 4289/Y2-32880
	cd: sony SMK 60695

33CX 1030/orchestral works by tchaikovsky/american columbia
recorded in carnegie hall new york on 3 november 1947 and in columbia studios new york in november 1949 respectively/producer goddard lieberson/ lp matrix numbers XLP 431 and 2103

stokowski	**francesca da rimini**
new york	*american columbia issues*
philharmonic	78: M 806
	lp: ML 4071/ML 4381/P 14137
	cd: cala CACD 0533
	romeo and juliet
	american columbia issues
	78: M 898
	lp: ML 4273/ML 4381

33CX 1031/string quintets by mozart/american columbia
recorded in liederkranz hall new york on 11-12 december 1946/producers richard gilbert and paul turner/ lp matrix numbers XLP 974-975

budapest	**quintet in c minor k406**
string quartet	cd: sony SM3K 46527
trampler,	*american columbia issues*
viola	78: M 830
	lp: ML 4143
	quintet in d k593
	cd: sony SM3K 46527
	american columbia issues
	78: M 708
	lp: ML 4143

33CX 1032/chopin the 14 valses
recorded in geneva radio studio on 3-12 july 1950/producer walter legge/published in april 1953/lp matrix numbers XAX 108-109

lipatti, piano
- 78: LX 1341-1346/LFX 959-964/LNX 2005-2010
- lp: FCX 156/FCX 492/FCX 30097/QCX 156/VCX 531/ WCX 1032/C 80643
- *other lp issues:* american columbia ML 4522/3216 0058/ emi HLM 7075/2C061 00167/1C047 00167/ 1C197 53780-53786M
- cd: emi CDC 747 8902/CDH 769 8022/CDH 566 2222/ CDM 566 9042/CZS 767 1632
- *selections from the complete recording*
- 45: SEB 3506/SEB 3508/SEB 3509/SEB 3511/SEL 1660/ SEL 1668/SEBQ 130/SEBQ 131/SEBQ 141/SEBQ 144/ ESBF 130/ESBF 163/ESBF 164/ESBF 17111/ ESBF 17112/ESBF 17113/ESBF 17114/ESBF 17115
- lp: angel seraphim 60207

33CX 1033/orchestral works by handel and tchaikovsky
recorded in kingsway hall london on 26-31 april 1952 and 30 july 1952 respectively/ producer walter legge/published in september 1953/lp matrix numbers XAX 198-199

karajan
philharmonia

water music, suite arranged by harty
- 78: LX 8945-8946
- lp: FCX 164/QCX 164
- *other lp issues:* angel 35004/toshiba EAC 37001-37019
- cd: emi CMS 763 4642
- *recording completed in july 1952*

casse noisette, standard ballet suite
- lp: FCX 164/FCX 25013/QCX 164/VCX 528
- *other lp issues:* angel 35004/toshiba EAC 37020-37038
- cd: emi CMS 763 4602
- *excerpts from casse noisette suite*
- 78: LX 1599/LX 1602
- 45: SCB 116/SEDQ 682/SCBQ 3059
- lp: FC 25136

33CX 1034/mahler symphony no 4/american columbia
recorded in new york on 10 may 1945 / lp matrix numbers XLP 298-299
walter   78: LX 949-954/LVX 21-26
new york   lp: FCX 198
philharmonic   *american columbia issues*
halban   78: M 589
                     lp: ML 4031/3216 0026
                     other lp issues: philips NBL 5038/L09406L/philips classical
                           favourites GBL 5608/G03587L/cbs 61357-61358/
                           78222
                     cd: sony MPK 46450/SMK 64450/naxos 811.0876

33CX 1035/beethoven symphony no 7
recorded in kingsway hall london 28 november 1951 / producer walter legge / published in february 1953 / lp matrix numbers XAX 168-169
karajan   lp: FCX 160/QCX 10007/VCX 519/WCX 1035/C 90304
philharmonia   *other lp issues:* angel 35003/world records SH 143-149/
                           toshiba EAC 37001-37019/emi SLS 5053/
                           1C181 01830-01836Y/eterna 820 030
                     cd: emi CMS 763 3102
                     recording completed in april and may 1952

33CX 1036/dvorak symphony no 8/american columbia
recorded in new york on 28 november 1947 / lp matrix numbers XLP 443-444
walter   78: GQX 11465-11468
new york   lp: QCX 10011
philharmonic   *american columbia issues*
                     78: M 770
                     lp: ML 4119
                     other lp issues: philips A01336L/ABL 3288/A01433L

33CX 1037/orchestral works by bizet and tchaikovsky
recorded in columbia studios new york on 21-22 december 1949/lp matrix numbers XLP 2101-2102

beecham
 columbia
 symphony
	carmen, suite
	 lp: FCX 330/QCX 10012/VCX 521
	 american columbia issues
	 78: X 333
	 lp: ML 4287/3216 0117
	 other 45 issue: philips fontana CFE 15019/496 017CE
	 other lp issues: philips fontana KFR 4001/676 001KR/
	  philips classical favourites GL 5720/G03632L/
	  cbs 54035
	 cd: sony MH2K 63366
	 capriccio italien
	 78: LX 8924-8925
	 lp: FCX 330/QCX 10012/VCX 521
	 american columbia issues
	 78: X 334
	 lp: ML 4287/3216 0117
	 other 45 issue: philips fontana CFE 15028/496 025CE
	 other lp issues: philips fontana KFR 4001/676 001KR/
	  philips classical favourites GL 5720/G03632L/
	  cbs 54035
	 cd: sony MH2K 63366

33CX 1038/symphonies by mozart and haydn
recorded in kingsway hall london on 9 march 1951 and 24 april 1950 respectively/producer lawrance collingwood/lp matrix numbers XAX 174-175

beecham	**symphony no 31 "paris"**
royal	lp: FCX 329/QCX 10032/WCX 1038
philharmonic	*other lp issues:* american columbia ML 4474/philips SBL 5226/ S04644L/S06685R/philips classical favourites GL 5742/ GBR 6525/G03643L/G05610R/philips fontana EFL 2503/697 206EL/699 023CL
	cd: sony SMK 89808
	recording completed in abbey road studios on 9 may 1951
	symphony no 93
	78: LX 1361-1363/GQX 11472-11474
	other 78rpm issue: american columbia M 991
	lp: FCX 329/QCX 10032/WCX 1038
	other lp issues: american columbia ML 5437/Y-33285/ philips NBL 5037/N02136L/philips classical favourites GL 5632/G03614L
	cd: sony SMK 89890
	recording completed on 1 june 1950

33CX 1039/symphonies by schubert and beethoven
recorded in kingsway hall london on 15 and 24 january 1951 and on 18 may 1951 respectively/producers p.de jongh and lawrance collingwood/lp matrix numbers XAX 178-179

beecham	**schubert symphony no 8 "unfinished"**
royal	78: LX 8942-8944
philharmonic	lp: FCX 236/VCX 517/WCX 1039
	other lp issues: american columbia ML 4474/philips fontana EFL 2505/CFL 1004/697 201EL/699 003CL/ philips classical favourites GL 5730/G03638L
	cd: emi CDM 763 3982/sony SMK 87876
	recording completed in may and july 1951
	beethoven symphony no 8
	lp: QCX 10040/WCX 1039/VCX 517
	other lp issues: american columbia ML 4681/philips fontana EFL 2507/EFR 2020/CFL 1004/697 205EL/ 664 012ER/699 003CL/699 038CL/philips classical favourites GL 5745/G03642L
	cd: emi CDM 763 3982/sony SMK 89888
	recording completed in october, november and december 1951

33CX 1040/schubert 12 lieder
recorded in abbey road studios london on 4-7 october 1952/producer walter legge/
published in september 1953/lp matrix numbers 259-260

schwarzkopf	lp: FCX 181/FCX 30307/QCX 10214/WCX 1040/C 90305
e.fischer,	*other lp issues:* angel 35022/emi ALP 3843/2C053 00404/
piano	1C137 53032-53036M
	cd: emi CDC 747 3262/CDH 764 0262/CDH 567 4942'
	562 7542
	selections from the complete recording
	45: SEL 1564/SEL 1570/SEL 1582/C 50581
	another 45rpm selection: electrola E 50157

33CX 1041-1042/catalogue nos. appear not to have been allocated

33CX 1043/chamber and instrumental works by beethoven/american columbia
recorded in new york on 1-15 december 1947/lp matrix numbers XLP 748-749

serkin, piano	**piano trio no 4 "ghost"**
a.busch, violin	*american columbia issues*
h.busch, cello	78: M 804
	lp: ML 4128/3216 0361
	cd: sony MPK 46447
serkin, piano	**piano sonata no 24; fantasia op 77**
	american columbia issues
	78: M 816
	lp: ML 4128

33CX 1044/lieder by bach, gluck, mozart, beethoven, schubert, schumann, brahms, wolf and richard strauss
recorded in abbey road studios london on 4-11 january 1954/producer walter legge/published in june 1954/lp matrix numbers XAX 200-201

schwarzkopf	lp: FCX 182/WCX 1044/C 90306
moore, piano	*other lp issues:* angel 35023/emi RLS 763/1C151 43160-43163M
	selections from the complete recording
	78: LX 1577
	lp: emi 154 6133
	cd: emi CDM 763 6542/CMS 763 7902/CHS 565 8602/
	CMS 567 6342/585 1052

33CX 1045/schumann symphony no 3 "rhenish"/american columbia
recorded in carnegie hall new york on 4 february 1941/lp matrix numbers XLP 269-270

walter 78: LZX 230-233
new york lp: FCX 147
philharmonic *american columbia issues*
  78: M 464
  lp: ML 4040
  other lp issues: philips A01336L/parnassus 7205/
    discocorp BWS 709
  cd: sony SMK 64488/grammofono AB 78532/iron needle
    IN 1357/arlecchino ARLA 53/historical performers HP17/
    history 205.244/205.241

33CX 1046/beethoven symphony no 3 "eroica"
recorded in kingsway hall london between 20 november and 1 december 1952/producer walter legge/published in june 1953/lp matrix numbers XAX 264-265

karajan lp: FCX 204/QCX 10013/WCX 1046/C 90307
philharmonia *other lp issues:* angel 35000/world records SH 143-149/
    emi SLS 5053/1C181 01830-01836Y/SHZE 133/
    toshiba EAC 37001-37019
  cd: emi CMS 763 3102
  also unofficially published on a cd by pickwick, who describe it as a performance by dresden symphony orchestra under fritz schreiber

33CX 1047/orchestral works by sibelius
recorded in kingsway hall london on 1 december 1951 and 29-31 july 1952 respectively/ producer walter legge/published in june 1953/lp matrix numbers XAX 251-252

karajan **symphony no 5**
philharmonia lp: FCX 192/QCX 10019/VCX 520/WCX 1047/C 90308
  other lp issues: angel 35002/toshiba EAC 37020-37038
  cd: emi CDM 566 6002/557 7540
  recording completed on 29 july 1952
  finlandia
  78: LX 1593/GQX 11536/LOX 831
  45: SCD 2115
  lp: FCX 192/QCX 10019/VCX 520/WCX 1047/C 90308
  other lp issues: angel 35002/toshiba EAC 37020-37038
  cd: emi CMS 763 4642/CDM 566 6002/557 7540

33CX 1048/brahms piano concerto no 1
recorded in kingsway hall london on 6-9 february 1953/producer geraint jones/published in november 1953/lp matrix numbers XAX 262-263
rieger lp: QCX 10062/WCX 1048
philharmonia *other lp issues:* angel 35014
malcuzynski, piano

33CX 1049/orchestral works by prokofiev, falla, ravel and dukas
recorded in abbey road studios london on 14 november 1951 (prokofiev and falla) and 12-13 september 1952/producer walter legge/published in june 1953/lp matrix numbers XAX 287-288

markevitch **prokofiev symphony no 1 "classical"**
philharmonia lp: FCX 203/FC 25040/QCX 10015/QIMX 7002/ WCX 1049/C 90309
  other lp issues: angel 35008/emi XLP 30001
  cd: testament SBT 1107
  recording completed in september 1952
  falla el sombrero de 3 picos, ballet suite
  lp: FCX 203/QCX 10015/WCX 1049/C 90309
  other lp issues: angel 35008/emi XLP 30001
  cd: testament SBT 1105
  excerpts
  lp: 33CX 1198/FCX 358/WCX 1198
  other lp excerpts: angel 35152
  recording completed in september 1952
  ravel la valse
  lp: FCX 203/QCX 10015/WCX 1049/C 90309
  other lp issues: angel 35008/emi XLP 30001
  cd: testament SBT 1060
  dukas l'apprenti sorcier
  45: ESBF 17043/SEBQ 147
  lp: FCX 203/FC 25087/QCX 10015/QIMX 7002/ WCX 1049/C 90309
  other lp issues: angel 35008/emi XLP 30001

33CX 1050/schumann piano quintet op 44/american columbia
recorded in new york on 28-29 april 1951/lp matrix numbers XLP 7106-7107
budapest lp: QCX 10023
string quartet *american columbia issues*
curzon, piano lp: ML 4426/3226 0019
  cd: archipel ARPCD 0241

33CX 1051-1052/lehar die lustige witwe
recorded in kingsway hall london on 16-21 april 1953/producer walter legge/published in june 1953/lp matrix numvers XAX 305-308

ackermann	lp: FCX 237-238/QCX 10050-10051/VCX 515-516/WCX 1051-1052/WSX537-538/C90310-90311/C80516-80517
philharmonia	
bbc chorus	*other lp issues:* angel 3501/emi SXDW 3045/1C153 00001-00002/1C149 03116-03117M
schwarzkopf	
loose	cd: emi CDH 769 5202/CHS 567 5292/585 8222
gedda	*excerpts*
niessner	78: LX 1597
kunz	45: SEL 1559/SCB 113/SCD 2083/SCBQ 3019
o.kraus	lp: 33CX 1712/WSX 563/C 80587
schmidinger	*other lp excerpts:* emi RLS 763/1C147 03580-03581M/ 1C151 43160-43163M
	cd: emi CDM 763 6572/CMS 763 7902

33CX 1053/brahms symphony no 1
recorded in kingsway hall london on 5 may 1952/producer walter legge/published in february 1954/lp matrix numbers XAX 272-273

karajan	lp: FCX 162/QCX 10044/WCX 1053/C 90312
philharmonia	*other lp issues:* angel 35001/CBX 78/toshiba EAC 37020-37038
	cd: emi CMS 763 4562
	recording completed in july 1952

33CX 1054/bartok concerto for orchestra
recorded in kingsway hall london on 28-29 november 1952/producer walter legge/ published in november 1953/lp matrix numbers XAX 253-254

karajan	lp: FCX 199/QCX 10052/WCX 1054/C 90313
philharmonia	*other lp issues:* angel 35003/toshiba EAC 37020-37038
	cd: emi CMS 763 4642/CDM 566 5962
	recording completed in july 1953

33CX 1055/piano sonatas by beethoven
recorded in kongresshalle zürich on 17-22 june 1951/published in september 1953/ lp matrix numbers XZX 4-5

gieseking, piano

sonata no 21 "waldstein"
lp: QCX 10069/WCX 1055/C 90314
other lp issues: angel 35024/american columbia 3216 0314/emi 3C153 52384-52393
cd: emi CDM 567 5852

sonata no 23 "appassionata"
lp: QCX 10069/WCX 1055/C 90314
other lp issues: angel 35024/american columbia 3216 0314/emi 3C153 52384-52393/ SMVP 8042
cd: emi CDM 567 5852

33CX 1056-1057/t.s. eliot murder in the cathedral
recorded in abbey road studios london on 13-15 may 1953/producer robert helpmann/ published in september 1953/lp matrix numbers XAX 320-323

old vic theatre company
donat

lp: angel 3505

33CX 1058-1060/bellini i puritani
recorded in basilica santa euphemia milan on 24-30 march 1953/producer dino olivieri/ published in november 1953

serafin
la scala
orchestra
and chorus
callas
cattelani
di stefano
mercuriali
panerai
rossi-lemeni
forti

lp: QCX 10016-10018/WCX 1058-1060/C 90315-90317
other lp issues: angel 3502/emi SLS 5140/EX 29 08743/ 2C163 00406-00408/2C163 52780-52787/ 3C163 00406-00408
cd: emi CDS 747 3088/CDS 566 2752/CMS 252 9432/ 585 6472/naxos 811.0259-0260
excerpts
45: SEL 1550/SEL 1554
lp: 33CX 1540/WSX 523/WSX 566/C 80448/C80602
other lp excerpts: angel 35304/36940/3743/emi SLS 856/ SLS 5057/SLS 5104/OVB 2171-2174/ 1C191 01433-01434M/1C191 01593-01594M/ 3C063 01510/3C065 01016/3C065 17902
cd: emi CDM 769 5432/CDC 754 0162/CDS 754 1032/ CMS 763 2442/CMS 565 5342/CZS 252 1642

33CX 1061/string quartets by haydn/american columbia
recorded in liederkranz hall new york on 2 may 1947 and in hollywood cbs studios on 31 october 1947 respectively/ lp matrix numbers XLP 1385-1386

budapest string quartet
- **string quartet op 64 no 5 "lark"**
  lp: QCX 10022
  american columbia issues
  78: M 853
  lp: ML 4216
- **string quartet op 76 no 4 "sunrise"**
  lp: QCX 10022
  american columbia issues
  78: M 864
  lp: ML 4216

33CX 1062/beethoven symphony no 6 "pastoral"
recorded in abbey road studios london between 7 and 19 december 1951/producer lawrance collingwood/ lp matrix numbers XAX 192-193

beecham
royal philharmonic
lp: QCX 10020
other lp issues: american columbia ML 4828/philips fontana KFR 4003/EFL 2505/676 003KR/697 201EL/philips classical favourites GL 5745
cd: sony SMK 89888
recording completed on 5 may 1952

33CX 1063/a garland for the queen: songs for mixed voices
recorded in abbey road studios london on 11-12 june 1953/ lp matrix numbers XAX 332-333

cambridge university madrigal society

33CX 1064/franck symphony in d minor
recorded in théatre des champs-élysées paris on 9-10 march 1953/producer rené challan/ published september 1953/ lp matrix numbers XLX 139-140

cluytens
orchestre national
lp: FCX 191/QCX 10033/WCX 1064/C 90318
other lp issues: angel 35029
cd: testament SBT 1237/SBT 7247

33CX 1065/ballet suites by tchaikovsky
recorded in kingsway hall london between 24 november and 1 december 1952/producer walter legge/published september 1953/lp matrix numbers XAX 266-267

karajan	**swan lake**
philharmonia	lp: FCX 202/FCX 30002/QCX 202/WCX 1065/C 90319
	other lp issues: angel 35006/toshiba EAC 37020-37038
	cd: emi CMS 763 4602/priory BL 013
	excerpts
	45: SEL 1537/SCBQ 3059/SEBQ 135/SEDQ 682
	lp: FC 25136
	sleeping beauty
	lp: FCX 202/FCX 30002/QCX 202/WCX 1065/C 90319
	other lp issues: angel 35006/toshiba EAC 37020-37038
	cd: emi CMS 763 4602/priory BL 013
	excerpts
	45: SEL 1532/SEBQ 132
	lp: FC 25136

this recording remained available as the mono equivalent to the later stereo re-make of this coupling on columbia SAX 2306

33CX 1066/works by chopin
recorded in abbey road studios london on 28 february-1 march 1953 and 10 march 1953 respectively/producer lawrance collingwood/published in september 1953/lp matrix numbers XAX 274-275

kletzki	**piano concerto no 2**
philharmonia	lp: FCX 154/QCX 10034/WCX 1066/C 90320
malcuzynski,	*other lp issues:* angel 35030
piano	*not to be confused with an earlier 78rpm recording of the work with the same participants and re-issued on lp by american columbia and on cd by dante and pearl*
malcuzynski,	**fantasy in f minor**
piano	lp: FCX 154/QCX 10034/WCX 1066/C 90320
	other lp issues: angel 35030

33CX 1067/goldmark rustic wedding symphony
recorded in abbey road studios london on 5-8 may 1952/producer lawrance collingwood/ lp matrix numbers XAX 212-213

beecham	*american columbia issue*
royal	lp: ML 4626
philharmonic	*other lp issues:* philips NBL 5041/N02140L/philips classical favourites GL 5719/G03631L
	cd: sony SMK 87780

32
33CX 1068/mahler symphony no 1/american columbia
recorded in minneapolis on 4 november 1940
mitropoulos   78: LOX 530-535
minneapolis   lp: QCX 10065/WCX 1068
symphony   *american columbia issues*
                       78: M 468
                       lp: ML 4251/RL 3120/P 14157
                       cd: sony MHK 62342/grammofono AB 78566/AB 78646-
                           78649/theorema TH 121.152/biddulph WHL 031-032/
                           sirio SO 5300.30/music master 37093/arkadia 78583
this was the first gramophone recording of the symphony

33CX 1069/mozart arias from don giovanni, le nozze di figaro and idomeneo
recorded in kingsway hall london 1-5 july 1952/producer walter legge/published in november 1953/lp matrix numbers XAX 210-211
pritchard   lp: FCX 183/QCX 10058/WCX 1069/C 90321
philharmonia   *other lp issues:* angel 35021/world records T 583/emi RLS 763/
schwarzkopf   1C151 43160-43163M/143 2221/2C051 43222
                       cd: emi CDH 763 7082
                       selections from the recital
                       78: LB 145/GQ 7260
                       45: SEL 1511/SEL 1515/SEBQ 124/ESBF 122
                       cd: emi CDC 747 9502/CDM 565 5772/notablu 93.509112
                       recordings completed in september 1952

33CX 1070/beethoven piano concerto no 5 "emperor"/american columbia
recorded in philadelphia on 19 november 1950/lp matrix numbers XLP 4346-4347
ormandy   lp: QCX 10041
philadelphia   *american columbia issue*
orchestra   lp: ML 4373
serkin, piano   *other lp issues:* philips fontana EFR 2014/664 011ER/
                           697 207EL/philips classical favourites GL 5748/
                           G03644L
                       cd: sony SM3K 47269

33CX 1071/violin concerti by mendelssohn and mozart/american columbia
recorded in philadelphia on 30 october 1950 and in new york on 28 march 1950 respectively/ lp matrix numbers XLP 3954 and 3132

ormandy	mendelssohn violin concerto
philadelphia	lp: FCX 210/QCX 10042/WCX 1071
orchestra	*american columbia issue*
stern, violin	lp: ML 4363
	other lp issues: philips fontana EFL 2526/697 211EL/philips classical favourites GL 5749/G03646L
stern	mozart violin concerto no 3 k216
columbia	lp: FCX 210/QCX 10042/WCX 1071
symphony	*american columbia issue*
stern, violin	lp: ML 5248
	other lp issues: philips fontana CFL 1013/699 019CL/ 697 203EL

33CX 1072/piano works by schumann and brahms
recorded in abbey road studios london on 23-25 april 1953/producer walter legge/published in october 1953/lp matrix numbers XAX 310-311

anda, piano   **études symphoniques**
                       lp: FCX 283/WCX 1072/C 90322
                       other lp issues: angel 35046
                       cd: testament SBT 1069
                       variations on a theme by paganini
                       lp: FCX 283/WCX 1072/C 90322
                       other lp issue: angel 35046
                       cd: testament SBT 1068

33CX 1073/beethoven sonatas nos 8 "pathétique" and 14 "moonlight"
recorded in kongresshalle zürich in june 1951/published in october 1953/lp matrix numbers XZX 1-2

gieseking,   lp: FC 1024/QCX 10080/WCX 1073/C 90323
piano   *other lp issues:* angel 35025/emi 3C053 00823

33CX 1074/organ works by bach/american columbia
recorded in parish church günsbach in september 1952/lp matrix numbers XLP 9332-9333

schweitzer,   **toccata adagio and fugue in c**
organ   *american columbia issue* lp: SL 223
                  other lp issue: philips A01109L
                  fugue in a minor
                  american columbia issue lp: SL 223
                  45rpm issue: philips ABE 10000/409 000AE
                  other lp issue: philips A01109L
                  fantasia and fugue in g minor
                  american columbia issue lp: SL 223
                  other lp issues: philips A01109L/philips classical favourites GBL 5509/G03515L

33CX 1075/cherubini requiem mass in c minor
recorded in rome in 1952/producer dino olivieri/published in november 1953/ lp matrix numbers XBX 1-2

giulini   lp: FCX 231/QCX 10045/WCX 1075/C 90324
santa cecilia   *other lp issues:* angel 35042/emi 3C053 01569
orchestra
and chorus

33CX 1076/ravel l'heure espagnole
recorded in théatre du champs-élysées paris between 9 and 14 october 1952/published in november 1953/lp matrix numbers XLX 114-115

cluytens   lp: FCX 172/QCX 172/WCX 1076
opéra-comique   *other lp issues:* angel 35018
orchestra   cd: emi CDM 565 2692
duval   *recording completed on 21 november 1952*
giraudeau

33CX 1077/beethoven symphony no 5/american columbia
recorded in new york on 13 february 1950/lp matrix numbers XLP 2524-2525

walter   lp: FCX 211/QCX 211
new york   *american columbia issues*
philharmonic   lp: ML 4297/ML 4790/CL 918
                     other lp issues: philips ABL 3239/A01300L/L09400L/philips
                                classical favourites GL 5615/G03593L/cbs 77511

33CX 1078-1079/delius a mass of life
recorded in abbey road studios london between 8 november and 13 december 1952/ producer lawrance collingwood/lp matrix numbers XAX 326-329

beecham   *american columbia issue*
royal   lp: SL 197
philharmonic   *other lp issues:* philips fontana CFL 1005-1006/699 004-
london   699 005CL/cbs 61182-61183
philharmonic   cd: sony SM2K 89432
choir   *recording completed between january and may 1953*
fisher/raisbeck
sinclair
craig
boyce

33CX 1080/beethoven piano concerto no 3/american columbia
recorded in philadelphia on 24 december 1947/lp matrix numbers XLP 2355-2356

ormandy   lp: FCX 142/QCX 10075
philadelphia   *american columbia issues*
orchestra   78: M 917
arrau, piano   lp: ML 4302/Y-34601
                 other lp issues: philips SBR 6252/S06681R
                 cd: dante HPC 124/history 205236.303/205235.324

33CX 1081/bach 7 chorale preludes/american columbia
recorded in parish church günsbach in september 1952/published in november 1953/
lp matrix numbers XLP 9334-9335

schweitzer,   *american columbia issue*
organ   lp: SL 223
                 selection from the recording
                 lp: philips classical favourites GBL 5509/G03513L

33CX 1082/symphonies by schubert and mozart/american columbia
recorded in philadelphia on 2 march 1947 and in new york on 23 january 1945 respectively/
lp matrix numbers XOX 1-2

walter   **schubert symphony no 8 "unfinished"**
philadelphia   lp: QCX 10079
orchestra   *american columbia issues*
                     78: M 699
                     lp: ML 2010/ML 4880
                     cd: grammofono AB 78805-78806/history 205243/205241

walter   **mozart symphony no 41 "jupiter"**
new york   lp: QCX 10079
philharmonic   *american columbia issue*
                     lp: ML 4880
                     cd: dante LYS 338

33CX 1083/stravinsky le sacre du printemps/american columbia
recorded in liederkranz hall new york on 29 april 1940/producer goddard lieberson/
lp matrix numbers XLP 550-551

stravinsky   78: LOX 494-497
new york   lp: QCX 10066
philharmonic   *american columbia issues*
                     78: M 417
                     lp: ML 4092/ML4882
                     other lp issues: philips A01307L
                     cd: dante LYS 271-273/andante 1979-1981

33CX 1084/organ works by bach and mendelssohn/american columbia
recorded in parish church günsbach in september 1952/published in december 1953/
lp matrix numbers XLP 9336-9337

schweitzer, organ	**bach prelude in c; canzona in d minor; mendelssohn organ sonata no 6**

american columbia issues
lp: SL 223/ML 4602
other lp issue: philips A01111L
bach prelude in d
american columbia issues
lp: SL 223/ML 4602
45rpm issue: philips ABE 10000/409 000AE
other lp issue: philips A01111L

33CX 1085/sibelius symphony no 1
recorded in abbey road studios london on 23 may 1951/producer lawrance collingwood/
lp matrix numbers XAX 338-339

beechan royal philharmonic	lp: QCX 10071 *american columbia issue* lp: ML 4653 *other lp issues:* philips SBR 6245/S06708R/philips classical favourites GL 5716/G03628L cd: sony SMK 87798 *recording completed between november 1951 and may 1952*

33CX 1086/beethoven symphony no 3 "eroica"
recorded in abbey road studios london in 20-21 december 1951/producer lawrance collingwood/lp matrix numbers XAX 285-286

beecham royal philharmonic	*american columbia issue* lp: ML 4698 *other lp issues:* philips SBL 5233/S05648L cd: sony SMK 89887 *recording completed on 13 august 1952*

33CX 1087 / orchestral works by franck and rimsky-korsakov
recorded in kingsway hall london on 9 march 1951 and between 9 and 24 january 1951 respectively / producer lawrance collingwood / lp matrix numbers XAX 171 and 209

beecham	**le chasseur maudit**
royal	78: LX 8813-8814/GQX 11489-11490
philharmonic	lp: QCX 10085
	american columbia issue
	lp: ML 4474
	other lp issues: philips fontana KFR 4000/676 000KR/ CFL 1042/699 041CL
	cd: sony SMK 87964
	le coq d'or, suite
	lp: QCX 10085
	american columbia issue
	lp: ML 4474
	other lp issues: philips fontana KFR 4000/676 000KR/ philips classical favourites GL 5692/G03636L
	cd: sony SMK
	american columbia lp excerpts: ML 5321/Y-33288
	other excerpts
	45: philips fontana CFE 15030/496 036CE
	lp: philips fontana CFL 1021/699 041CL/cbs 61655

33CX 1088 / orchestral works by mozart
recorded in théatre municipal perpignan on 2 july 1951 and 21-22 june 1951 respectively / producer lawrance collingwood / lp matrix numbers XAX 224-225

casals	**symphony no 29**
perpigan	lp: FCX 223
festival	*american columbia issue*
orchestra	lp: ML 4563
	cd: pearl GEMS 0167
	serenade no 13 "eine kleine nachtmusik"
	lp: FCX 223
	american columbia issue
	lp: ML 4563
	cd: pearl GEMS 0167

33CX 1089/mozart sinfonia concertante k364
recorded in théatre municipal perpignan on 5-8 july 1951/producer lawrance collingwood/ lp matrix numbers XAX 226-227

casals	lp: FCX 224
perpignan	*american columbia issue*
festival	lp: ML 4564
orchestra	*other lp issues:* philips fontana CFL 1013/699 019CL
stern, violin	cd: sony SMK 58983/pearl GEMS 0167
primrose, viola	

33CX 1090/works by mozart
recorded in théatre municipal perpignan on 22-23 june 1951/producer lawrance collingwood/lp matrix numbers XAX 228-229

casals	**divertimento no 11 k251**
perpigan	lp: FCX 227
festival	*american columbia issue*
orchestra	lp: ML 4566
	recording completed on 2-3 july 1951

tabuteau, oboe	**oboe quartet k370**
stern, violin	lp: FCX 227
primrose, viola	*american columbia issue*
tortelier, cello	lp: ML 4566

33CX 1091/mozart piano concerto no 9 k271
recorded in théatre municipal perpignan on 6-7 july 1951/producer lawrance collingwood/lp matrix numbers XAX 230-231

casals	lp: FCX 225
perpignan	*american columbia issue*
festival	lp: ML 4568
orchestra	*other lp issue:* philips A01351L
hess, piano	

33CX 1092/mozart piano concerto no 22 k482
recorded in théatre municipal perpignan on 26 july 1951/producer lawrance collingwood/lp matrix numbers XAX 232-233

casals	lp: FCX 226
perpignan	*american columbia issue*
festival	lp: ML 4569
orchestra	*other lp issue:* philips A01352L
serkin, piano	cd: sony SMK 66570

33CX 1093/instrumental music by beethoven
recorded in théatre municipal perpignan on 31 july 1951/producer lawrance collingwood/
lp matrix numbers XAX 234-235

casals, cello **cello sonata op 5 no 2**
serkin, piano *american columbia issues*
lp: ML 4572/ML 4877/SL 201/3236 0016
other lp issues: philips ABL 3222/A01285L
cd: sony MPK 46725/SM2K 58985/515 3042
**variations on mozart's bei männern welche liebe fühlen;
variations on mozart's ein mädchen oder weibchen**
american columbia issues
lp: ML 4572/ML 4877/SL 201/3236 0016
other lp issues: philips A01351-01352L
cd: sony MPK 46724/SM2K 58985/515 3042

33CX 1094-1095/puccini tosca
*recorded in teatro alla scala milan on 10-21 august 1953/producer walter legge/
published in december 1953/lp matrix numbers XBX 7-10*

de sabata   lp: FCX 253-254/QCX 10028-10029/WCX 1094-1095/
la scala   C 90325-90326
orchestra   *other lp issues:* angel 3508/emi SLS 825/EX 29 00393/
and chorus   1C191 00410-00411M/2C163 00410-00411/
callas   3C163 00410-00411
di stefano   cd: emi CDS 747 1758/CDS 556 3042/CMS 252 9432/
gobbi   585 6442/naxos 811.0256-0257/regis RRC 2065
excerpts
45: SEL 1526/SEL 1530/SEL 1543/SEL 1569/SELW 1526/
    SELW 1530/SELW 1543/C 50149/C 50150/C 50153/
    SCB 3037/SEBQ 122/SEBQ 126/SEBQ 145/SEBQ 167/
    SEBQ 268/ESBF 177/ESBF 1332/
other 45rpm issues of excerpts: hmv 7ERQ 271/7RQ 3001
lp: 33CX 1725/33CX 1784/33CX 1893/FCX 802/FCX 929/
    QCX 10403/QCX 10415/QCX 10444/WSX 561/C 80585
other lp issues of excerpts: angel 3699/36940/36966/emi SLS 856/
    SLS 5104/SHZE 173/1C061 00741/1C191 01433-01434M/
    1C191 01593-01594M/3C063 00841/3C065 01480
cd: emi CDM 769 5432/CDS 754 1032/CMS 763 2442/
    CMS 565 5342/CMS 565 9522/CZS 252 6142/
    CMS 764 4182/CMS 557 0622/562 7942

33CX 1096-1097/humperdinck hänsel und gretel
recorded in kingsway hall london between 27 june and 2 july 1953/producer walter legge/ published in december 1953/lp matrix numbers XAX 334-337

karajan lp: FCX 286-287/QCX 10048-10049/WCX 1096-1097/
philharmonia C 90327-90328
loughton and *other lp issues:* angel 3506/hmv LALP 207-208/emi SLS 5145/
bancrofts choirs EX 769 2931/world records OC 187-188
schwarzkopf cd: emi CMS 763 2932/CMS 763 7902/naxos 811.0897-0898
grümmer *excerpts*
felbermayer 45: SEL 1694
schürhoff lp: 33CX 1819/WSX 545/C 80528
metternich *other lp excerpts:* world records OH 189
 cd: emi CDM 763 6572/CMS 763 7902

33CX 1098/debussy préludes 1er livre
recorded in abbey road studios london on 15 august 1953/producer geraint jones/published in december 1953/lp matrix numbers XAX 376-377

gieseking, lp: FCX 185/QCX 10063/WCX 1098/C 90329
piano *other lp issues:* angel 35006/emi RLS 752/2C061 00412/
 3C053 01026/3C153 52331-52440M/F667 473-478M
 cd: emi CDH 761 0042/CHS 556 5852/CHS 556 8552

33CX 1099/orchestral works by ravel and debussy
recorded in kingsway hall london on 16-17 july and 20-22 july 1953 respectively/producer walter legge/published in december 1953/lp matrix numbers XAX 371 and 386

karajan **rapsodie espagnole**
philharmonia lp: FCX 298/QCX 10059/C 90330
 other lp issues: angel 35081/toshiba EAC 37020-37038
 cd: emi CMS 763 4642
 la mer
 lp: FCX 298/QCX 10059/C 90330
 other lp issues: angel 35081/toshiba EAC 37020-37038
 cd: emi CMS 763 4642

33CX 1100/works by stravinsky/american columbia
recorded in carnegie hall new york and in columbia studio hollywood between february 1945 and august 1946/lp matrix numbers XLP 2758-2759

stravinsky new york philharmonic	**fireworks** lp: FCX 212/QCX 212 *american columbia issues* 78: M 653 lp: ML 4398 *further issues* lp: philips A01516L cd: andante 1979-1981
	norwegian impressions 78: LZX 240/LOX 607 lp: FCX 212/QCX 212 *american and canadian columbia issues* 78: 12371D lp: ML 4398 *further issues* lp: philips A01516L cd: andante 2990
	circus polka lp: FCX 212/QCX 212 *american columbia issue* lp: ML 4398 *further issues* lp: philips A01516L cd: andante 2990
	ode lp: FCX 212/QCX 212 *american columbia issues* lp: ML 4398 *further issues* lp: philips A01516L cd: andante 2990
stravinsky woody herman orchestra	**ebony concerto** lp: FCX 212/QCX 212 *american and canadian columbia issues* 78: 7479M/25019 lp: ML 4398 *further issues* lp: philips A01516L cd: andante 2990
szigeti, violin stravinsky, piano	**russian maiden's song** lp: FCX 212/QCX 212 *american columbia issues* 78: 72495D lp: ML 4398 *further issues* lp: philips A01516L cd: sony SMK 64136

33CX 1101/string quartets by boccherini
recorded in milan on 6-8 october 1953/published in december 1953/lp matrix numbers XBX 121-122

quartetto italiano	**quartet op 39 no 3** lp: FCX 262/QCX 10024/WCX 1101/C 90331 *further lp issue:* angel 35062 **quartet op 58 no 3** lp: FCX 262/QCX 10024/WCX 1101/C 90331 *further lp issue:* angel 35062 cd: testament SBT 1124

33CX 1102/mozart string quartets no 14 k387 and no 15 k421
recorded in milan on 6-8 october 1953/published in december 1953/lp matrix numbers XBX 119-120

quartetto italiano	lp: FCX 261/QCX 10025/WCX 1102/C 90332 *further lp issue:* angel 35063

33CX 1103/beethoven string quartet no 13 op 130
recorded in milan on 6-8 october 1953/published in december 1953/lp matrix numbers XBX 117-118

quartetto italiano	lp: FCX 260/QCX 10026/WCX 1103/C 90333

33CX 1104/symphonies by haydn
recorded in abbey road studios london on 13-14 july 1951 and in kingsway hall london on 29 january-1 february 1951 respectively/producer lawrance collingwood/lp matrix numbers XAX 172-173

beecham
royal
philharmonic
	symphony no 94 "surprise"
	78: LX 1499-1501
	lp: FCX 328/QCX 10060
	american columbia issue
	lp: ML 4453
	further lp issues: philips NBL 5037/N02136L/S04623L/
	    philips classical favourites GL 5632/G03614L
	cd: sony SMK 89890
	recording completed on 8 october 1951
	symphony no 103 "drum roll"
	lp: FCX 328/QCX 10060
	american columbia issue
	lp: ML 4453
	further lp issues: philips SBR 6253/S06710R/S04623L/
	    philips fontana 699 036CL
	cd: sony SMK 89890

33CX 1105/orchestral works by handel and mozart
recorded in kingsway hall london on 24 april 1950 and 18 april 1950 respectively/ producer lawrance collingwood/ lp matrix numbers XAX 309 and 358

beecham	**the faithful shepherd, suite arranged by beecham**
royal	*american columbia issues*
philharmonic	78: M 990
	lp: ML 5437/Y-33285
	further lp issues: philips fontana CFL 1008/699 007CL
	cd: sony SMK 87780
	excerpts from the suite
	78: LX 1600
	american columbia excerpts from the suite
	lp: ML 5226
	other excerpts from the suite
	45: philips CFE 15031/496 037CE
	recording completed on 28 september 1950
	symphony no 38 "prague"
	78: LX 1517-1519
	lp: FCX 235
	american columbia issues
	78: M 934
	lp: ML 4313/3216 0023/3236 0009
	other lp issues: philips SBL 5226/S04644L/philips fontana EFL 2503/697 206EL/699 023CL/philips classical favourites GL 5742/G03643L
	cd: sony SMK 87963

33CX 1106/works by liszt
recorded in abbey road studios london between 2 and 9 march 1953/producer geraint jones/ published in december 1953/ lp matrix numbers XAX 299-300

susskind	**piano concerto no 2**
philharmonia	lp: FCX 195/QCX 10067
malcuzynski,	*other lp issue:* angel 35031
piano	
malcuzynski,	**piano sonata in b minor**
piano	lp: FCX 195/QCX 10067
	other lp issue: angel 35031

33CX 1107/works for soprano and orchestra by richard strauss
recorded in town hall watford in 25-26 september 1953/producer walter legge/published in december 1953/lp matrix numbers XAX 380-381

ackermann	**4 letzte lieder**
philharmonia	lp: FCX 294/WCX 1107/C 90334
schwarzkopf	*other lp issues:* angel 35084/38266/emi RLS 751/100 8651/ 2C061 01208
	cd: emi CDH 761 0012/585 8252/notablu 935 0923
	capriccio, closing scene
	lp: FCX 294/WCX 1107/C 90334
	other lp issues: angel 35084/38266/emi RLS 751/100 8651
	cd: emi CDH 761 0012/585 8252/notablu 935 0923

33CX 1108/bach orchestral suites
recorded in église saint pierre prades on 20-21 june and 20-21 may 1950 respectively/ producer lawrance collingwood/lp matrix numbers XAX 216-217

casals	**suite no 1**
prades	*american columbia issue*
festival	lp: ML 4348
orchestra	cd: pearl
	suite no 2
	american columbia issue
	lp: ML 4348
	other lp issue: philips A01513L
	cd: pearl

33CX 1109/concerti by bach
recorded in église saint pierre prades on 6 and 15 june 1950 respectively/producer lawrance collingwood/lp matrix numbers XAX 220-221

casals	**piano concerto bwv 1056**
prades	*american columbia issues*
festival	lp: ML 4353/76082
orchestra	*other lp issue:* philips A01511L
haskil, piano	cd: sony SMK 58982/pearl GEMS 0202

casals	**violin concerto bwv 1061**
prades	*american columbia issues*
festival	lp: ML 4353/76082/SL 169-170
orchestra	*other lp issue:* philips A01511L
stern, violin	cd: sony SMK 58982/pearl GEMS 0202

33CX 1110/instrumental music by bach
recorded in église saint pierre prades in june 1950/producer lawrance collingwood/lp matrix numbers XAX 223-224

casals, cello	**gamba sonata bwv 1029**
baumgartner, piano	*american columbia issue*
	lp: ML 4350
	cd: sony MPK 46445

serkin, piano	**italian concerto; chromatic fantasy and fugue bwv 903**
	american columbia issues
	lp: ML 4350/MP 39761

33CX 1111/violin sonatas by franck and debussy/american columbia
recorded in new york on 26 april 1946/lp matrix numbers XLP 1175-1176

francescatti, violin	**franck violin sonata in a**
casadesus, piano	lp: FCX 125
	american columbia issues
	78: 72367-72370D
	lp: ML 4178
	cd: sony 5033 852/dante LYS 378/pearl GEMMCD 9250
	recording completed on 7 may 1947
	debussy violin sonata in g minor
	lp: FCX 125
	american columbia issues
	78: 72045-72046D
	lp: ML 4178
	cd: sony 5033 842/dante LYS 378

33CX 1112/delius appalachia
recorded in abbey road studios london on 29 october 1952/producer lawrance collingwood/lp matrix numbers XAX 330-331

beecham	*american columbia issue*
royal	lp: ML 4915/Y-33283/61354
philharmonic	*other lp issues:* philips A01335L/philips classical favourites
rpo chorus	GL 5690/G03634L/philips fontana CFL 1009/
	699 009CL
	cd: sony SMK 89429/SX5K 87342
	recording completed in november and december 1952

33CX 1113/concerti by bach

recorded in église saint pierre prades between 27 may and 16 june 1950/producer lawrance collingwood/lp matrix numbers XAX 218-219

casals	**violin concerto bwv 1052**
prades	*american columbia issue*
festival	lp: ML 4352
orchestra	cd: pearl GEMS 0202
szigeti, violin	

casals	**concerto for flute, violin and piano bwv 1044**
prades	*american columbia issue*
festival	lp: ML 4352
orchestra	cd: pearl GEMS 0202
wummer, flute	
schneider, violin	
horszowski, piano	

33CX 1114-1115/lehar das land des lächelns

recorded in kingsway hall london on 17-20 april 1953/producer walter legge/published in december 1953/lp matrix numbers XAX 367-370

ackermann	lp: FCX 288-289/WCX 1114-1115/WSX 535-536/ C 90335-90336/C 80514-80515
philharmonia	
bbc chorus	*other lp issues:* angel 3507/emi SXDW 3044/1C147 03580-03581/1C149 03047-03048
schwarzkopf	
loose	cd: emi CHS 763 5232/CHS 567 5292/585 8222
gedda	*excerpts*
kunz	45: SEL 1556
o.kraus	lp: 33CX 1712/WSX 563/C 80587
	other lp issues of excerpts: emi RLS 763/SLS 5250/ 1C151 43160-43163M
	recording completed in 28 june 1953

33CX 1116/saint-saens symphony no 3 "organ"/american columbia
recorded in new york on 10 november 1947/lp matrix numbers XLP 668-669
munch 78: LFX 901-904/GQX 11358-11359/LHX 8003-8006
new york lp: FCX 166/QCX 166
philharmonic *american columbia issues*
nies-berger, 78: M 747
organ lp: ML 4120

33CX 1117/beethoven symphony no 3 "eroica"/american columbia
recorded in carnegie hall new york on 21 march 1949/lp matrix numbers XLP 1470-1471
walter lp: FCX 232/QCX 10061
new york *american columbia issues*
philharmonic 78: X 858
45: A 1072
lp: ML 4228/77511
other lp issues: philips ABL 3242/A01303L/L09403L/
philips classical favourites GBL 5618/G03596L
cd: palladio PD 4163/historical performers HP 15

33CX 1118/works for piano and orchestra/american columbia
recorded in new york on 20 december 1948 and in abbey road studios london on 21 october 1949 respectively/lp matrix numbers XLP 2325-2326
munch **d'indy symphony on a french mountain song**
new york lp: FCX 119/QCX 119
philharmonic *american columbia issues*
casadesus, 78: M 911
piano lp: ML 4298

weldon **franck variations symphoniques**
philharmonia 78: LX 8800-8801
casadesus, lp: FCX 119/QCX 119
piano *american columbia issue*
lp: ML 4298

33CX 1119/mélodies by ravel and poulenc/american columbia
recorded in new york/lp matrix numbers XLP 2575-2576
bernac lp: FCX 141
poulenc, piano *american columbia issue*
lp: ML 4333
cd: testament SBT 3161

33CX 1120/beethoven symphony no 7/american columbia
recorded in new york on 12 march 1951/lp matrix numbers XLP 6450-6451
walter lp: FCX 233/QCX 10072/WCX 1120
new york *american columbia issues*
philharmonic lp: ML 4414/77511
        other lp issues: philips ABL 3242/A01303L/L09403L/
        philips classical favourites GBL 5618/G03596L
        cd: palladio PD 4163/histotical performers HP 15

33CX 1121-1123/bach mass in b minor
recorded in musikvereinssaal vienna on 2-7 november 1952 (choruses) and in abbey road studios london on 23-30 november 1952/producer walter legge/published in february 1954/lp matrix numbers XHAX 57-62
karajan lp: FCX 291-293/QCX 10055-10057/WCX 1121-1123/
philharmonia   C 90337-90339
wiener *other lp issues:* angel 3500/world records T 854-856/
singverein   emi RLS 746/EX 29 09743/1C181 01791-01793
schwarzkopf cd: emi CHS 763 5052
höffgen *excerpts*
gedda lp: WSX 544/C 80527
rehfuss *recording completed in london on 16 july 1953*

vienna sessions for the above recording were accompanied by members of the vienna symphony orchestra described as orchester der gesellschaft der musikfreunde

33CX 1124/beethoven symphony no 6 "pastoral"
recorded in kingsway hall london on 9-10 july 1953/producer walter legge/published in april 1954/lp matrix numbers XAX 395-396
karajan lp: FCX 234/QCX 10093/WCX 1124/C 90340
philharmonia *other lp issues:* angel 35080/world records SM 143-149/
        toshiba EAC 37001-37019/emi SLS 5053/
        1C181 01830-01836Y/SHZE 196
        cd: emi CMS 763 3102
        also published in an unofficial cd edition by javelin with orchestra incorrectly described as london philharmonic

33CX 1125/orchestral works by sibelius
recorded in kingsway hall london on 6-7 july 1953 and on 14-15 july 1953 respectively/ producer walter legge/ published in march 1954/ lp matrix numbers XAX 363-364
karajan symphony no 4
philharmonia lp: FCX 280/QCX 10078/WCX 1125/C 90341
    other lp issues: angel 35082/toshiba EAC 37020-37038
    cd: emi CMS 763 4642/CDM 566 6002/557 7540
tapiola
lp: FCX 280/QCX 10078/WCX 1125/C 90341
other lp issues: angel 35082/toshiba EAC 37020-37038
cd: emi CMS 763 4642/CDM 566 6002

33CX 1126-1127/oscar wilde the importance of being earnest
recorded in abbey road studios london on 25-27 may 1953/ producers alan dent and john gielgud/ lp matrix numbers XAX 372-373
edith evans   *other lp issue:* angel 3504
john gielgud

33CX 1128/mozart piano sonata no 16 k570; variations k24, k25 and k180; rondo in a minor k616; allegro k3; various minuets and trios
recorded in abbey road studios london between 7 and 18 august 1953/ producers walter legge, walter jellinek and geraint jones/ published in february 1954/ lp matrix numbers XAX 402-403
gieseking, lp: FCX 311/WCX 1128/C 90342
piano   *other lp issues:* angel 35068/3511/3C153 00997-01007M/
    1C197 43020-43024M
    cd: emi CHS 763 6882

33CX 1129/wagner tannhäuser overture and venusberg music; tristan und isolde prelude and liebestod
recorded in kingsway hall london between 15 and 23 june 1953/ published in february 1954/ producer geraint jones/ lp matrix numbers XAX 342-343
kletzki lp: FCX 275/QCX 10073/WCX 1129/C 90343
philharmonia *other lp issue:* angel 35059

33CX 1130/operatic arias by massenet, bizet, gounod, flotow, cilea, auber, donizetti, tchaikovsky, ponchielli and verdi
recorded in kingsway hall london between 10 and 17 april 1953/ producers walter legge and geraint jones/ published in july 1954/ lp matrix numbers XAX 420-421
galliera lp: FCX 302/WCX 1130/C 90344
philharmonia *other lp issue:* angel 35096
gedda   cd: emi CMS 567 4452
   selections from the recital
   78: LX 1614/LX 1617
   lp: FC 25098
   other lp selections: emi SLS 5250/1C137 78233-78236

33CX 1131-1132/donizetti lucia di lammermoor
recorded in teatro communale florence on 29 january-6 february 1953/producer dino olivieri/ published in march 1954/lp matrix numbers XBX 3-6

serafin	lp: FCX 259-259/QCX 10030-10031/WCX 1131-1132/
maggio	C 90345-90346
musicale	*other lp issues:* angel 3503/angel seraphim 6032/emi 1C137
orchestra	00942-00943M/2C163 00942-00943/3C165 00942-00943
and chorus	cd: emi CMS 769 9802/562 7472/566 4382/586 1072/
callas	regis RRC 2066/naxos 811.0131-0132
canali	*excerpts*
di stefano	45: SEL 1522
natali	lp: 33CX 1385/WSX 607/C 80112
gobbi	*other lp excerpts:* emi 1C153 52287-52288/3C065 17902
	cd: emi CMS 763 2442/CMS 565 5342/CZS 252 6142/
arié	CMS 764 4182/CMS 557 0622

33CX 1133/tchaikovsky symphony no 5
recorded in kingsway hall london in may and july 1952/producer walter legge/published in december 1954/lp matrix numbers XAX 352-353

karajan	lp: FCX 161/QCX 10098/WCX 1133/C 90347
philharmonia	*other lp issues:* angel 35055/toshiba EAC 37020-37038
	cd: emi CMS 763 4602
	recording completed on 19 june 1953

33CX 1134/orchestral works by ravel
recorded in the théatre des champs-élysées paris between 16 and 25 june 1953/producer rené challan/published in march 1954/lp matrix numbers XLX 179-180

cluytens	alborada del gracioso
orchestre	45: SEL 1524
national	lp: FCX 218/WCX 1134/C 90348
	other lp issue: angel 35054
	cd: testament SBT 1238

cluytens	daphnis et chloé, first and second suites
orchestre	lp: FCX 218/WCX 1134/C 90348
national	*other lp issue:* angel 35054
briclot choir	cd: testament SBT 1238

33CX 1135/works by prokofiev
recorded in paris on 24 january 1953 (concerto) and 4 april 1953/producer rené challan/ published in march 1954/lp matrix numbers XLX 141-142

cluytens	**piano concerto no 3**
orchestre	lp: FCX 218/WCX 1135/C 90349
national	*other lp issue:* angel 35045
francois, piano	cd: emi CZS 573 1772/CZS 762 9512/585 2462
	recording completed on 23 september 1953

francois, piano	**visions fugitives; toccata**
	lp: FCX 218/WCX 1135/C 90349
	other lp issue: angel 35045
	cd: emi CZS 762 9512/585 2462

33CX 1136/orchestral works by beethoven
recorded in kingsway hall london on 21 november 1953, 20 june 1953 and 13-14 july 1953 respectively/producer walter legge/published in september 1954/lp matrix numbers XAX 442-443

karajan	**symphony no 1**
philharmonia	lp: FCX 250/QCX 10099/WC 515/WCX 1136/C 70367/ C 90350
	other lp issues: angel 35097/world records SM 143-149/emi SLS 5053/1C181 01830-01836Y/toshiba EAC 37001-37019
	cd: emi CMS 763 3102
	egmont overture
	lp: FCX 250/FC 25107/QCX 10099/WC 511/WCX 1136/ C 70363/C 90350
	other lp issues: angel 35097/emi SLS 5053/SHZE 169/ 1C181 01830-01836Y/toshiba EAC 37001-37019
	cd: emi CMS 763 3102
	recording completed on 15 july 1953
	leonore no 3 overture
	lp: FCX 250/QCX 10099/WC 511/WCX 1136/C 70363/ C 90350
	other lp issues: angel 35097/emi SLS 5053/1C181 01830-01836Y/toshiba EAC 37001-37019
	cd: emi CMS 763 4562

33CX 1137/debussy images books 1 and 2; estampes; pour le piano
recorded in abbey road studios london on 12-17 august 1953/producer geraint jones/
published in march 1954/lp matrix numbers XAX 378-379

gieseking,   lp: FCX 282/WCX 1137/C 90351
piano   *other lp issues:* angel 35063/emi RLS 752/2C061 00413/
                         3C053 01025/3C153 52331-52440M/F667 473-478M
                cd: emi CHS 556 5852/CHS 556 8552
                estampes and images only
                cd: emi 562 7982

33CX 1138/chopin selection of mazurkas and polonaises
recorded in abbey road studios london on 3-6 march 1953/producer geraint jones/
published in april 1954/lp matrix numbers XAX 270-271

malcuzynski,   lp: FCX 197/WCX 1138/C 90352
piano   *other lp issue:* angel 35284
                selections from the recital
                78: LX 1461
                45: SEL 1561

33CX 1139/tchaikovsky symphony no 4
recorded in kingsway hall london between 4 and 16 july 1953/producer walter legge/
published in november 1954

karajan   lp: FCX 274/QCX 10106/WCX 1139
philharmonia   *other lp issues:* angel 35099/toshiba EAC 37020-37038
                cd: emi CMS 763 4602

33CX 1140/mozart the four horn concerti
recorded in kingsway hall london between 12 and 23 november 1953/producer walter legge/
piblished in october 1954/lp matrix numbers XAX 464-465

karajan   lp: FCX 251/QCX 10100/WCX 1140/C 90354
philharmonia   *other lp issues:* angel 35092/toshiba EAC 37001-27019/
brain, horn   emi ASD 1140/1C063 00414/2C051 00414/
                         3C053 00414
                cd: emi CDH 761 0132/CDM 566 8982/CDC 555 0872

33CX 1141/khachaturian violin concerto
recorded in abbey road studios london on 2-3 december 1953/producer walter legge/
published in april 1954/lp matrix numbers XAX 448-449

goossens   lp: QCX 10126/WCX 1141/C 90355
philharmonia   *other lp issues:* angel 35100/emi MFP 2050
i.oistrakh,
violin

33CX 1142/mozart piano sonatas k282 and k331; fantasia k397; variations k265; minuet k355; suite k399; andantino k236
recorded in abbey road studios london between 2 and 19 august 1953/producers walter legge, walter jellinek and geraint jones/published in april 1954/lp matrix numbers XAX 404-405

gieseking,	lp: FCX 312/QCX 10125/WCX 1142/C 90356
piano	*other lp issues:* angel 35069/3511/emi 1C197 43020-43024M/ 3C153 00997-01007M
	cd: emi CHS 763 6882

33CX 1143/works by rachmaninov
recorded in abbey road studios london on 13-15 october 1953 and between 4 and 11 january 1954 respectively/producer walter legge/published in september 1954/lp matrix numbers XAX 466-467

galliera	**piano concerto no 2**
philharmonia	lp: FCX 281/QCX 10178/WSX 601/C 80109
anda, piano	*other lp issue:* angel 35093
	cd: testament SBT 1064

anda, piano	**preludes op 23 no 5 and op 32 no 5**
	78: LX 1603
	45: SCB 117
	lp: FCX 281/QCX 10178/WSX 601/C 80109
	other lp issue: angel 35093
	cd: testament SBT 1064

33CX 1144/piano works by beethoven, bach and brahms
recorded in abbey road studios london on 21-28 june 1951/published in april 1954/ lp matrix numbers XAX 341-342

malcuzynski,	lp: FCX 228
piano	*selections from the recital*
	78: LX 1459-1461

33CX 1145/fauré requiem
recorded in église saint roch in paris on 14-17 september 1950/producer rené challan/ published in may 1954/lp matrix numbers XLX 106-107

cluytens	lp: FCX 108/WCX 1145
chanteurs et	*other lp issue:* angel 35019
orchestre de	cd: testament SBT 1240/SBT 7247
st. eustache	
angelici	
noguéra	
duruflé, organ	

33CX 1146-1148/handel messiah
recorded in town hall huddersfield on 10-16 january 1954/producer lawrance collingwood/ published in april 1954/lp matrix numbers XAX 480-485

sargent
liverpool
philharmonic
huddersfield
choral society
morison
thomas
lewis
walker

lp: QCX 10082-10084
other lp issues: angel 3510/emi XLP 30050-30052
excerpts
45: SEL 1512/SEL 1513/SEL 1517/SEL 1518/
    SEL 1519/SEL 1520/SCB 115/SCD 2017
lp: 33CX 1613
other lp excerpts: angel 35551/emi XLP 30096/HQM 1115

33CX 1149/short piano pieces by debussy
recorded in abbey road studios london between 12 and 20 august 1953/producers walter jellinek and geraint jones/published in may 1954/lp matrix numbers XAX 384-385

gieseking,
piano

lp: FCX 296/WCX 1149/C 90357
other lp issues: angel 35026/emi 2C061 01546/3C065 01204/
    3C153 52331-52440M/F667 473-478M
cd: emi CHS 556 5852/CHS 556 8552
selections from the recital
78: LX 1618
45: SEL 1548/SEL 1552/ESBF 102
lp: emi HQM 1225
cd: emi 562 7982

33CX 1150-1152/offenbach les contes d'hoffmann
recorded in théatre des champs-élysées paris on 11-26 march 1948/producer michel de bry/ published in may 1954/lp matrix numbers XLX 3-8

cluytens
opéra-comique
orchestra
and chorus
doria, bovy,
boué, revoil.
jobin, bourdin,
musy, pernet

78: LFX 794-809
lp: FCX 137-139/WCX 1150-1152/C 90358-90360
other lp issues: american columbia SL 106/
    emi 2C153 14151-14153
cd: emi CMS 565 2602

33CX 1153/orchestral works by bizet
recorded in théatre des champs-élysées paris on 15 june 1951 and 8 october 1953 respectively/ producer rené challan/published in july 1954/lp matrix numbers XPTX 219-210

cluytens · l'arlésienne suites nos 1 and 2
orchestre · lp: DTX 145/FCX 264/QTX 103/QCX 10081/
national · WCX 1153/C 90361
other lp issue: angel 35048
cd: testament SBT 1235/SBT 7247
la jolie fille de perth suite
lp: DTX 145/QCX 10081/WCX 1153/C 90361
other lp issue: angel 35048
cd: testament SBT 1238/SBT 7247

33CX 1154/songs by schubert, brahms, wolf, hahn, fauré and chausson
recorded in abbey road studios london on 14-17 july 1953/producer walter legge/published in may 1954/lp matrix numbers XAX 458-459

dobbs · lp: FCX 299/QCX 10097
moore, piano · *other lp issue:* angel 35094
cd: testament SBT 1137

33CX 1155/string quartets by french composers
recorded in milan on 6-8 october 1953/published in july 1954/lp matrix numbers XBX 113-114

quartetto · **debussy string quartet**
italiano · lp: FCX 309/QCX 10054/WCX 1155/C 90362
cd: emi CDZ 574 7922
milhaud string quartet
lp: FCX 309/QCX 10054/WCX 1155/C 90362
cd: emi CDZ 574 7922/testament SBT 1123

33CX 1156/works by tchaikovsky and délibes
recorded in abbey road studios london on 12-15 october 1953 and on 4 january 1954 respectively/producer walter legge/published in november 1954/lp matrix numbers XAX 472-473

galliera · **piano concerto no 1**
philharmonia · lp: FCX 295/QCX 10095/WC 519/WCX 1156/
anda, piano · C 70375/C 90363
other lp issue: angel 35083
cd: testament SBT 1064

anda, piano · **waltz from coppélia, arranged for piano by dohnanyi**
45: SEL 1516/SEBQ 118/ESBF 121
lp: FCX 295/QCX 10095/WCX 1156/C 90363
other lp issue: angel 35083
cd: testament SBT 1067

33CX 1157/schubert incidental music from rosamunde
recorded in kingsway hall london on 7-9 july 1952/producer geraint jones/published in may 1954/lp matrix numbers XAX 470-471
kletzki   lp: FCX 279/QCX 10086
philharmonia   *other lp issue:* emi XLP 30041
                 excerpts
                 45: SEL 1502/SEBQ 103
                 lp: 33SX 1394

33CX 1158/saint-saens symphonic poems: la jeunesse d'hercule; danse macabre; phaeton; le rouet d'omphale
recorded in théatre des champs-élysées paris on 17-18 february 1953/published in july 1954/lp matrix numbers XLX 126-127
fourestier   lp: FCX 165
colonne   *other lp issue:* angel 35058
orchestra   cd: emi 585 2102

33CX 1159/britten variations on a theme of frank bridge; vaughan williams fantasia on a theme of thomas tallis
recorded in kingsway hall london between 10 and 23 november 1953/producer walter legge/ published in october 1954/lp matrix numbers XAX 450-451
karajan   lp: QCX 10109/WCX 1159/C 90364
philharmonia   *other lp issues:* angel 35142/toshiba EAC 37020-37038/
                     emi XLP 60002/1C053 03827M
                cd: emi CMS 763 3162/CDM 566 6012

33CX 1160/mozart piano sonatas nos 2 k280 and no 8 k310; adagio k540; variations k54 and k179
recorded in abbey road studios london between 1 and 19 august 1953/producers walter legge, walter jellinek and geraint jones/published in september 1954/lp matrix numbers XAX 406-407
gieseking,   lp: FCX 313/QCX 10127/WCX 1160/C 90365
piano   *other lp issues:* angel 35070/3511/emi 1C197 43020-43024M/
                   3C153 00997-01007M
                cd: emi CHS 763 6882

33CX 1161/rachmaninov piano concerto no 3
recorded in abbey road studios london on 26 april 1949/producer walter legge/published in july 1954/lp matrix numbers XAX 54-55
kletzki   78: LX 1352-1356/LX 8767-8771 auto/LVX 16-20
philharmonia   lp: FCX 104/WCX 1161/C 90366
malcuzynski,   *other lp issue:* american columbia ML 4369
piano   cd: dante HPC 144

33CX 1162/lieder by hugo wolf
recorded in abbey road studios london on 3-8 may 1953/producer walter legge/published in july 1954/lp matrix numbers XAX 422-423
hotter   lp: WCX 1162/C 90367
moore, piano   *other lp issue:* angel 35057
                  cd: testament SBT 1197
                  selections from the recording
                  lp: angel seraphim 6051/emi 1C147 01633-01634

33CX 1163/concerti by marcello, albinoni, gabrieli and vivaldi
recorded in milan in february 1954/published in october 1954/lp matrix numbers XBX 127-128
i musici   lp: QCX 10039
                  other lp issue: angel 35088

33CX 1164/orchestral works by tchaikovsky, smetana and ravel
recorded in kingsway hall london on 8-10 july 1952, 24 june 1953 and 23 june 1953 respectively/published in july 1954/producer geraint jones/lp matrix numbers XAX 345 and 488
kletzki   **serenade for strings**
philharmonia   lp: FCX 356/WCX 1164/C 90368
                  other lp issue: emi MFP 2045
                  excerpt
                  45: SEL 1535
                  the bartered bride overture
                  78: LX 1594
                  45: SEL 1510
                  lp: WCX 1164/C 90368
                  other lp issue: emi MFP 2045
                  boléro
                  lp: WCX 1164/C 90368
                  other lp issue: emi MFP 2045

33CX 1165/brahms violin concerto
recorded in kingsway hall london on 15-17 february 1954/producer walter legge/published in october 1954/lp matrix numbers XAX 524-525

kletzki	lp: QCX 10102/WCX 1165/C 90369
philharmonia	*other lp issue:* angel 35137
martzy, violin	cd: testament SBT 1037

33CX 1166/menotti amelia al ballo
recorded in milan in march 1954/published in october 1954/lp matrix numbers XBX 139-140

sanzogno	lp: QCX 10070/WCX 1166/C 90370
la scala	*other lp issue:* angel 35140
orchestra	cd: testament SBT 1179
and chorus	
carosio, prandelli,	
panerai, campi	

33CX 1167/orchestral works by borodin and ippolitov-ivanov
recorded in kingsway hall london on 3 february 1954 and between 16 and 23 june 1953 respectively/producer geraint jones/published in october 1954/lp matrix numbers XAX 523 and 344

kletzki	**borodin symphony no 2**
philharmonia	*other lp issue:* angel 35145
	cd: testament SBT 1048
	ippolitov-ivanov caucasian sketches
	lp: FCX 356
	other lp issue: angel 35145

33CX 1168/beethoven string quartets op 18 nos 1 and 2
recorded in studio magellan paris on 8 december 1953 and 15-17 november 1953 respectively/producer norbert gamsohn/published in october 1954/lp matrix numbers XAX 503-504

hungarian	lp: FCX 240/WCX 1168/C 90371
string quartet	*other lp issue:* angel 35106
	cd: emi CZS 767 2362

33CX 1169/ catalogue number appears not to have been allocated

33CX 1170/various concerti by vivaldi
recorded in milan in february 1954/published in september 1954/lp matrix numbers XBX 125-126

i musici	lp: QCX 10038
	other lp issue: angel 35087

33CX 1171/works by scarlatti, cimarosa and paisiello
published in september 1954/lp matrix numbers XBX 111-112
caracciolo   lp: QCX 10036
orchestra   *other lp issue:* angel 35141
alessandro
scarlatti

33CX 1172/beethoven string quartets op 18 nos 3 and 4
recorded in studio magellan paris on 15-16 october 1953 and 6-8 december 1953 respectively/producer norbert gamsohn/published in november 1954/lp matrix numbers XAX 505-506
hungarian   lp: FCX 241/WCX 1172/C 90372
string quartet   *other lp issue:* angel 35107
                  cd: emi CZS 767 2362

33CX 1173/orchestral works by bizet
recorded in théatre des champs elysées paris between 8 and 23 october 1953/producer rené challan/published in september 1954/lp matrix numbers XLX 196-197
cluytens   **symphony in c**
orchestre   lp: FCX 264/FCX 273/FC 25110/WCX 1173/C 90373
national   *other lp issue:* angel 35119
                   cd: emi CZS 575 1062/testament SBT 1235/SBT 7247
                   patrie overture
                   lp: FCX 273/WCX 1173/C 90373
                   other lp issue: angel 35119
                   cd: testament SBT 1235/SBT 7247

33CX 1174/mendelssohn a midsummer night's dream, incidental music
recorded in kingsway hall london on 4-5 february 1954/producer lawrance collingwood/ published in september 1954/lp matrix numbers XAX 534-535
kletzki   lp: FCX 366/WCX 1174/C 90374
philharmonia   *other lp issues:* angel 35146/emi XLP 30025
bbc chorus   *excerpts*
cole   78: LX 1615
mcloughlin   45: SEL 1534
                   lp: FC 25044
                   other lp excerpts: emi RLS 7701/1C141-43327-43229M

33CX 1175/works by britten and saint-saens
recorded in abbey road studios london on 11-13 september 1952 and 8 january 1954 respectively/producer walter legge/published in february 1955/lp matrix numbers XAX 495-496

markevitch	**young person's guide to the orchestra**
philharmonia	lp: FCX 376/QCX 10238
pears, narrator	*other lp issues:* angel 35135/emi XLP 30064
	recording completed on 8 june 1954

markevitch	**le carnaval des animaux**
philharmonia	lp: FCX 376/FC 25047/QCX 10238
anda and siki, pianos	*other lp issues:* angel 35135

33CX 1176/piano works by bartok
recorded in abbey road studios london on 11 january 1954 and 8-9 january 1955/producer walter legge/lp matrix numbers XAX 474-475

anda, piano **sonatina**
lp: FCX 347/WCX 1176/C 90375
other lp issue: angel 35126
cd: testament SBT 1067
for children, volume one
lp: FCX 347/WCX 1176/C 90375
other lp issue: angel 35126
cd: testament SBT 1065

33CX 1177/catalogue number appears not to have been allocated

33CX 1178/orchestral works by mozart
recorded in abbey road studios and kingsway hall london respectively on 17-18 november 1953/producer walter legge/published in november 1954/lp matrix numbers XAX 456-457

karajan	**sinfonia concertante k297b**
philharmonia	lp: FCX 308/QCX 10101/WCX 1178/C 90376
sutcliffe, oboe	*other lp issues:* angel 35098/toshiba EAC 37001-37019/
walton, clarinet	emi XLP 60004/RLS 7715/1C137 54364-54367M
james, bassoon	cd: emi CMS 763 3162
brain, horn	

karajan	**serenade no 13 "eine kleine nachtmusik"**
philharmonia	45: SELW 1812/C 50543
	lp: FCX 308/FC 25107/QCX 10101/WCX 1178/WC 537/
	C 90376/C 70391
	other lp issues: angel 35098/toshiba EAC 37001-37019
	cd: emi CMS 763 4562

33CX 1179-1181/bellini norma
recorded in teatro alla scala milan between 23 april and 3 may 1954/producer walter legge/ published in september 1954/lp matrix numbers XBX 143-148

serafin	lp: FCX 351-353/QCX 10088-10090/WCX 1179-1181/
la scala	C 90377-90379
orchestra	*other lp issues:* angel 3517/angel seraphim 6037/emi SLS 5115/
and chorus	EX 29 00663/2C163 00944-00946/2C163 03565-03567/
callas	2C163 52780-52787/3C163 00944-00946
stignani	cd: emi CDS 747 3048/CDS 556 2712/CMS 252 9432/
filippeschi	naxos 811.0325-0327
rossi-lemeni	*excerpts*
	45: SEL 1536/SEL 1550/SEL 1586/SELW 1550/C 50156/
	ESBF 17098/SEBQ 137/SEBQ 154/SEBQ 183/
	SCBQ 3041/SCBQ 3060
	lp: FCX 662/QCX 10255/WSX 521/C 80443
	other lp excerpts: angel 35379/3814/emi SLS 5057/SLS 5104/
	1C061 00741/1C053 01017M/1C191 01593-01594M/
	3C063 00741/3C063 01017
	cd: emi CDS 749 6002/CDS 754 1032/CMS 763 2442/
	CMS 764 4182/CMS 565 5342/CZS 252 1642/562 5642

33CXS 1182-33CX 1183/mascagni cavalleria rusticana
recorded in basilica santa eufemia milan between 16 and 25 june 1953/producer dino olivieri/published in october 1954/lp matrix numbers XBX 129-131

serafin	lp: FCX 266-257/QCX 10046-10047/WCX 1182-1183/
la scala	C 90380-90381
orchestra	*other lp issues:* angel 3509/3528/emi SLS 819/EX 29 12693/
and chorus	2C163 00415-00416/3C165 00415-00416
callas	cd: emi CDS 747 9818/CDS 556 2872/CMS 252 9432/
canali	notablu 93 5151
di stefano	*excerpts*
panerai	45: SEL 1549/SEL 1555/SEL 1563/SEL 1567
	lp: 33CX 1402/33CX 1725/WSX 520/C 80442
	other lp excerpts: angel 35345/36966/emi SLS 856/
	1C061 00741/1C063 00721/1C191 01433-01434M/
	3C063 00438/3C063 00741/3C065 17902
	cd: emi CDC 754 7022/CMS 763 2442/CMS 565 5342/
	CMS 565 7462/CZS 252 6142/562 5642/566 6882
	recording completed on 3-4 august 1953

33CX 1184/catalogue number appears not to have been allocated

33CX 1185/beethoven piano sonatas nos 31 and 32
recorded in abbey road studios london on 26 february-4 march 1954/producer walter jellinek/
published in september 1957/lp matrix numbers XAX 574-575
siki, piano

33CXS 1186-33CX 1187/j.strauss wiener blut
recorded in kingsway hall london between 21 and 31 may 1954/producer walter legge/
published in december 1954/lp matrix numbers XAX 576-578
ackermann   lp: WCX 1186-1187/WSX 539-540/C 90382-90383/
philharmonia   C 80518-80519
and chorus   *other lp issues:* angel 3519/emi SXDW 3042/
schwarzkopf   1C149 03180-03181
loose   cd: emi CDH 769 5292/CHS 567 5322
köth   *excerpts*
gedda   lp: WSX 608/C 80113
kunz   *other lp excerpts:* emi SMVP 6075/RLS 763/154 6133/
dönch   1C047 01954/1C147 03580-03581/1C151 43160-43163M

33CX 1188/beethoven piano concerto no 3
recorded in théatre des champs elysées paris on 9-10 march 1954/producer norbert gamsohn/
published in november 1954/lp matrix numbers XLX 244-245
cluytens   lp: FCX 300/FCX 30122/QCX 10220/WCX 1188/C 90384
conservatoire   *other lp issues:* angel 35131/emi 1C053 11626/
orchestra   2C045 11626
gilels, piano   cd: emi 483 4182

33CX 1189/tchaikovsky manfred symphony
recorded in kingsway hall london on 29 january 1954/producer lawrance collingwood/
published in november 1954/lp matrix numbers XAX 497-498
kletzki   lp: FCX 348
philharmonia   *other lp issues:* angel 35167/emi XLP 30015
                   cd: testament SBT 1048
                   recording completed on 12 february 1954

33CX 1190/franck variations symphoniques; d'indy symphony on a french mountain song
recorded in théatre des champs elysées paris between 15 and 29 june 1953/producer rené challan/published in november 1954/lp matrix numbers XLX 177-178

cluytens
conservatoire
orchestra
ciccolini, piano

lp: FCX 213
other lp issues: angel 35104/emi 2C045 11204
cd: emi CZS 573 1772/testament SBT 1237/SBT 7247

33CX 1191/beethoven string quartets op 18 nos 5 and 6
recorded in studio magellan paris between 9 and 15 december 1953/producer norbert gamsohn/published in january 1955/lp matrix numbers XAX 507-508

hungarian
string quartet

lp: FCX 242/WCX 1191/C 90385
other lp issue: angel 35108
cd: emi CZS 767 2362

33CX 1192/concerti by rossini, galuppi, tartini and marcello
recorded in milan in february 1954/published in november 1954/lp matrix numbers XBX 123-124

i musici   lp: FCX 303/QCX 10037

33CX 1193/christmas carols and sacred music
recorded in abbey road studios london between 22 february and 1 march 1954/producer alec robertson/published in november 1954/lp matrix numbers XAX 530-531

dykes bower
saint paul's
cathedral
choir

other lp issue: angel 3516
recording completed on 12 march 1954

33CX 1194/beethoven violin concerto
recorded in stockholm on 10-11 june 1954/producer edward fowler/published in december 1954/lp matrix numbers XCSX 103-104

ehrling
stockholm
festival
orchestra
oistrakh, violin

lp: FCX 354/FCX 30077/QCX 10126/WCX 1194/C 90386
other lp issues: angel 35162/hmv LALP 231
cd: testament SBT 1032

33CX 1195-1196/verdi messa da requiem
recorded in teatro alla scala milan between 18 and 27 june 1954/producer walter legge/ published in december 1954/lp matrix numbers XBX 160-163

de sabata	lp: FCX 361-362/QCX 10104-10105/WCX 1195-1196/
la scala	C 90387-90388
orchestra	*other lp issues:* angel 3520/emi 1C147 00937-00938/
and chorus	RLS 100 9373
schwarzkopf	cd: emi CHS 565 5062/teorema TH 121 123-124
dominguez	*excerpts*
di stefano	lp: emi 1C187 28985-28986M
siepi	cd: emi CDM 763 6572/CMS 763 7902

33CX 1197/homage to diaghilev volume one
recorded in abbey road studios london on 12 may 1954, 3 march 1954, 3 june 1954 and 23 april 1954 respectively/producers walter legge and walter jellinek/ published in november 1954/lp matrix numbers XAX 568-569

markevitch **satie parade**
philharmonia lp: FCX 357
other lp issue: angel 3518
cd: testament SBT 1060

weber aufforderung zum tanz, arranged by berlioz
lp: FCX 357/FC 25087
other lp issues: angel 3518/emi XLP 30007
cd: testament SBT 1105

debussy prélude a l'apres-midi d'un faune
lp: FCX 357
other lp issue: angel 3518
cd: testament SBT 1105

ravel daphnis et chloé, second suite
lp; FCX 357
other lp issue: angel 3518
cd: testament SBT 1105
recording completed on 3 june 1954

33CX 1198/homage to diaghilev volume two
recorded in abbey road studios london on 13-15 may 1954, 15 may 1954, 13 may 1954 and 14 november 1951/producers walter legge and walter jellinek/published in november 1954/lp matrix numbers XAX 570-571

markevitch	**tchaikovsky swan lake, ballet suite**
philharmonia	lp: FCX 358
	other lp issue: angel 3518
	cd: testament SBT 1107
	chopin mazurka from les sylphides, arranged by douglas
	lp: FCX 358
	other lp issue: angel 3518
	cd: testament SBT 1105
	tommasini the good-humoured ladies, ballet arranged by scarlatti
	lp: FCX 358
	other lp issue: angel 3518
	cd: testament SBT 1105
	falla miller's dance from el sombrero de 3 picos
	see 33CX 1049

33CX 1199/homage to diaghilev volume three
recorded in abbey road studios london on 27-29 april 1954 and 8 june 1954 (stravinsky)/ producers walter legge and walter jellinek/published in november 1954/lp matrix numbers XAX 572-573

markevitch	**prokofiev le pas d'acier, ballet suite**
philharmonia	lp: FCX 359
	other lp issue: angel 3518
	cd: emi CZS 762 6472
	liadov kikimora
	lp: FCX 359
	other lp issue: angel 3518
	cd: testament SBT 1060
	stravinsky danse russe, chez pétrouchka and fete populaire from petrushka
	lp: FCX 359
	other lp issue: angel 3518
	cd: emi CZS 762 6472

33CX 1200/catalogue number allocated to a pathé/french columbia recording of works by stravinsky and richard strauss with orchestre national and chorus conducted by jascha horenstein; according to deryk barker this was published only in france, usa and australia

33CX 1201/sonatas for violin and piano
recorded in stockholm in june 1953/producer edward fowler/published in march 1955/ lp matrix numbers XCSX 101-102

oistrakh, violin	**franck sonata in a**
yampolsky, piano	lp: FCX 355/FCX 30269/FC 25042/QCX 10160/ WCX 1201/C 90389
	other lp issues: angel 35163/hmv LALP 497
	szymanowski sonata no 1
	lp: FCX 355/FCX 30269/QCX 10160/WCX 1201/ C 90389
	other lp issues: angel 35163/melodiya D 05180-05181/ hmv LALP 497/bruno 14043/colosseum CRLP 190
	cd: testament SBT 1116

33CX 1202/piano works by liszt
recorded in abbey road studios london between 2 and 11 january 1954/producer walter legge/published in june 1955/lp matrix numbers XAX 476-477

anda, piano	**piano sonata; mephisto waltz; la campanella, arranged by busoni**
	lp: FCX 331/QCX 10189/WCX 1202/C 90390
	other lp issue: angel 35127
	cd: testament SBT 1067
	étude de concert no 3
	45: SEL 1516/SEBQ 118/ESBF 121
	lp: FCX 331/QCX 10189/WCX 1202/C 90390
	other lp issue: angel 35127
	cd: testament SBT 1067

33CX 1203/beethoven string quartet op 59 no 1
recorded in studio magellan paris on 22-23 september 1953/producer norbert gamsohn/ published in february 1955/lp matrix numbers XAX 509-510

hungarian string quartet	lp: FCX 243/WCX 1203/C 90391
	other lp issue: angel 35109
	cd: emi CZS 767 2362

33CX 1204/puccini arias from manon lescaut, turandot, gianni schicchi, la boheme and madama butterfly and suor angelica
recorded in town hall watford on 15-21 september 1954/producer walter legge/published in december 1954/lp matrix numbers XAX 602-603

serafin
philharmonia
callas

lp: FCX 377/FCX 30079/QCX 10108/WCX 1204/C 90392
other lp issues: angel 35195/emi ALP 3799/1C053 00417/ 2C057 00417/2C165 54178-54188/3C065 00417
cd: emi CDC 747 9662/CDS 749 4532/562 7942/566 6182
selections from the recital
45: SEL 1533/SEL 1546/SCD 2140/SELW 1533/ SELW 1546/C 50151/C 50154/SEBQ 127/ SEBQ 159/ESBF 173/ESBF 17060
lp: FC 25059/C 90413
other lp selections: angel 36930/emi SLS 5057/SLS 5104
cd: emi CDS 749 6002/CDC 754 7022/CDS 754 1032/ CDC 555 0162/CZS 252 6142/CDM 565 7472/ CMS 565 7462/CMS 565 9522/CMS 565 5342/ CMS 557 0622/562 5642

33CX 1205/bliss music for strings; miracle in the gorbals ballet suite
recorded in kingsway hall london on 26-28 january 1954/producer alec robertson/published in january 1955/lp matrix numbers XAX 528-529

bliss
philharmonia

other lp issues: angel 35136/emi HQM 1009

33CX 1206/berlioz symphonie fantastique
recorded in kingsway hall london between 7 and 21 july 1954/producer walter legge/ published in april 1955/lp matrix numbers XAX 639-640

karajan
philharmonia

lp: FCX 396/QCX 10136/WCX 1206/C 90393
other lp issues: angel 35202/world records TP 625/toshiba EAC 37001-37019/emi RLS 7715/1C137 54364-54367M
cd: emi CMS 763 3162/CDM 566 5982

33CX 1207/mahler symphony no 1
recorded in tel aviv on 10-12 may 1954/producer lawrance collingwood/published in april 1955/lp matrix numbers XTVX 1-2

kletzki
israel
philharmonic

lp: FCX 378/WCX 1207/C 90394
other lp issues: angel 35180/emi MFP 2051
recording completed on 25-27 may 1954

33CX 1208/orchestral works by tchaikovsky, mussorgsky and borodin
recorded in salle de la mutualité paris in 1954/producer rené challan/published in june 1955/ lp matrix numbers XLX 248-249

markevitch	**romeo and juliet; night on bare mountain**
orchestre	lp: FCX 349/WCX 1208/C 90395
national	*other lp issue:* angel 35144

markevitch	**polovtsian dances/prince igor**
orchestre	lp: FCX 349/WCX 1208/C 90395
national	*other lp issue:* angel 35144
and chorus	

33CX 1209-1210/catalogue numbers appear not to have been allocated

33CXS 1211-33CX 1212/leoncavallo i pagliacci
recorded in teatro alla scala milan on 12-17 june 1954/producer walter legge/published in september 1955/lp matrix numbers XBX 157-159

serafin	lp: FCX 410-411/QCX 10132-10133/WCX 1211-1212/
la scala	C 90396-90397
orchestra	*other lp issues:* angel 3527/3528/emi SLS 819/2C163 00418-
and chorus	00419/3C163 00418-00419
callas	cd: emi CDS 747 9818/CDS 556 2872/CMS 252 9432/
di stefano	notablu 93 5152
monti	*excerpts*
gobbi	45: SEL 1555/SELW 1555/SELW 1562/C 50482/C 50484/
panerai	SEBQ 157/SEBQ 172/SEBQ 174
	lp: 33CX 1402/FCX 929/FCX 30152/QCX 10230/
	QCX 10441/QCX 10447/WSX 520/WSX 622/WC 610/
	C 80442/C 80689/C 70400
	other lp excerpts: angel 35345/3814/emi SLS 5104/1C187
	28985-28986M/1C191 01593-01594M/3C063 00438
	cd: emi CDC 555 2162/CMS 565 7462

33CX 1213/songs by debussy, bachelet, fauré, chausson, duparc and bizet
recorded in abbey road studios london on 6 july 1954/producers walter legge and alec robertson/published in march 1955/lp matrix numbers XAX 583-584

merriman	*other lp issue:* angel 35217
moore, piano	cd: testament SBT 1134

33CX 1214/catalogue number appears not to have been allocated

33CX 1215-1216/rossini l'italiana in algeri
recorded in teatro alla scala milan on 5-12 august 1954/producer walter legge/published in february 1955/lp matrix numbers XBX 168-171

giulini	lp: FCX 388-389/QCX 10111-10112/WCX 1215-1216/
la scala	C 90398-90399
orchestra	*other lp issues:* angel 3529/angel seraphim 6119/emi RLS 747/
and chorus	3C163 00981-00982
simionato	cd: emi CHS 764 0412
sciutti	*excerpts*
masini, valletti,	lp: emi 3C053 18031
petri, campi	

33CX 1217/works by saint-saens and mozart
recorded in théatre des champs elysées paris on 11 march 1954 /producer peter de jongh/ published in february 1955/lp matrix numbers XLX 246-247

cluytens	**saint-saens piano concerto no 2**
conservatoire	lp: FCX 301/FC 25033/QCX 301/WCX 1217/C 90400
orchestra	*other lp issue:* angel 35132
gilels, piano	cd: testament SBT 1029
gilels, piano	**mozart piano sonata no 16 k570**
	lp: FCX 301/QCX 301/WCX 1217/C 90400
	other lp issues: angel 35132/emi 1C153 11627-11628M
	cd: testament SBT 1089

33CX 1218/poulenc les mamelles de tirésias
recorded in théatre des champs elysées paris between 14 and 25 september 1953/producer rené challan/published in february 1955/lp matrix numbers XLX 220-221

cluytens	lp: FCX 230
opéra comique	*other lp issue:* angel 35090
orchestra	cd: emi CDM 565 5652
and chorus	
duval	
giraudeau	

33CX 1219/orchestral works by mendelssohn
recorded in tel aviv on may 9-10 1954/producer lawrance collingwood/published in april 1955/lp matrix numbers XTVX 3-4

kletzki	**symphony no 3 "scotch"**
israel	lp: FCX 381
philharmonic	*other lp issue:* angel 35183
	meeresstille glückliche fahrt overture
	lp: FCX 381
	other lp issue: angel 35183
	cd: emi CZS 575 4682
	recordings completed on 25 may 1954

33CX 1220/mozart piano sonatas nos 13 k333 and 14 k457; variations k353; fantasia k475
recorded in abbey road studios london between 4 and 19 august 1953/producers walter legge, walter jellinek and geraint jones/published in march 1955/lp matrix numbers XAX 408-409

gieseking,	lp: FCX 314/WCX 1220/C 90401
piano	*other lp issues:* angel 35071/3511/emi 1C197 03133-03137M/ 3C153 00997-01007M
	cd: emi CHS 763 6882

33CX 1221/works by manuel de falla
recorded in maison de la murualité paris on 18 december 1953/producer rené challan/published in june 1955/lp matrix numbers XLX 238-239

halffter	**noches en los jardines de espana**
orchestre	lp: FCX 272
national	*other lp issue:* angel 35134
ciccolini, piano	cd: emi CZS 569 2352
halffter	**homenajes para orquesta**
orchestre	lp: FCX 272
national	*other lp issue:* angel 35134
	cd: emi CZS 569 2352

33CXS 1222-33CX 1223/schubert winterreise
recorded in abbey road studios london on 26-29 may 1954/producers walter legge and walter jellinek/published in april 1955/lp matrix numbers XAX 564-566
hotter
moore, piano
                lp: WCX 1222-1223/C 90402-90403
                other lp issues: angel 3521/angel seraphim 6051/ emi XLP 30102-30103/1C147 01274-01275M
                cd: emi CDM 566 9852
                selection from the cycle
                lp: C 70479

33CX 1224-1225/j.strauss eine nacht in venedig
recorded in kingsway hall london on 25-31 may 1954/producer walter legge/published in september 1955/lp matrix numbers XAX 618-621
ackermann
philharmonia
and chorus
schwarzkopf
loose
gedda
kunz
dönch
                lp: WCX 1224-1225/WSX 531-532/C 90404-90405/ C 80510-80511
                other lp issues: angel 3530/emi SXDW 3043/1C149 03171-01372/5C181 03049-03050
                cd: emi CDH 769 5302/CHS 567 5322
                excerpts
                lp: emi SMVP 6075/RLS 763/1C151 43160-43163M/ 1C047 01954/2C053 00478
                recording completed on 25 september 1954

33CX 1226/arabella, scenes from the opera
recorded in kingsway hall london between 27 september and 6 october 1954/producer walter legge/published in march 1955/lp matrix numbers XAX 606-607
matacic
philharmonia
schwarzkopf
felbermayer
gedda
metternich
schlott
                lp: 33CX 1897/FCX 385/WCX 1226/WSX 571/ C 80619/C 90406
                other lp issues: angel 35094/world records OH 199/ emi RLS 751/1C037 03297
                excerpts
                45: SEL 1579/SCBW 802/C 30166
                lp: emi RLS 154 6133
                cd: emi CDH 761 0012/CDM 565 5772/585 8252

33CX 1227/orchestral works by beethoven
recorded in kingsway hall london on 12-13 november 1953 and 20 june 1953 respectively/ producer walter legge/ published in february 1956/ lp matrix numbers XAX 579-580

karajan   **symphony no 2**
philharmonia   lp: FCX 420/QCX 10185/WCX 1227/C 90407
other lp issues: angel 35196/world records SM 143-149/ emi SLS 5053/1C181 01830-01836Y/toshiba EAC 37001-37019
cd: emi CMS 763 3102
recording completed on 23 november 1953

coriolan overture
lp: FCX 420/FC 25107/QCX 10185/WCX 1227/WC 511/ C 90407/C 70363
other lp issues: angel 35196/emi SLS 5053/1C181 01380-01386Y/ toshiba EAC 37001-37019
cd: emi CMS 763 3102
recording completed on 15 july 1953

33CX 1228/orchestral works by stravinsky
recorded in salle de la mutualité paris on 12-13 march 1954 and 22 march 1954 respectively/ producer rené challan/.published in march 1955/ lp matrix numbers XLX 250-251

markevitch   **le baiser de la fée**
orchestre   lp: FCX 350
national   *other lp issue:* angel 35143

pulcinella suite
lp: FCX 350
other lp issue: angel 35143
cd: emi CZS 762 6472

33CX 1229/debussy 3 nocturnes; prélude a l'apres-midi d'un faune; marche écossaise
recorded in théatre des champs-élysées paris on 7-8 april 1953/producer rené challan/ published in march 1955/ lp matrix numbers XLX 149-150

inghelbrecht   lp: FCX 216
orchestre   *other lp issue:* angel 35103
national   cd: testament SBT 1212
and chorus

33CX 1230/haydn string quartets op 3 no 5 and op 76 no 2
recorded in august 1954/published in march 1955/lp matrix numbers XBX 155-156
quartetto   lp: QCX 10114/WCX 1230/C 90408
italiano   *other lp issue:* angel 35297

33CX 1231/operatic arias by boito, giordano, cilea, catalani, verdi, rossini, délibes and meyerbeer
recorded in town hall watford on 17-20 september 1954/producer walter legge/published in september 1955/lp matrix numbers XAX 622-623
serafin   lp: FCX 430/FCX 30088/QCX 10129/WCX 1231/C 90409
philharmonia   *other lp issues:* angel 35233/emi ALP 3824/1C053 01013/
callas   3C065 01013/2C165 54178-54188
                 cd: emi CDC 747 2822/CDS 749 4532/566 6182
                 selections from the recital
                 45: SEL 1581/SELW 1817/C 50550/SCBQ 3035/SEBQ 177/
                     SEBQ 265/ESBF 17110
                 lp: FC 25029
                 other lp selections: emi SLS 869/SLS 5018/SLS 5057/
                     1C187 01398-01399
                 cd: emi CDC 555 0162/CDC 555 2162/CDC 754 7022/
                     CDM 565 7472/CMS 565 5342/CMS 565 7462/
                     CMS 565 9522/CMS 763 2442/CZS 252 6142/
                     CMS 557 0622/562 5642

33CX 1232-1233/bizet les pecheurs de perles
recorded in maison de la mutualité paris on 22-30 june 1954/producer rené challan/published in may 1955/lp matrix numbers XLX 285-288
cluytens   lp: FCX 344-345/WCX 1232-1233/C 90410-90411
opéra comique *other lp issue:* angel 3524
orchestra   cd: emi CMS 565 2662
and chorus
angelici
legay
dens
noguéra

33CX 1234/catalogue number allocated to a recording of bach solo sonatas and partitas by johanna martzy which was subsequently not passed for release; martzy recorded the works later (see 33CX 1286-1288)

33CX 1235/piano concerti by mozart
recorded in abbey road studios london on 22-24 august 1953/producer walter legge/ published in october 1955/lp matrix numbers XAX 631 and 638

rosbaud	**concerto no 20 k466**
philharmonia	lp: FCX 30003/QCX 10181/WCX 1235/C 90412
gieseking,	*other lp issue:* angel 35215
piano	cd: emi CHS 763 7092
	concerto no 25 k503
	lp: FCX 30003/FC 25114/QCX 10181/WCX 1235/C 90412
	other lp issue: angel 35215
	cd: emi CHS 763 7092

33CX 1236/beethoven string quartets op 59 no 2 and op 95
recorded in studio magellan paris on 9-10 september 1953 and 28 september 1953 respectively/producer norbert gamsohn/published in april 1955/lp matrix numbers XAX 511-512

hungarian	lp: FCX 244/WCX 1236/C 90413
string quartet	*other lp issue:* angel 35110
	cd: emi CZS 767 2362

33CX 1237/madrigals and sacred music
recorded in abbey road studios london on 22 february-1 march 1954/producer alec robertson/ published in april 1955/lp matrix numbers XAX 532-533

dykes bower	*other lp issue:* angel 3516
saint paul's	*recording completed on 12 march 1954; section of the philharmonia*
cathedral	*orchestra accompanies sections from haydn nelson mass*
choir	

33CX 1238/piano concerti by chopin and liszt
recorded in maison de la mutialité paris on 28 may-1 june 1954 and 28 november 1954 respectively/producer rené challan/published in april 1955/lp matrix numbers XLX 281-282

tzipine	**chopin piano concerto no 1**
conservatoire	lp: FCX 341
orchestra	*other lp issue:* angel 35168
francois, piano	cd: emi CZS 762 9512
	liszt piano concerto no 1
	lp: FCX 341
	other lp issue: angel 35168

33CX 1239-1240/bach the four orchestral suites
recorded in kingsway hall london between 19 november and 4 december 1954/producers walter legge, john hughes and alan melville/published in april 1955/lp matrix numbers XAX 643-646
klemperer lp: FCX 433-434/QCX 10137 and 10139/WCX 1239-1240/
philharmonia C 90414-90415
other lp issue: angel 3536
cd: testament SBT 2131

33CX 1241/orchestral works by hindemith and brahms
recorded in kingsway hall london on 7-8 october 1954/producers walter legge and walter jellinek/published in november 1955/lp matrix numbers XAX 628-629
klemperer **nobilissima visione**
philharmonia lp: FCX 418/WCX 1241/WC 514/C 90416/C 70366
other lp issues: angel 35221/angel seraphim 60004
cd: emi CMS 763 8352
haydn variations
lp: FCX 418/WCX 1241/WC 514/C 90416/C 70366
other lp issues: angel 35221/angel seraphim 60004
cd: emi CDH 764 1462/562 7422

33CX 1242/mozart piano sonatas nos 1 k279 and 9 k311; variations k613; fantasia and fugue k394
recorded in abbey road studios london between 1 and 10 august 1953/producers walter legge, walter jellinek and geraint jones/published in may 1955/lp matrix numbers XAX 410-411
gieseking, lp: FCX 315/QCX 10346/WCX 1242/C 90417
piano *other lp issues:* angel 35072/3511/emi 1C197 03133-03137M/
3C153 00997-01007M
cd: emi CHS 763 6882

33CX 1243/recital of spanish songs
recorded in abbey road studios london on 8-9 july 1954/producer alec robertson/published in may 1955/lp matrix numbers XAX 585-586
merriman *other lp issue:* angel 35208
moore, piano cd: testament SBT 1134

33CX 1244/brahms string quartet op 67
recorded in august 1954/published in may 1955/lp matrix numbers XBX 153-154
quartetto lp: QCX 10113/WCX 1244/C 90418
italiano *other lp issue:* angel 35184

33CX 1245/bartok string quartets nos 1 and 2
recorded in wigmore hall london on 2-10 july 1954/producer alan melville/published in april 1956/lp matrix numbers XAX 662-663

vegh string	lp: WCX 1245/C 90419
quartet	*other lp issue:* angel 35240

33CX 1246/lalo symphonie espagnole
recorded in abbey road studios london on 13-14 november 1954/producers walter legge and lawrance collingwood/published in may 1955/lp matrix numbers XAX 651-652

martinon	lp: FCX 427/QCX 10151/WCX 1246/C 90420
philharmonia	*other lp issues:* angel 35205/angel seraphim 60332/
oistrakh,	emi XLP 30109
violin	cd: testament SBT 1116

33CX 1247-1248/elgar the dream of gerontius
recorded in town hall huddersfield on 4-6 november 1954/producer lawrance collingwood/published in may 1955/lp matrix numbers XAX 658-661

sargent	*other lp issue:* angel 3543
liverpool	cd: emi CHS 763 3762
philharmonic	
huddersfield	
choral society	
thomas	
lewis	
cameron	

33CX 1249/bach chorale preludes
recorded in église sainte aurélie strasbourg on 16 march 1937/producer walter legge/published in may 1955/lp matrix numbers XLX 33-34

schweitzer,	78: ROX 158-164/ROX 8018-8024
organ	*other 78rpm issue:* american columbia M 310
	selections from the recording
	lp: emi HLM 7003/1C047 01265M

this recording formed one of the pre-war columbia society editions

33CX 1250-1251/mahler symphony no 9; schoenberg verklärte nacht
recorded in tel aviv on 16-24 may 1954/producer lawrance collingwood/published in may 1955/lp matrix numbers XTVX 3-6

kletzki lp: FCX 379-380/WCX 1250-1251/C 90422-90423
israel *other lp issue:* angel 3526
philharmonic

33CX 1252/le groupe des six volume one
recorded in maison de la mutualité paris on 6-10 november 1953/producer rené challan/ published in june 1955/lp matrix numbers XLX 226-227

tzipine **tailleferre ouverture; honegger prelude fugue et postlude**
conservatoire lp: FCX 264
orchestra *other lp issue:* angel 3515
 cd: emi 585 2042

tzipine **poulenc sechéresses**
conservatoire lp: FCX 264
orchestra *other lp issue:* angel 3515
brasseur choir cd: emi 585 2042

tzipine **durey le printemps au fond de la mer**
conservatoire lp: FCX 264
orchestra *other lp issue:* angel 3515
duval cd: emi 585 2042

33CX 1253/le groupe des six volume two
recorded in maison de la mutualité paris on 6-10 november 1953/producer rené challan/ published in june 1955/lp matrix numbers XLX 228-229

tzipine **auric phedre; milhaud symphony no 2**
conservatoire lp: FCX 265
orchestra *other lp issue:* angel 3515
 cd: emi 585 2042

33CX 1254/beethoven string quartets op 59 no 3 and op 74
recorded in studio magellan paris on 28 september-1 october 1953 and 11 september 1953 respectively/producer norbert gamsohn/published in june 1955

hungarian lp: FCX 245/WCX 1254/C 90424
string quartet *other lp issue:* angel 35111
 cd: emi CZS 767 2362
 recording of op 74 completed on 1 october 1953

33CX 1255/brahms klavierstücke op 76; fantasien op 116
recorded in kongresshalle zürich on 20-23 june 1951/producer walter legge/published in june 1955/lp matrix numbers XZX 16-17

gieseking, lp: FCX 200/QCX 200/WCX 1255/C 90425
piano
other lp issues: angel 35028/angel seraphim 6117/
    emi 1C147 01575-01576/3C153 52434-52441
intermezzo op 116 no 4 also issued in 78rpm format on LX 1586 and GQX 11534

33CX 1256/piano music by brahms
recorded in kongresshalle zürich on 20-23 june 1951/producer walter legge/published in june 1955/lp matrix numbers XZX 9 and 18

gieseking, **klavierstücke op 118**
piano
lp: FCX 201/QCX 201/WCX 1256/C 90426/C 70489
other lp issues: angel 35029/angel seraphim 6117/
    emi 1C147 01575-01576/3C153 52434-52441

klavierstücke op 119
78: LB 135 and LX 1581
lp: FCX 201/QCX 201/WCX 1256/C 90426/C 70489
other lp issues: angel 35029/angel seraphim 6117/
    emi 1C147 01575-01576/3C153 52434-52441

2 rhapsodien op 79
78: LX 1561 and LX 1586
lp: FCX 201/QCX 201/WCX 1256/C 90426
other lp issues: angel 35029/angel seraphim 6117/
    emi 1C147 01575-01576/3C153 52434-52441

brahms piano music on 33CX 1255-1256 also published on cd by toshiba in japan

33CX 1257/symphonies by mozart
recorded in kingsway hall london on 5-9 october 1954/producers walter legge and walter jellinek/published in october 1955/lp matrix numbers XAX 626-627

klemperer **symphony no 41 "jupiter"**
philharmonia
lp: FCX 426/FC 25105/QCX 10177/WCX 1257/
    WSX 610/WC 516/C 90427/C 80115/C 70368
other lp issue: angel 35209
cd: testament SBT 1093
recording completed on 24 november 1954

symphony no 29
lp: FCX 426/QCX 10177/WCX 1257/WCX 523/
    C 90427/C 91148
other lp issue: angel 35209
cd: testament SBT 1093

columbia in germany appear to have issued symphony no 29 in stereophonic versions numbered STC 90548 and STC 91069, making this chronologically the earliest stereophonic columbia recording to have been published (information from michael gray)

33CX 1258-1260/verdi la forza del destino
recorded in teatro alla scala milan on 19-27 august 1954/producer walter legge/published in june 1955/lp matrix numbers XBX 172-177

serafin	lp: FCX 393-395/QCX 10122-10124/WCX 1258-1260/
la scala	C 90428-90430
orchestra	*other lp issues:* angel 3531/angel seraphim 6088/emi SLS 5120/
and chorus	1C153 00966-00968M/2C163 00966-00968/EX 29 09213
callas	cd: emi CDS 747 5818/CDS 556 3252/CMS 252 9432
nicolai	*excerpts*
tucker	45: SEL 1536/SEBQ 137/SEBQ 235/SCBQ 3047
tagliabue	lp: 33CX 1503/33CX 1681/FCX 816/FCX 30156/
capecchi	QCX 10304/WSX 522/C 80444
rossi-lemeni	*other lp excerpts:* angel 35432/35759/emi SLS 5104/
	1C053 01507M/3C063 01507
	cd: emi CMS 565 5342/CZS 252 6142/palladio PD 4182-4183

33CX 1261/debussy piano works
recorded in abbey road studios london on 7-11 december 1954 and 16 april 1955 respectively/ producers walter legge and geraint jones/published in february 1957/lp matrix numbers XAX 740-741

gieseking,	**études**
piano	lp: FCX 483/FCX 30020/QCX 10260/WCX 1261/C 90431
	other lp issues: angel 35250/emi 2C061 01028/3C053 01028/
	3C153 52331-52440M/F 667 473-478M
	cd: emi CHS 556 5852/CHS 556 8662
	d'un cahier d'esquisses
	lp: FCX 483/QCX 10260/WCX 1261/C 90431
	other lp issues: angel 35250/3C153 52331-52440M/
	F667 473-478M

33CX 1262-1264/mozart cosi fan tutte
recorded in abbey road studios london on 13-21 july 1954/producer walter legge/published in september 1955/lp matrix numbers XAX 596-601

karajan	lp: FCX 484-486/QCX 10146-10148/WCX 1262-1264/
philharmonia	C 90432-90434
chorus	*other lp issues:* angel 3522/world records OC 195-197/
schwarzkopf	emi RLS 7709/1C147 01748-01750M/2C153 01748-
merriman	01750/3C153 01748-01750/1C197 54200-54208M
otto	cd: emi CHS 769 6352/CMS 567 0642
simoneau	*excerpts*
panerai	lp: WSX 557/C 80574
bruscantini	*other lp excerpts:* world records OH 198/emi 1C063 00838
	cd: emi CDM 763 6572/CMS 763 7902/CDEMX 2211
	recording completed on 6 november 1955; overture recorded in kingsway hall london on 13 july 1954

33CX 1265/opera intermezzi by mascagni, massenet, leoncavallo, offenbach, kodaly, puccini, bizet, mussorgsky, granados and verdi
recorded in kingsway hall london on 22-24 july 1954/producer walter legge/published in september 1955/lp matrix numbers XAX 616-617

karajan
philharmonia
brain, organ

cavalleria rusticana
45: SEL 1551/SCBQ 3049
lp: FCX 407/FC 25106/QCX 10150/WCX 1265/C 90435
other lp issues: angel 35207/3554/toshiba EAC 37020-37038
cd: emi CDM 566 6032

karajan
philharmonia
parikian, violin

méditation/thais
45: SEL 1547/SCD 2242/SEBQ 149/SCBQ 3055
lp: FCX 407/FC 25106/QXC 10150/WCX 1265/C 90435
other lp issues: angel 35207/3554/toshiba EAC 37020-37038

karajan
philharmonia

i pagliacci
45: SEL 1551/SEBQ 152
lp: FCX 407/QCX 10150/WCX 1265/C 90435
other lp issues: angel 35207/3554/toshiba EAC 37020-37038
cd: emi CDM 566 6032

barcarolle/les contes d'hoffmann
45: SEL 1547/SCD 2130/SEBQ 149/SCBQ 3055
lp: FCX 407/FC 25106/QCX 10150/WCX 1265/C 90435
other lp issues: angel 35207/toshiba EAC 37020-37038
cd: emi CDM 566 6032

hary janos
lp: FCX 407/QCX 10150/WCX 1265/C 90435
other lp issues: angel 35207/toshiba EAC 37020-37038
cd: emi CMS 763 4642/CDM 566 5962

manon lescaut
lp: FCX 407/QCX 10150/WCX 1265/C 90435
other lp issues: angel 35207/toshiba EAC 37020-37038
cd: emi CDM 566 6032

33CX 1265/opera intermezzi/concluded
karajan carmen act four
philharmonia 45: SEL 1547/SCD 2130/ESBF 170/SEBQ 149
lp: FCX 407/QCX 10150/WCX 1265/C 90435
other lp issues: angel 35207/toshiba EAC 37020-37038
khovantschina act four
45: SEBQ 255
lp: FCX 407/QCX 10150/WCX 1265/C 90435
other lp issues: angel 35207/toshiba EAC 37020-37038
cd: emi CDM 566 6032
goyescas
45: SEL 1551/SEBQ 152
lp: FCX 407/FC 25106/QCX 10150/WCX 1265/C 90435
other lp issues: angel 35207/toshiba EAC 37020-37038
la traviata act three
45: SEL 1551/SEBQ 152
lp: FCX 407/QCX 10150/WCX 1265/C 90435
other lp issues: angel 35207/3554/toshiba EAC 37020-37038
cd: emi CDM 566 6032
l'amico fritz
45: SCBQ 3047
lp: FCX 407/QCX 10150/WCX 1265/C 90435
other lp issues: angel 35207/3554/toshiba EAC 37020-37038
cd: emi CDM 566 6032

33CX 1266/works by beethoven
recorded in kingsway hall london on 9-10 november 1954 and in town hall watford on 20 september 1954 respectively/producer walter legge/published in november 1955/lp matrix numbers XAX 702-703
karajan **symphony no 5**
philharmonia lp: FCX 454/FCX 30093/QCX 10186/WCX 1266/
WC 517/C 90436/C 70369
other lp issues: angel 35231/world records SM 143-149/
toshiba EAC 37001-37019/emi SLS 5053/SHZE 169/
1C181 01380-01386Y
cd: emi CMS 763 3102

karajan **abscheulicher wo eilst du hin?/fidelio**
philharmonia lp: FCX 454/FCX 30093/QCX 10186/WCX 1266/C 90436
schwarzkopf *other lp issues:* angel 35231/toshiba EAC 37001-37019/
emi RLS 7715/154 5133/1C137 54364-54367M
cd: emi CDH 763 2012

33CX 1267/bartok string quartets nos 3 and 4
recorded in wigmore hall london on 12-20 july 1954/producer alan melville/published in june 1956/lp matrix numbers XAX 664-665

vegh string quartet	lp: WCX 1267/C 90437
	other lp issue: angel 35241

33CX 1268/violin concerti by bruch and prokofiev
recorded in abbey road studios london on 17-20 november 1954/published in september 1955/ lp matrix numbers XAX 655-656

matacic   **bruch violin concerto no 1**
london
symphony   lp: FCX 419/FCX 30245/FC 25119/QCX 10248/ WCX 1268/WS 523/C 90438/C 60548
oistrakh, violin   *other lp issues:* angel 35243/hmv LALP 255/emi SLS 5004/ XLP 30109/SMVP 8028/1C047 50510/ HC 126/melodiya D 021421-021422
cd: emi CDM 769 2612

prokofiev violin concerto no 1
lp: FCX 419/FCX 30245/QCX 10248/WCX 1268/WS 531/ C 90438/C 91395/C 70430
other lp issues: angel 35243/hmv LALP 255
cd: emi 562 8882/testament SBT 1116

33CX 1269/schubert schwanengesang
recorded in abbey road studios london on 28-30 may 1954/producers walter legge and walter jellinek/published in september 1955/lp matrix numbers XAX 612-613

hotter	lp: WCX 1269/C 90439
moore, piano	*other lp isues:* angel 3521/angel seraphim 6051/ emi XLP 30102-30103
	cd: emi CDH 565 1962

33CX 1270/beethoven overtures
recorded in kingsway hall london between 17 and 24 november 1954/producer walter jellinek/published in september 1955/lp matrix numbers XAX 673-674

klemperer	**fidelio**
philharmonia	lp: FCX 446/QCX 10237/WCX 1270/C 90440
	other lp issues: angel 35258/emi SLS 873/EX 29 04573/ 1C191 01526-01528
	leonore no 1
	lp: FCX 446/QCX 10237/WCX 1270/C 90440
	other lp issues: angel 35258/emi SLS 873/EX 29 04573/ 1C191 01526-01528
	cd: emi CDM 764 1432
	leonore no 2; leonore no 3
	lp: FCX 446/QCX 10237/WCX 1270/C 90440
	other lp issues: angel 35258/emi SLS 873/EX 29 04573/ 1C191 01526-01528
	cd: emi CDM 763 8552

33CX1271/mozart piano sonata no 6 k284; fugue k401; rondo k494; allegro k312; allegro and andante k533
recorded in abbey road studios london between 2 and 20 august 1953/producers walter legge, walter jellinek and geraint jones/published in september 1955/lp matrix numbers XAX 412-413

gieseking,	lp: FCX 316/WCX 1271/C 90441
piano	*other lp issues:* angel 35073/3511/emi 1C197 03133-03137M/3C153 00997-01007M
	cd: emi CHS 763 6882

33CX 1272/beethoven string quartets op 127 and op 135
recorded in studio magellan paris on 7 september 1953 and 17 october 1953 respectively/ producer norbert gamsohn/published in september 1955

hungarian	lp: FCX 254/WCX 1272/C 90442
string quartet	*other lp issue:* angel 35112
	cd: emi CZS 767 2362

33CX 1273/a portrait of the waltz
recorded in abbey road studios london on 12 september 1952 (chabrier), 12 january 1954 (tanzwalzer) and 2-3 march 1954/producers walter legge and walter jellinek/ published in september 1955/lp matrix numbers XAX 587-588

markevitch
philharmonia

busoni tanzwalzer; liszt mephisto waltz
lp: FCX 417/FCX 30084/QCX 10172
other lp issue: angel 35154
cd: testament SBT 1060

stravinsky valse/suite no 2
lp: FCX 417/FCX 30084/QCX 10172
other lp issue: angel 35154
cd: testament SBT 1107

sibelius valse triste
45: SEL 1539/SCD 2136/SEBQ 147
lp: FCX 417/FCX 30084/FC 25087/QCX 10172
other lp issue: angel 35154

mozart german dance k605 no 3
lp: FCX 417/FCX 30084/QCX 10172
other lp issue: angel 35154

berlioz danse des sylphes/la damnation de faust
45: SEL 1539/SCD 2136/ESBF 137/SEBQ 142
lp: FCX 417/FCX 30084/QCX 10172
other lp issue: angel 35154
recording completed on 15 may 1954

saint-saens danse macabre
45: SEL 1539/ESBF 17084/SEBQ 142
lp: FCX 417/FCX 30084/FC 25087/QCX 10172
other lp issue: angel 35154
recording completed on 15 may 1954

chabrier fete polonaise/le roi malgré lui
45: SEL 1544
lp: FCX 417/FCX 30084/QCX 10172
other lp issue: angel 35154

33CXS 1274-33CX 1275/bruckner symphony no 4 "romantic"
recorded in kingsway hall london on 12-13 october 1954/producer walter legge/published in september 1955/lp matrix numbers XAX 713-715

matacic
philharmonia

lp: WCX 1274-1275/C 90443-90444
other lp issue: angel 3548
cd: testament SBT 1050
recording completed on 11-14 december 1954

angel and testament also include bruckner overture in g minor recorded on 16 january 1956 but never published by columbia in uk

85

33CX 1276/vivaldi concerti in a and d minor; leo concerto in d; sacchini edipo a colono overture
published in october 1955/lp matrix numbers XBX 178 and 180
caracciolo lp: QCX 10140/WCX 1276/C 90445
alessandro *other lp issue:* angel 35254
scarlatti
orchestra

33CX 1277/lully ballet suite; cimarosa oboe concerto; tartini concerto in f
published in october 1955/lp matrix numbers XBX 179 and 181
caracciolo lp: QCX 10138/WCX 1277/C 90446
alessandro *other lp issue:* angel 35255
scarlatti
orchestra

33CX 1278/works by beethoven
recorded in kingsway hall london on 13-16 november 1953 and in town hall watford on 20 september 1954 respectively/producer walter legge/published in september 1955/ lp matrix numbers XAX 604-605
karajan **symphony no 4**
philharmonia lp: QCX 10149/WCX 1278/C 90447
  other lp issues: angel 35203/world records SM 143-149/
    toshiba EAC 37001-37019/emi SLS 5053/
    1C181 01830-01836Y
  cd: emi CMS 763 3102

karajan **ah perfido!, concert aria**
philharmonia lp: QCX 10149/WCX 1278/C 90447
schwarzkopf *other lp issues:* angel 35203/toshiba EAC 37001-37019/
    emi RLS 7715/154 6133/1C137 54364-54367M
  cd: emi CDH 763 2012

33CX 1279/tchaikovsky string quartet no 2
recorded in abbey road studios london on 26 november 1954/producer lawrance collingwood/published in october 1955/lp matrix numbers XAX 649-650
armenian *other lp issue:* angel 35238
state string
quartet

33CX 1280/orchestral works by balakirev
recorded in kingsway hall london on 11-14 december 1954/producer walter legge/published in november 1955/lp matrix numbers XAX 696-697

matacic **russia, symphonic poem**
philharmonia *also known as second overture on russian themes*
lp: QCX 10187
other lp issues: angel 35291/emi XLP 30107
cd: emi CZS 568 5502/testament SBT 1331
thamar, symphonic poem
lp: QCX 10187
other lp issue: angel 35291
islamey, oriental fantasy arranged by schalk
lp: QCX 10187
other lp issue: angel 35291
cd: testament SBT 1331

33CX 1281/violin concerti by glazunov and paganini
recorded in kingsway hall london on 15-17 december 1954/producers walter legge and alec robertson/published in october 1955/lp matrix numbers XAX 691-692

matacic **glazunov violin concerto**
philharmonia lp: WCX 1281/C 90448
rabin, violin *other lp issue:* angel 35259
cd: emi CMS 764 1232
paganini violin concerto no 1
lp: WCX 1281/WC 524/C 90448/C 70379
other lp issues: angel 35259
cd: emi CMS 764 1232/CDF 300 0212

33CX 1282/debussy childrens corner and la boite a joujoux, suites arranged by caplet
recorded in maison de la mutualité paris between 15 and 29 april 1954/producer rené challan/published in october 1955/lp matrix numbers XLX 189 and 262

cluytens lp: FCX 307
orchestre *other lp issue:* angel 35172
national cd: testament SBT 1236/SBT 7247
recording of childrens corner completed on 13 may 1954

33CX 1283/schumann kreisleriana; carnaval
recorded in abbey road studios london on 4-7 january 1955/producer walter legge/published in october 1955/lp matrix numbers XAX 679-680
anda, piano   lp: QCX 10182/WCX 1283/C 90449
                      other lp issue: angel 35247
                      cd: testament SBT 1069
                      recording of carnaval completed on 6 february 1955

33CX 1284/schubert string quartet no 14 "der tod und das mädchen"
recorded in abbey road studios london on 29 november 1954/producer lawrance collingwood/published in november 1955/lp matrix numbers XAX 647-648
armenian   lp: WCX 1284/C 90450
state string   *other lp issue:* angel 35237
quartet

33CX 1285/bartok string quartets nos 5 and 6
recorded in wigmore hall london on 21-24 july 1954 and 4-10 november 1954 respectively/producers alan melville and walter jellinek/published in september 1956/lp matrix numbers XAX 660 and 667
vegh string   lp: WCX 1285/C 90451
quartet   *other lp issue:* angel 35242
                     recording od string quartet no 5 completed on 3 november 1954

33CX 1286/bach solo violin sonata no 1 bwv 1001; solo violin partita no 1 bwv 1002
recorded in abbey road studios london on 26-27 march 1954 and 27-30 april 1955 respectively/producer alan melville/published in october 1955/lp matrix numbers XAX 731 and 744
martzy, violin   lp: WCX 1286/C 90452
                    other lp issue: angel 35280

33CX 1287/bach solo violin sonata no 2 bwv 1003; solo violin partita no 2 bwv 1004
recorded in abbey road studios london on 29 march-2 april 1955 and 24-26 july 1954 respectively/producers walter legge, alan melville and alec robertson/published in november 1955/lp matrix numbers XAX 615 and 732
martzy, violin   lp: WCX 1287/C 90453
                    other lp issue: angel 35281

33CX 1288/bach solo violin sonata no 3 bwv 1005; solo violin partita no 3 bwv 1006
recorded in abbey road studios london on 1 may 1954 and 15-18 may 1955 respectively/ producer walter jellinek/published in movember 1955/lp matrix numbers XAX 614 and 764

martzy, violin	lp: WCX 1288/C 90454
	other lp issue: angel 35282
	recording of sonata no 3 completed on 1-3 june 1954

solo sonatas and partitas on 33CX 1286-1288 are also issued on cd by toshiba in japan

33CXS 1289-33CX 1291/rossini il turco in italia
recorded in teatro alla scala milan on 31 august-8 september 1954/producers walter legge and walter jellinek/published in october 1955/lp matrix numbers XBX 11-15

gavazzeni	lp: QCX 10153-10155/WCX 1289-1291/C 90455-90457
la scala	*other lp issues:* angel 3535/angel seraphim 6095/emi SLS 5148/
orchestra	2C163 03456-03457/3C063 01019-01021
callas	cd: emi CDS 749 3442/CDS 556 3132/CZS 252 9432
gedda	*excerpts*
calabrese	lp: angel 3743/emi SLS 5104
rossi-lemeni	cd: emi CMS 763 2442/CMS 565 5342/CZS 252 6142
stabile	

33CX 1292-1294/strauss ariadne auf naxos
recorded in kingsway hall london on 30 june-7 july 1954/producer walter legge/published in october 1955/lp matrix numbers XAX 746-751

karajan	lp: FCX 506-508/QCX 10168-10170/WCX 1292-1294/
philharmonia	C 90458-90460
schwarzkopf	*other lp issues:* angel 3532/emi RLS 760/EX 769 2961/
streich	1C153 03520-03522/2C153 03520-03522
seefried	cd: emi CMS 769 2962/CDS 555 1762/CMS 567 0772
schock	*excerpts*
dönch	cd: emi CDM 763 6572/CMS 763 7902/CDM 565 5772
prey	

33CX 1295/prokofiev string quartet no 2; malipiero string quartet no 2
recorded in 1955/published in november 1955/lp matrix numbers XBX 320-321

quartetto	lp: QCX 10145/WCX 1295/C 90461
italiano	*other lp issue:* angel 35296
	cd: testament SBT 1123

33CX 1296-1298/puccini madama butterfly
recorded in teatro alla scala milan on 1-6 august 1955/producer walter legge/published in november 1955/lp matrix numbers XBX 22-27

karajan	lp: FCX 472-474/QCX 10156-10158/WCX 1296-1298/
la scala	C 90462-90464
orchestra	*other lp issues:* angel 3523/emi SLS 5015/EX 29 12653/
and chorus	1C153 00424-00426/2C163 00424-00426/
callas	3C163 00424-00426
danieli	cd: emi CDS 747 9598/CDS 556 2982
gedda	*excerpts*
borriello	45: SEL 1617/SEL 1625/SEL 1629/SEL 1637/SEL 1641/
	ESBF 17102/SCBQ 3027/SCBQ 3048/SEBQ 159/
	SEBQ 202/SELW 1546/SELW 1625/C 50154/C 50510
	lp: 33CX 1787/FCX 30135/QCX 10471/WSX 546/
	WSX 622/C 80529/C 80689/C 70411
	other lp excerpts: emi SLS 5104/EX 29 01983/
	3C063 00550/SHZE 110
	cd: emi CMS 764 4182/762 7942/562 5642

33CX 1299-1301/gounod mireille
recorded in aix-en-provence on 27-30 july 1954/published in november 1955/lp matrix numbers XLX 293-298

cluytens	lp: FCX 363-365/C 90636-90638
conservatoire	*other lp issues:* angel 3533/emi 2C153 10613-10615
orchestra	cd: emi CMS 764 3822
aix festival	*excerpts*
chorus	lp: C 70411
vivalda	*other lp excerpts:* emi UCD 3162/SLS 5250/
gedda	1C137 78233-78236
dens	*recording completed in paris on 1 october 1954*

33CX 1302/works by beethoven
recorded in abbey road studios london on 2-7 january 1955/producer walter legge/published in november 1955/lp matrix numbers XAX 687-688

galliera	**piano concerto no 1**
philharmonia	lp: QCX 10194/WCX 1302/WC 533/C 90465/C 70431
anda, piano	*other lp issue:* angel 35248
anda, piano	**piano sonata no 14 "moonlight"**
	45: SEL 1623
	lp: QCX 10194/WCX 1302/C 90465
	other lp issue: angel 35248
	cd: testament SBT 1070

33CX 1303/khachaturian violin concerto
recorded in kingsway hall london on 26-27 november 1954/producer walter legge/published in november 1955/lp matrix numbers XAX 653-654

khachaturian lp: FCX 511/FCX 30291/QCX 10202/WCX 1303/C 90466
philharmonia *other lp issue:* angel 35244
oistrakh, violin cd: emi CDC 555 0352

33CX 1304/debussy préludes 2eme livre
recorded in abbey road studios london on 9-10 december 1954/producer walter legge/ published in november 1955/lp matrix numbers XAX 683-684

gieseking, lp: FCX 186/QCX 10221/WCX 1304/C 90467
piano *other lp issues:* angel 35249/emi RLS 752/2C061 00815/
    3C053 01027/3C153 52331-52440M/F667 473-478M
  cd: emi CDH 761 0042/CHS 556 5852/CHS 556 8552

33CX 1305/operatic arias and duets
recorded in kingsway hall london on 2-6 october 1953/producer walter legge/published in november 1955/lp matrix numbers XAX 752-753

galliera **verdi rigoletto, arias and duets**
philharmonia *other lp issue:* angel 35095
dobbs cd: testament SBT 1137
panerai

galliera **arias by rimsky-korsakov, massenet, bellini and**
philharmonia **délibes**
dobbs *other lp issue:* angel 35095
  cd: testament SBT 1137

33CX 1306-1307/pergolesi six concerti armonici; sonata in the style of a concerto; sinfonia for cello and strings, all arranged by giuranna
recorded in milan in october 1954/published in november 1955/lp matrix numbers XBX 190-193

i musici lp: QCX 10175-10176/WCX 1306-1307/
    C 90468-90469
  other lp issue: angel 3538

33CX 1308/spanish traditional and religious choral music
published in november 1955/lp matrix numbers XKX 55-56
capilla clasica   *other lp issue:* angel 35257
polifonica

33CX 1309-1310/j.strauss die fledermaus
recorded in kingsway hall london on 26-30 april 1953/producer walter legge/published in november 1955/lp matrix numbers XAX 765-768

karajan	lp: QCX 10183-10184/WCX 1309-1310/WSX 533-534/
philharmonia	C 90470-90471/C 80512-80513
and chorus	*other lp issues:* angel 3539/emi RLS 728/1C149 00427-00428/
schwarzkopf	2C181 00427-00428
streich	cd: emi CHS 769 5312/CMS 567 0742
gedda	*excerpts*
christ	45: SEL 1557
krebs	lp: 33CX 1516/WSX 602/C 80110
kunz	*other lp excerpts:* emi 1C047 01953/1C147 03580-03581M
	cd: emi CDM 763 5572/CDM 763 6572/CDM 565 5772/
	CMS 763 7902/585 1052

33CX 1311/sibelius symphony no 1
recorded in kingsway hall london on 18-19 july 1955/producer walter legge/published in may 1956/lp matrix numbers XAX 809-810

kletzki	lp: QCX 10204/WCX 1311/C 90472
philharmonia	*other lp issue:* angel 35313
	cd: testament SBT 1049

angel 35313 also contained sibelius symphony no 3 which was recorded at the same time but which remained unpublished in uk

33CX 1312/catalogue number appears not to have been allocated

33CX 1313/walton troilus and cressida, scenes
recorded in kingsway hall london on 18-20 april 1955/producer walter legge/published in november 1955/lp matrix numbers XAX 790-791

walton	lp: QCX 10173
philharmonia	*other lp issues:* angel 35278/world records OH 217
schwarzkopf	cd: emi CDM 764 1992
sinclair	
lewis	

33CX 1314/catalogue number appears not to have been allocated

33CX 1315/mozart piano sonatas nos 3 k281 and 19 k135a; gigue k574; variations k398, k500 and k573; rondo k511
recorded in abbey road studios london between 1 and 20 august 1953/producers walter legge, walter jellinek and geraint jones/published in february 1956/lp matrix numbers XAX 414-415

gieseking,   lp: FCX 317/QCX 10350/WCX 1315/C 90473/C 80658
piano   *other lp issues:* angel 35074/3511/emi 1C197 03133-03137M
                cd: emi CHS 763 6882

33CX 1316/bartok for children volume two
recorded in abbey road studios london on 8-9 january 1955/producer walter legge/published in may 1956/lp matrix numbers XAX 681-682

anda, piano   lp: WCX 1316/C 90474
                other lp issue: angel 35246
                cd: testament SBT 1065

33CX 1317/an evening with robert burns
published in january 1956/lp matrix numbers XAX 675-676

saltire music
group

33CX 1318-1320/verdi aida
recorded in teatro alla scala milan on 10-24 august 1955/producer walter legge/published in january 1956/lp matrix numbers XBX 28-33

serafin   lp: FCX 570-572/QCX 10165-10167/WCX 1318-1320/
la scala   C 90475-90477
orchestra   *other lp issues:* angel 3525/emi SLS 5108/EX 29 09763/
and chorus   1C153 00429-00431/2C163 00429-00431/
callas   3C163 00429-00431
barbieri   cd: emi CDS 749 0308/CDS 556 3162/CMS 252 9432
tucker   *excerpts*
gobbi   lp: 33CX 1681/FCX 816/FCX 30157/QCX 10352/
zaccaria   QCX 10442/WSX 566/C 80567
modesti   *other lp excerpts:* angel 35759/35938/3814/emi SLS 5104/
                 2C053 01676
                 cd: emi CDC 555 2162/CMS 565 5342/CMS 565 7462/
                 CZS 252 6142/palladio PD 4182-4183

33CX 1321/mozart song recital
recorded in abbey road studios london on 13-16 april 1955/producer walter legge/published in february 1956/lp matrix numbers XAX 784-785

schwarzkopf   lp: FCX 30116/QCX 10303/WCX 1321/C 90478
gieseking,   *other lp issues:* angel 35270/emi ASD 3858/2C061 01578/
piano   3C153 52700-52705M
                   cd: emi CDH 763 7022
                   selections from the recital
                   45: ESBF 17122
                   lp: melodiya M10 43861-43862
                   cd: emi CDC 747 3262/585 1052

33CX 1322/piano quintets by mozart and beethoven
recorded in abbey road studios london on 14-16 april 1955/producer walter legge/ published in january 1956/lp matrix numbers XAX 822-823

gieseking,   **mozart piano quintet k452**
piano   lp: FCX 543/QCX 10248/WCX 1322/C 90479
sutcliffe, oboe   *other lp issues:* angel 35303/emi 1C047 01242/
james, bassoon   3C153 52700-52705M
walton, clarinet   cd: emi CHS 763 7092/testament SBT 1091
brain, horn   **beethoven piano quintet in e flat**
                   lp: FCX 543/QCX 10248/WCX 1322/C 90479
                   other lp issues: angel 35303/emi 1C047 01242/
                   3C153 52700-52705M

33CX 1323/rachmaninov piano concerto no 3
recorded in théatre des champs elysées paris on 13 june 1955/producer norbert gamsohn/ published in january 1956/lp matrix numbers XLX 372-373

cluytens   lp: FCX 432/QCX 10197/WCX 1323/C 90480
conservatoire   *other lp issues:* angel 35230/emi 1C153 11627-11628
orchestra   cd: testament SBT 1029
gilels, piano

33CXS 1324-33CX 1326/verdi rigoletto
recorded in teatro alla scala milan on 3-16 september 1955/producers walter legge and walter jellinek/published in february 1956/lp matrix numbers XBX 38-42

serafin	lp: FCX 532-534/QCX 10216-10218/WCX 1324-1326/
la scala	C 90481-90483
orchestra	*other lp issues:* angel 3537/emi SLS 5018/EX 29 09283/
and chorus	1C153 01346-01347M/2C163 00432-00434/
callas	2C163 03227-03228/3C163 00432-00434
lazzarini	cd: emi CDS 747 4698/CDS 556 3272/CMS 252 9432
di stefano	*excerpts*
gobbi	45: SEL 1650/SEL 1656/SEL 1659/SEL 1676/SEBQ 221/
zaccaria	SEBQ 225/SEBQ 230/SEBQ 231/SCBQ 3065/C 50556
	lp: 33CX 1582/33CX 1681/FCX 816/FCX 929/FCX 30155/
	QCX 10313/QCX 10352/QCX 10441/QCX 10477/
	WSX 518/WSX 622/WC 610/C 80431/C 80689/C 70400
	other lp excerpts: angel 35518/35759/36929/36940/emi
	SLS 856/SLS 5057/SLS 5104/1C053 00483M/
	1C187 28985-28986M/1C191 01433-01434M/
	2C161 01433-01434M/3C063 00483/3C065 17902
	cd: emi CDC 749 5022/CDC 754 7022/CDC 252 9382/
	CDM 769 5432/CMS 565 5342/CMS 565 7462/
	CMS 565 9522/CZS 252 6142

33CX 1327/ballet music from the operas
recorded in kingsway hall london 5-8 november 1954/producer walter legge/published in february 1956/lp matrix numbers XAX 739 and 861

karajan ponchielli dance of the hours/la gioconda
philharmonia
    45: SCD 2171/SEBQ 256
    lp: FC 25106/QCX 10192/WCX 1327/C 90484
    other lp issues: angel 35307/toshiba EAC 37020-37038
    cd: emi CDM 566 6032
    wagner venusberg music/tannhäuser
    lp: QCX 10192/WCX 1327/C 90484
    other lp issues: angel 35307/toshiba EAC 37020-37038
    verdi ballet music from act two/aida
    lp: QCX 10192/WCX 1327/C 90484
    other lp issues: angel 35307/toshiba EAC 37020-37038
    cd: emi CDM 566 6032
    mussorgsky dance of the persian slaves/khovantschina
    45: SEBQ 255
    lp: QCX 10192/WCX 1327/C 90484
    other lp issues: angel 35307/toshiba EAC 37020-37038
    cd: emi CDM 566 6032
    borodin dance of the polovtsian maidens and polovtsian dances/prince igor
    lp: FCX 579/QCX 10192/WCX 1327/C 90484
    other lp issues: angel 35307/toshiba EAC 37020-37038

33CX 1328/tchaikovsky romeo and juliet; strauss tod und verklärung
recorded in kingsway hall london on 15-16 march 1955/producer walter legge/published in february 1957/lp matrix numbers XAX 828-829

galliera lp: WCX 1328/C 90485
philharmonia *other lp issue:* angel 35410

33CX 1329-1330/j.strauss der zigeunerbaron
recorded in kingsway hall london on 18-21 may 1954/producer walter legge/published in october 1958/lp matrix numbers XAX 608-611

ackermann lp: WSX 541-542/C 80520-80521
philharmonia *other lp issues:* angel 3566/emi SXDW 3046/2C149 03051-
chorus   03052/5C181 03051-03052
schwarzkopf cd: emi CHS 769 5262/CHS 567 5352
köth *excerpts*
sinclair lp: emi SLS 5250/RLS 763/1C151 43160-43163M
gedda *recording completed on 31 may and 25 september 1954*
kunz
prey

33CX 1331/dvorak klänge aus mähren; carissimi four cantatas; monteverdi four madrigals
recorded in abbey road studios london on 25-27 may 1955/producer walter legge/ published in march 1956/lp matrix numbers XAX 847-848
schwarzkopf   lp: FCX 515/WCX 1331/C 90486
seefried   *other lp issues:* angel 35290/angel seraphim 60376/emi
moore, piano   HLM 7267
                 cd: emi CDH 769 7932

33CX 1332/sibelius symphony no 2
recorded in kingsway hall london on 16 july 1955/producer walter legge/published in june 1956/lp matrix numbers XAX 804-805
kletzki   lp: SAX 2280/QCX 10228/WCX 1332/C 90487
philharmonia   *other lp issues:* angel 35314/emi XLP 30031/SXLP 30031
                 cd: emi CZS 767 7262
this was the first complete columbia lp in the 33CX series to have an equivalent stereo version; however, SAX 2280 was not published until three years later

33CX 1333/beethoven piano concerto no 4
recorded in kingsway hall london on 30-31 may 1955/producer walter jellinek/published in march 1956/lp matrix numbers XAX 849-850
galliera   lp: QCX 10196/WCX 1333/C 90488
philharmonia   *other lp issues:* angel 35300/quintessence PMC 7074
arrau, piano   cd: emi CZS 767 3792/pantheon D 15070

33CX 1334/borodin string quartet no 2; shostakovich string quartet no 1
recorded in abbey road studios london on 10 november 1954/producer lawrance collingwood/published in march 1956/lp matrix numbers XAX 668-669
armenian   *other lp issue:* angel 35239
string quartet

33CX 1335/philharmonia promenade concert
recorded in kingsway hall london on 8-9 july 1955, 23 july 1954 (schwanda) and 17-21 july 1953 (espana and les patineurs)/producer walter legge/published in march 1956/ lp matrix numbers XAX 792-793

karajan philharmonia
waldteufel les patineurs, waltz; chabrier espana
45: SEL 1528/SEBQ 129
lp: FCX 512/FCX 30103/QCX 10198/WSX 528/C 80464
other lp issues: angel 35327/toshiba EAC 37020-37038
chabrier marche joyeuse
45: ESBF 135
lp: FCX 512/FCX 30103/QCX 10198/WSX 528/C 80464
other lp issues: angel 35327/toshiba EAC 37020-37038
j.strauss I radetzky march; j.strauss tritsch-tratsch polka; j.strauss thunder and lightning polka
45: SEL 1568/SEBQ 171
lp: FCX 512/FCX 30103/QCX 10198/WSX 528/C 80464
other lp issues: angel 35327/toshiba EAC 37020-37038
offenbach orfée aux enfers, overture; weinberger schwanda the bagpiper, polka
lp: FCX 512/FCX 30103/QCX 10198/WSX 528/C 80464
other lp issues: angel 35327/toshiba EAC 37020-37038
suppé light cavalry, overture
45: SEL 1557/SEBQ 162
lp: FCX 512/FCX 30103/QCX 10198/WSX 528/C 80464
other lp issues: angel 35327/toshiba EAC 37020-37038

karajan's only lp recording with the philharmonia orchestra not yet to have been transferred to cd, presumably because the identical programme was remade on 33CX 1758 with a stereo equivalent

33CX 1336/catalogue number appears not to have been allocated

33CX 1337/piano sonatas by chopin and enescu
recorded in abbey road studios london on 1-4 march 1947 and in bern on 18 october 1943 respectively/producer walter legge (chopin)/published in march 1956/ lp matrix numbers XAX 66 and XZX 19

lipatti, piano
chopin piano sonata no 3
78: LX 994-996/LX 8560-8562/LFX 766-768/GQX11123-25
lp: FCX 493/FCX 30098/QCX 10213/WCX 1337/ C 90490/C 60624
other lp issues: american columbia ML 4721/3216 0369/emi RLS 749/HQM 1163/1C047 01282M/1C061 01282/ 1C197 53780-53786M
cd: emi CDH 763 0382/CZS 767 1632/CDM 567 5662
enescu piano sonata in d
other lp issues: angel 35931/emi 2C051 01696
cd: emi CZS 767 1632/CDM 567 5662

33CX 1338/chopin recital
recorded in paris on 17 october 1955/producer norbert gamsohn/published in march 1956/ lp matrix numbers XLX 390-391
malcuzymski,   *other lp issue:* angel 35171
piano

33CX 1339/respighi fontane di roma; impressioni brasiliane
recorded in kingsway hall london on 18-21 march 1955/producer walter legge/published in april 1956/lp matrix numbers XAX 830-831
galliera   lp: QCX 10206
philharmonia   *other lp issues:* angel 35405/emi MFP 2055

33CX 1340/pergolesi la serva padrona
recorded in teatro alla scala milan on 29 may-1 june 1955/producer walter legge/published in april 1956/lp matrix numbers XBX 16-17
giulini   lp: QCX 10152/WCX 1340/C 90491
la scala   *other lp issues:* angel 35279/angel seraphim 60333/
orchestra   emi 2C063 01335
carteri
rossi-lemeni

33CX 1341/symphonies by sibelius
recorded in kingsway hall london on 4-6 july 1955/producer walter legge/published in april 1956/lp matrix numbers XAX 826-827
karajan   **symphony no 6**
philharmonia   lp: QCX 10195
   other lp issues: angel 35316/toshiba EAC 37020-37038
   cd: emi CMS 763 4642/CDM 566 6022
   symphony no 7
   lp: QCX 10195
   other lp issues: angel 35316/toshiba EAC 37020-37038/
      emi SXLP 30430/1C053 03791
   cd: emi CMS 763 4642/CDM 566 6022
   symphony no 7 also published unofficially on cd by palladio

33CX 1342/violin sonatas by prokofiev and karen khachaturian
recorded in salle coloniale brussels on 21-23 may 1955/producer walter legge/published in april 1956

oistrakh,	**prokofiev violin sonata no 2**
violin	lp: FCX 514/FCX 30012/QCX 10202
yampolsky,	*other lp issues:* angel 35306/melodiya D 024427-024428/
piano	bruno 14006/colosseum CRLP 252
	cd: emi 562 8882/testament SBT 1113
	karen khachaturian violin sonata
	lp: FCX 514/FCX 30012/QCX 10202
	other lp issues: angel 35306/melodiya D 024427-024428/
	bruno 14006/colosseum CRLP 252
	cd: testament SBT 1113

33CX 1343/beethoven piano sonata no 21 "waldstein"; prokofiev piano sonata no 4; scriabin 2 poems
recorded in abbey road studios london on 15-19 november 1955/published in november 1956/lp matrix numbers XAX 892-893
malinin, piano   *other lp issue:* angel 35402

33CX 1344/piano works by chopin, debussy, paderewski, prokofiev, rachmaninov, scriabin and szymanowski
recorded in paris on 18 october 1955/producer norbert gamsohn/published in april 1956/ lp matrix numbers XLX 395-396

malcuzynski,	lp: QCX 10207
piano	*other lp issue:* angel 35348

33CX 1345/mozart piano sonatas no 5 k283 and no 17 k576; variations k264 and k455
recorded in abbey road studios london between 2 and 19 august 1953/producers walter legge, walter jellinek and geraint jones/published in april 1956/lp matrix numbers XAX 444-445

gieseking,	lp: FCX 318/WCX 1345/C 90492
piano	*other lp issues:* angel 35075/3511/emi 1C197 03133-03137M/
	3C153 00997-01007M
	cd: emi CHS 763 6882

33CX 1346/beethoven symphony no 3 "eroica"
recorded in kingsway hall london on 3-4 october 1955/producer walter legge/published in june 1956/lp matrix numbers XAX 870-871

klemperer   lp: FCX 557/WCX 1346/C 90493
philharmonia   *other lp issues:* angel 35328/emi SLS 873/EX 29 04573/
                     1C191 01526-01528
             cd: emi CDM 763 8552/567 7402
             recording completed on 17 december 1955

33CX 1347-1348/handel israel in egypt
recorded in town hall huddersfield on 10-13 june 1955/producer lawrance collingwood/published in april 1956/lp matrix numbers XAX 818-821

sargent   *other lp issue:* angel 3550
liverpool   cd: dutton CDLX 7045
philharmonic
huddersfield
choral society
morison
sinclair
lewis

33CX 1349/orchestral works by schubert and brahms
recorded in kingsway hall london on 17-19 may 1955/producer walter legge/published in may 1957/lp matrix numbers XAX 808-808

karajan   symphony no 8 "unfinished"
philharmonia   lp: FCX 594/QCX 10281/WCX 1349/WC 536/
                 C 90494/C 70390
             other lp issues: angel 35299/toshiba EAC 37001-37019/
                 emi SXLP 30513/1C053 43052/1C047 01441M/
                 2C059 43355/3C053 01574
             cd: emi CDM 769 2272
             haydn variations
             lp: FCX 594/QCX 10281/WCX 1349/C 90494
             other lp issues: angel 35299/toshiba EAC 37001-37019/
                 emi 3C053 01574
             cd: emi CMS 763 4562

33CXS 1350-33CX 1352/ravel works for solo piano: le tombeau de couperin; sonatine; valses nobles et sentimentales; gaspard de la nuit; pavane pour une infante défunte; jeux d'eau; a la maniere de chabrier; a la maniere de borodine; menuet sur le nom de haydn; miroirs; menuet antique; prélude
recorded in abbey road studios london between 7 and 17 december 1954/producers walter legge and geraint jones/published in may 1956/lp matrix numbers XAX 726-730

gieseking, piano	lp: FCX 528-530/FCX 30026-30027/QCX 10251-10253/ WCX 1350-1352/C 90495-90497
	other lp issues: angel 3541/emi 2C061 01565-01566/ 3C053 01248-01250/3C153 52331-52340M
	cd: teorema TH 112.1163-1164
	selections from the recordings
	45: SEL 1697/SEL 1701
	lp: 33CX 1761
	other lp selections: angel seraphim 60210/emi HQM 1225/ RLS 143 6203

33CX 1353/works by contemporary french and italian composers
recorded in studio albert paris on 7 june 1951 (delage) and in rome in 1955 (dallapiccola)/producer rené challan (delage)/published in may 1956

cluytens instrumental ensemble angelici	**delage 4 poemes hindous; berceuse phoque from chants de la jungle**
	78: hmv DA 5054-5055
	45: hmv 7RF 113-114
	other lp issues: angel 35228/hmv FBLP 1014
	cd: testament SBT 1135
markevitch santa cecilia orchestra and chorus	**dallapiccola canti di prigonia**
	other lp issues: angel 35228/hmv FBLP 1029
pascal string quartet	**guarnieri string quartet no 2**
	other lp issue: angel 35228

33CX 1354/respighi gli uccelli; trittico botticelliano
recorded in june 1955/published in may 1956/lp matrix numbers XBX 356-357
caracciolo lp: QCX 10163
orchestra *other lp issue:* angel 35310
alessandro
scarlatti

33CX 1355/brahms symphony no 2
recorded in kingsway hall london on 24-25 may 1955/producer walter legge/published in november 1957/lp matrix numbers XAX 762-763
karajan lp: FCX 586/QCX 10231/WCX 1355/C 90498
philharmonia *other lp issues:* angel 35218/toshiba EAC 37020-37038/
    emi SXLP 30513/1C053 43052
  cd: emi CDM 769 2272

33CX 1356/orchestral works by borodin and rimsky-korsakov
recorded in kingsway hall london on 6-8 april 1955 and 16-17 march 1955 respectively/producer walter legge/published in november 1956/lp matrix numbers XAX 855-856
galliera **borodin symphony no 1**
philharmonia *other lp issues:* angel 35346/emi XLP 30107
  rimsky-korsakov capriccio espagnol
  45: SEL 1614
  lp: FC 25092
  other lp issue: angel 35346

33CX 1357/concerti by corelli, vivaldi and martini
recorded in october 1954/published in june 1956/lp matrix numbers XBX 194-195
i musici lp: QCX 10180
  other lp issue: angel 35253

33CX 1358/mozart piano sonatas no 12 k332 and no 15 k545; fantasy k396; variations k354 and k460
recorded in abbey road studios london between 4 and 18 august 1953/producers walter jellinek and geraint jones/ published in june 1956/lp matrix numbers XAX 416-417
gieseking, lp: FCX 319/WCX 1358/C 90499
piano *other lp issues:* angel 35076/3511/emi 1C197 03133-03137M/
    3C153 00997-01007M
  cd: emi CHS 763 6882

33CX 1359/schubert violin sonatinas d384 and d385
recorded in electrola studio berlin on 23-26 february 1955/producer fritz ganss/published in november 1956/lp matrix numbers XRX 204-205
martzy, violin   lp: WCX 1359/WC 503/C 80756/C 70079
antonietti,   *other lp issue:* angel 35364
piano

33CX 1360/catalogue number appears not to have been allocated

33CX 1361/orchestral works by mozart
recorded in abbey road studios london on 9-10 july 1955/producer walter legge/published in february 1957/lp matrix numbers XAX 682-683
karajan   **symphony no 39**
philharmonia   lp: FCX 740/QCX 10256/WCX 1361/C 90500/
                      C 90633/C 91304
                 other lp issues: angel 35323/35739/toshiba
                      EAC 37001-37019
                 cd: emi CMS 763 4562
                 recording completed in kingsway hall london on 11 october 1955

karajan   clarinet concerto
philharmonia   lp: FCX 740/QCX 10256/WCX 1361/C 90500
walton,   *other lp issues:* angel 35323/emi XLP 60004/
clarinet   toshiba EAC 37001-37019
                 cd: emi CMS 763 3162
                 excerpt
                 lp: 33SX 1394

33CX 1362/brahms symphony no 4
recorded in kingsway hall london on 26 may 1955/producer walter jellinek/published in september 1956/lp matrix numbers XAX 802-803
karajan   lp: FCX 538/QCX 10201/WCX 1362/C 90501
philharmonia   *other lp issues:* angel 35298/toshiba EAC 37020-37038/
                     emi SXLP 30505/1C053 03604
                 cd: emi CDM 769 2282

33CX 1363/orchestral works by schubert and grieg
recorded in abbey road studios on 25-26 november 1955 (schubert) and 17-19 november 1955 (grieg)/producer lawrance collingwood/published in september 1956/lp matrix numbers XAX 900-901

beecham	**schubert symphony no 6**
royal	lp: FCX 526/QCX 10247/WCX 1363/C 90502
philharmonic	*other lp issues:* angel 35339/emi ENC 108/XLP 30028/ world records T 909/ST 909
	cd: emi CDM 769 7502
	grieg in autumn, overture; old norwegian romance with variations
	lp: FCX 526/QCX 10247/WCX 1363/C 90502
	other lp issues: angel 35339/emi ENC 108/XLP 30028 world records T 909/ST 909
	recordings of all three works completed on 15 december 1955

33CX 1364/chopin piano sonata no 2; shostakovich three preludes and fugues
recorded in new york on 19-20 october 1955/producer john coveney/published in september 1956/lp matrix numbers USC 199-200

gilels, piano	lp: FCX 487/QCX 10223
	other lp issues: angel 35308/angel seraphim 60010/ emi 1C153 11626-11628
	prelude and fugue no 5 only
	cd: testament SBT 1029

33CX 1365/vivaldi le quattro stagioni
recorded in abbey road studios london on 29 september-2 october 1955/producers walter legge, alec robertson and geraint jones/published in september 1956/lp matrix numbers XAX 868-869

giulini	lp: FCX 525/QCX 10215/WCX 1365/C 90503
philharmonia	*other lp issues:* angel 35216/emi XLP 30058/TRI 31110
parikian, violin	cd: testament SBT 1155
dart, harpsichord	

33CX 1366/liszt piano concerto no 1; hungarian fantasia
recorded in abbey road studios london on 7-9 may 1955/producer walter legge/published in september 1956/lp matrix numbers XAX 771-772
ackermann   lp: QCX 10258/WCX 1366/C 90504
philharmonia   *other lp issue:* angel 35268
anda, piano   cd: testament SBT 1071

33CX 1367/schubert string quartet d32; mozart string quartet k458
recorded in milan in 1956/published in september 1956/lp matrix numbers XBX 366-367
quartetto   lp: QCX 10199/WCX 1367/C 90505
italiano   *other lp issue:* angel 35351
    cd: testament SBT 1125

33CX 1368/piano music by mozart, schubert, chopin, debussy, liszt and granados
recorded in paris in 1956/published in july 1957/lp matrix numbers XLX 64-65
iturbi, piano   lp: FCX 509/QCX 10235
    other lp issue: angel 35347

33CX 1369/works by rachmaninov and chopin
recorded in kingsway hall london on 28-29 november 1955/producer walter jellinek/published in september 1956/lp matrix numbers XAX 890-891
ackermann   rachmaninov piano concerto no 2
philharmonia   lp: WCX 1369/C 90506
malinin, piano

malinin, piano   chopin nocturne op 27 no 2
    lp: WCX 1369/C 90506

33CX 1370-1371/verdi la traviata
recorded in teatro alla scala milan on 15-21 september 1955/producer walter jellinek/published in september 1956/lp matrix numbers XBX 34-37
serafin   lp: FCX 574-575/QCX 10211-10212/WCX 1370-1371/
la scala   C 90507-90508
orchestra   *other lp issues:* angel 3545/emi 1C163 00972-00973/
and chorus   3C163 00972-00973
stella   cd: testament SBT 2211
di stefano   *excerpts*
gobbi   45: SEL 1566/SEBQ 131
zaccaria   lp: QCX 10159/33CX 1376/C 90511
    other lp excerpts: angel 35265/emi 3C063 01522

33CX 1372/schubert rondo brillant d895; fantasie d934
recorded in electrola studio berlin on 23-26 february 1955/producer fritz ganss/ published in october 1957/ matrix numbers XRX 207-208
martzy, violin   *other lp issue:* angel 35366
antonietti.
piano

33CX 1373/works by bach
recorded in kingsway hall and abbey road studios between 16 and 25 november 1955/ producer geraint jones/published in september 1956/ lp matrix numbers XAX 884-885

ackermann	**double violin concerto bwv 1043**
philharmonia	lp: WCX 1373/C 90509/C 70427
kogan and	*other lp issue:* angel 35343
elisaveta	cd: testament SBT 1223/SBT6 1248
kogan, violins	

ackermann	**violin concerto bwv 1042**
philharmonia	lp: WCX 1373/C 90509/C 70427
kogan, violin	*other lp issue:* angel 35343
	cd: testament SBT 1223/SBT6 1248

kogan, violin	**sarabande from the second solo partita**
	lp: WCX 1373/C 90509
	other lp issue: angel 35343
	cd: testament SBT 1223/SBT6 1248

33CX 1374/beethoven piano sonatas nos 30 op 109 and 32 op 110
recorded in abbey road studios london on 31 august-1 september 1955/producer walter jellinek/published in november 1956/ lp matrix numbers XAX 842-843
gieseking,   lp: WCX 1374/C 90510
piano   *other lp issues:* angel 35363/emi 3C153 52384-52393

33CX 1375/shakespeare sonnets and scenes from as you like it
published in september 1956/ lp matrix numbers XAX 632-633
evans   *other lp issue:* angel 35220
redgrave

33CX 1376/verdi choruses from nabucco, i lombardi, ernani, la traviata, il trovatore, otello and aida
recorded in teatro alla scala milan on 6-7 june 1955/producer walter legge/published in october 1956/lp matrix numbers XBX 18-19

serafin	lp: QCX 10159/WCX 1376/C 90511
la scala	*other lp issue:* angel 35265
orchestra	*selections from the recording*
and chorus	45: SEL 1566/SEL 1571/SEBQ 131/SEBQ 169
modesti	*excerpts from la traviata are probably taken from the complete recording of the opera on 33CX 1370-1371*

33CX 1377/tchaikovsky symphony no 6 "pathétique"
recorded in kingsway hall london on 17-22 may 1955/producer walter legge/published in april 1959/lp matrix numbers XAX 767 and 760

karajan	lp: FCX 576
philharmonia	*other lp issues:* emi SXLP 30534/1C037 00935/769 4161/ toshiba EAC 37020-37038
	cd: emi CMS 763 4602/CZS 252 1432
	recording completed on 18 june 1956

33CX 1378/haydn symphonies nos 86 and 92 "oxford"
recorded in july 1955/published in october 1956/lp matrix numbers XBX 354-355

caracciolo	lp: QCX 10174
alessandro	*other lp issue:* angel 35325
scarlatti	*recording completed in november 1955*
orchestra	

33CX 1379/beethoven symphony no 7
recorded in kingsway hall london on 5-6 october 1955/producer walter legge/published in october 1956/lp matrix numbers XAX 862-863

klemperer	lp: FCX 587/WCX 1379/C 90512
philharmonia	*other lp issues:* angel 35330/emi SLS 873/EX 29 04573/ 1C191 01526-01528
	cd: emi CDM 769 1832/CDM 763 8682/567 8512
	recording completed on 17 december 1955

33CX 1380/piano sonatas by mozart and beethoven
recorded in paris/published in june 1957/lp matrix numbers XLX 498-499

iturbi, piano	**mozart sonatas k331 and k332**
	lp: FC 1047/QCX 10270
	other lp issue: angel 35378
	beethoven sonata no 14 "moonlight"
	lp: QCX 10270
	other lp issue: angel 35378

33CX 1381/brahms violin sonatas nos 1 and 2
recorded in abbey road studios london on 15-20 november 1955/producer walter jellinek/ published in october 1956/lp matrix numbers XAX 876-877
kogan, violin   *other lp issue:* angel 35332
mitnik, piano

33CX 1382/brahms variations and fugue on a theme of handel; intermezzo op 118 no 6; rhapsody op 79 no 2
recorded in paris on 18 october 1955/producer norbert gamsohn/published in october 1956/ lp matrix numbers XLX 392-393
malcuzynski,   *other lp issue:* angel 35349
piano

33CX 1383/string quartets by haydn
recorded in milan in 1956/published in october 1956/lp matrix numbers XBX 364-365
quartetto   **op 33 no 3 "the bird"**
italiano   lp: WCX 1383/C 90513
           other lp issue: angel 35185
           cd: testament SBT 1125
           op 76 no 4 "the sunrise"
           lp: WCX 1383/C 90513
           other lp issue: angel 35185

33CX 1384/scenes from eighteenth century comedy
published in october 1956/lp matrix numbers XAX 634-635
evans   *other lp issue:* angel 35213
gielgud

33CX 1385/see 33CX 1131-1132

33CX 1386/piano works by bach, scarlatti, chopin and ravel
recorded in abbey road studios london on 20 february and 27 september 1947 (scarlatti) and on 17-21 april 1948 (chopin and ravel) and in geneva radio studio on 6-10 july 1950 (bach)/ producer walter legge/lp re-issue published in september 1957/lp matrix numbers XAX 716-717
lipatti, piano   **bach ich ruf zu dir and nun komm der heiden heiland, chorale preludes arranged by busoni**
           78: LX 1247/LFX 992/GQX 11500/LZX 263
           45: SEL 1631/SCD 2142/ESBF 112/ESBF 17036/SEBQ 139
           lp: FCX 494/FC 25009/QCX 10276/WCX 1386/C 90514
           other lp issues: american columbia ML 4633/3216 0320/
              emi RLS 749/HQM 1210/1C047 01406M/2C061 01963/
              1C197 53780-53786M
           cd: emi CDC 747 5172/CDH 769 8002/CZS 767 1632/
              CDM 566 9882

33CX 1386/piano works by bach, scarlatti, chopin and ravel/concluded
lipatti, piano   **bach jesu meine freude, chorale prelude srranged by hess; siciliano from second flute sonata, arranged by kempff**
78: LB 109/GQ 7232/GQ 7248
45: SEL 1631/SCD 2110/ESBF 112/ESBF 17036/
    SCBF 110/SEBQ 139/SCBQ 3008
lp: FCX 494/FC 25009/QCX 10276/WCX 1386/C 90514
other lp issues: american columbia ML 4633/3216 0320/
    emi RLS 749/HQM 1163/1C047 01406M/
    2C061 01963/1C197 53780-53786M
cd: emi CDC 747 5172/CDH 769 8002/CZS 767 1632/
    CDM 566 9882

scarlatti sonata in e/longo 23
78: LB 113/GQ 7247
lp: FCX 495/QCX 10276/WCX 1386/C 90514
other lp issues: american columbia ML 2216/emi RLS 749/
    HQM 1163/1C047 01406M/2C051 01696/
    1C197 53780-53786M
cd: emi CDC 747 5172/CDH 769 8002/CZS 767 1632/
    CDM 566 9882

scarlatti sonata in d/longo 413
78: LB 113/LC 30/LF 253/GQ 7232/GQ 7247/LZ 9
lp: FCX 495/QCX 10276/WCX 1386/C 90514
other lp issues: american columbia ML 2216/emi RLS 749/
    HQM 1163/1C047 01406M/2C051 01696/
    1C197 53780-53786M
cd: emi CDC 747 5172/CDH 769 8002/CZS 767 1632/
    CDM 566 9882

chopin barcarolle in f sharp minor
78: LX 1437/LFX 1024
lp: FCX 493/FCX 30098/QCX 10276/WCX 1386/C 90514
other lp issues: american columbia ML 4721/emi RLS 749/
    HQM 1163/1C047 01282M/2C061 01282/
    1C197 53780-53786M
cd: emi CDC 747 3902/CDH 769 8022/CDM 566 2222/
    CZS 767 1632/CDM 566 9882

alborada del gracioso/miroirs
78: LB 70/LF 269
45: SEB 3501/ESBF 108/SEBQ 106
lp: FCX 495/QCX 10276/WCX 1386/C 90514
other lp issues: american columbia ML 2216/emi RLS 749/
    HQM 1163/HLM 7008/1C049 01811M/
    2C051 01696/1C197 53780-53786M
cd: emi CDH 763 0382/CZS 767 1632/CDM 567 5662

33CX 1387-1389/sheridan the school for scandal
recorded in abbey road studios london on 9 september 1953/published in november 1956/ lp matrix numbers XAX 779-783

bloom	*other lp issue:* angel 35292-35294
evans	*performance of the play included music by boyce played by the*
parker	*philharmonia orchestra conducted by walter jellinek*

33CX 1390/taneyev suite de concert
recorded in kingsway hall london on 24-25 february 1956/producer walter legge/published in november 1956/lp matrix numbers XAX 913-914

malko	*other lp issues:* angel 35355/emi SLS 5004/bruno 14013/
philharmonia	melodiya D 021509-021510
oistrakh, violin	cd: emi CDM 565 4192

33CX 1391-1392/symphonies by beethoven
recorded in musikvereinssaal vienna on 24-29 july 1955 and in kingsway hall london on 19-20 may 1955 respectively/producer walter legge/published in november 1956/ lp matrix numbers XHAX 63-65 and XAX 814

karajan	**symphony no 9 "choral"**
philharmonia	lp: FCX 448-449/QCX 10190-10191/WCX 1391-1392/
wiener	C 90515-90516
singverein	*other lp issues:* angel 3544/world records SM 143-149
schwarzkopf	toshiba EAC 37001-37019/emi SLS 5053/HZE 107/
höffgen	1C063 01200M/3C053 01200/1C181 01380-01386M
haefliger	cd: emi CMS 763 3102
edelmann	

karajan	**symphony no 8**
philharmonia	lp: FCX 449/QCX 10191/WCX 1392/WC 512/
	C 90516/C 70364
	other lp issues: angel 3544/toshiba EAC 37001-37019
	separate stereo performance
	lp: world records SM 143-149/emi SLS 5053/toshiba EAC 37001-37019
	cd: emi CMS 763 3102

33CX 1481

33CX 1572

33CX 1393/works by johann and josef strauss
recorded in kingsway hall london on 6-9 july 1955/producer walter legge/published in november 1956/lp matrix numbers XAX 794-795

karajan kaiserwalzer; an der schönen blauen donau;
philharmonia **delirienwalzer**
lp: FCX 531/FCX 30105/QCX 10205/WCX 1393/
WSX 527/C 90572/C 80463
other lp issues: angel 35342/toshiba EAC 37020-37038
cd: emi CMS 763 4562
der zigeunerbaron overture
45: SEL 1557
lp: FCX 531/FCX 30105/QCX 10205/WCX 1393/
WSX 527/C 90572/C 80463
other lp issues: angel 35342/toshiba EAC 37020-37038
cd: emi CMS 763 4562
künstlerleben waltz
45: EW 22/SELW 1503/C 50142
lp: FCX 531/FCX 30105/QCX 10205/WCX 1393/
WSX 527/C 90572/C 80463
other lp issues: angel 35342/toshiba EAC 37020-37038
cd: emi CMS 763 4562
pizzicato polka
45: SEL 1568/SEBQ 171
lp: FCX 531/FCX 30105/QCX 10205/WCX 1393/
WSX 527/C 90572/C 80463
other lp issues: angel 35342/toshiba EAC 37020-37038
cd: emi CMS 763 4562

33CX 1394/mendelssohn symphony no 4 "italian"; schubert symphony no 8 "unfinished"
recorded in maison de la mutualité paris on 12-18 january 1955/producer rené challan/ published in november 1956/lp matrix numbers XLX 325-326

markevitch lp: FCX 405/WCX 1395/C 90517
orchestre *other lp issue:* angel 35309
national cd: emi CZS 569 2122

33CX 1395/violin concerti by mozart and prokofiev
recorded in abbey road studios london on 23 november 1955 and 18 november 1955 respectively/producer geraint jones/published in november 1956/lp matrix numbers XAX 886-887

ackermann	mozart violin concerto no 3 k216
philharmonia	lp: WC 523/C 70378
kogan, violin	*other lp issue:* angel 35344

cameron	prokofiev violin concerto no 2
london	*other lp issue:* angel 35344
symphony	cd: testament SBT 1224/SBT6 1248
kogan, violin	

33CX 1396/beethoven string quartet no 10 op 74 "harp"
recorded in 1955-1956/published in november 1956/lp matrix numbers XBX 376-377

quartetto	lp: QCX 10209/WCX 1396/C 90573
italiano	*other lp issue:* angel 35367

33CX 1397-1398/handel solomon
recorded in abbey road studios london on 17-25 november 1955/producer lawrance collingwood/published in november 1956/lp matrix numbers XAX 961-964

beecham	lp: SAX 2499-2500/FCX 966-967/SAXF 966-967
royal	*other lp issues:* angel 3546/angel seraphim 6039/emi SLS 5163/
philharmonic	world records CM 82-83/SCM 82-83/T 82-83/ST 82-83
beecham	*excerpts*
choral society	45: hmv 7P 324
morison	lp: hmv ALP 1912/ASD 480/emi YKM 5007/
marshall	world records T 837/ST 837/angel seraphim 60134
young	*recording completed in december 1955 and january and may 1956*
cameron	

33CX 1399/schubert violin sonatina d408; violin sonata d574
recorded in electrola studio berlin on 7-13 november 1955 and 26 september 1955 respectively/producer fritz ganss/published in november 1956

martzy, violin	*other lp issue:* angel 35365
antonietti,	*recording of sonata d574 completed on 13 november 1955*
piano	

33CX 1400-1401/cornelius der barbier von bagdad
recorded in town hall watford on 11-14 may 1956 and in abbey road studios london on 15 may 1956/producers walter legge and walter jellinek/published in november 1957/ lp matrix numbers XAX 969-972

leinsdorf
philharmonia
chorus
schwarzkopf
g.hoffman
gedda
unger
wächter
prey

lp: WCX 1400-1401/C 90885-90886
other lp issues: angel 3553/emi 1C147 01448-01449M/ REG 2047-2048
cd: emi CMS 565 2842

33CX 1402/see 33CXS 1182-33CX 1183 and 33CXS 1211-33CX 1212

33CX 1403/bach concerto for two pianos bwv 1061; mozart concerto for two pianos k365
recorded in abbey road studios london on 24-26 april 1956/producers walter legge and walter jellinek/published in february 1957/lp matrix numbers XAX 925-926

galliera
philharmonia
haskil and
anda, pianos

lp: FCX 550/WCX 1403/C 90519
other lp issues: angel 35380/emi SXLP 30175/1C053 00439/ 2C051 00439
cd: emi CDH 763 4922

33CX 1404/songs by martini, mendelssohn, dvorak, hahn, tchaikovsky, jensen, grieg, sibelius, strauss, wolf and folksongs
recorded in abbey road studios london on 8-13 april and 18-19 may 1956/producer walter legge/published in february 1957/lp matrix numbers XAX 947-948

schwarzkopf
moore, piano

lp: SAX 2265/FCX 664/SAXF 145/WCX 1404/C 90545
other lp issues: angel 35383
selections from these recordings
45: SEL 1588/SEL 1589/SEL 1600/ESL 6255/ESL 6274/ SCD 2149/SELW 1805/C 50502/ESBF 17122
lp: emi RLS 154 6133
cd: emi CDM 763 6542/CMS 763 7902/ CHS 565 8602/585 1052
stereo lps SAX 2265 and SAXF 145 omitted the sibelius song schilf schilf säusle

33CX 1405/beethoven string quartet op 130; grosse fuge op 133
recorded in studio magellan paris on 15-18 september 1953/producer norbert gamsohn/ published in february 1957/lp matrix numbers XAX 517-518
hungarian   lp: FCX 247/WCX 1405/C 90521
string quartet   *other lp issue:* angel 35113
                  cd: emi CZS 767 2362

33CX 1406/hoffnung music festival
recorded in royal festival hall london on 13 november 1956/producer victor olof/published in february 1957/lp matrix numbers XAX 1058-1059
arnold   *other lp issues:* angel 35500/emi SLS 5069/
leonard   1C153 52125-52127
del mar
morley college
symphony
brain, horn

33CX 1407/works for cello and orchestra by schumann and tchaikovsky
recorded in kingsway hall london on 15-16 march 1956/producer walter jellinek/ published in february 1957/lp matrix numbers XAX 941-942
sargent   **schumann cello concerto**
philharmonia   lp: SAX 2282/FCX 744/QCX 10396/SAXQ 7279/
fournier, cello   WCX 1407/C 90522/C 70490/STC 70490
                other lp issues: angel 35397/emi 1A197 54430-54433
                tchaikovsky rococo variations
                lp: SAX 2282/FCX 744/QCX 10396/SAXQ 7279/
                    WCX 1407/C 90522
                other lp issue: angel 35397

33CX 1408/string quartets by galuppi, cambini and boccherini
recorded in milan in 1956/published in february 1957/lp matrix numbers XBX 394-395
quartetto   lp: QCX 10219/WCX 1408/C 90523
italiano   cd: testament SBT 1124

33CX 1409/songs by grieg and richard strauss
recorded in abbey road studios london on 4-7 july 1956/producers walter legge and walter jellinek/published in april 1957/lp matrix numbers XAX 1033-1034
nordmo-   *other lp issue:* angel 35590
lövberg
levin, piano

33CX 1410-1412/verdi falstaff
recorded in kingsway hall london on 21-29 june 1956/producer walter legge/published in march 1957/lp matrix numbers XAX 981-986

karajan	lp: SAX 2254-2256/QCX 10244-10246/WCX 1410-1412/
philharmonia	C 90524-90526
and chorus	*other lp issues:* angel 3552/emi SLS 5037/SLS 5211/
schwarzkopf	1C153 00442-00443/1C165 02125-02127/
merriman	2C167 03951-03952/3C153 00442-00443
moffo	cd: emi CDS 749 6682/CMS 567 0832
barbieri	*excerpts*
alva	lp: 33CX 1939/SAX 2578/WSX 528/C 80615
gobbi	*other lp excerpts:* emi 1C027 03903/1C063 02209
panerai	cd: emi CDM 769 3382/CZS 252 1592
zaccaria	

33CX 1413/saint-saens symphony no 3 "organ"
recorded in palais de chaillot paris on 19-21 september 1955/producer rené challan/ published in march 1957/lp matrix numbers XLX 386-387

cluytens	lp: FCX 447/QCX 10193/WCX 1413/C 90527
conservatoire	*other lp issue:* angel 35336
orchestra	cd: testament SBT 1240
roget, organ	

33CX 1414/malipiero symphony no 6; petrassi ritratto di don chisciotte
recorded in july 1955/published in march 1957/lp matrix numbers XBX 358-359

caracciolo	lp: QCX 10162/WCX 1414/C 90528
alessandro	*recording completed in november 1955*
scarlatti	
orchestra	

33CX 1415/violin sonatas by tartini and mozart
recorded in abbey road studios london on 16-17 february 1956/producer walter legge/ published in march 1957/ lp matrix numbers XAX 904-905

oistrakh, violin	**tartini sonata in g minor**
	45: ESBF 17119
yampolsky, piano	lp: FCX 654/QCX 10306/WCX 1415/C 90529
	other lp issues: angel 35356/hmv LALP 475/emi 1C147 52238-52239/melodiya D 028113-028114
	cd: emi 562 9142/testament SBT 1113
	mozart sonata no 32 k454
	lp: FCX 654/QCX 10306/WCX 1415/C 90529
	other lp issues: angel 35356/hmv LALP 475/emi 1C147 52238-52239/ melodiya D 012865-012866
	cd: testament SBT 1115

33CX 1416/liszt apres une lecture de dante; sonetti di petrarca nos 47, 104 and 123
recorded in abbey road studios london on 20-23 june 1955/producer walter jellinek/published in july 1957/ lp matrix numbers XAX 896-897
siki, piano

33CX 1417/beethoven piano sonatas nos 17 and 18 op 18 nos 2 and 3
recorded in abbey road studios london on 29 august-2 september 1955/producers walter legge and geraint jones/published in march 1957/ lp matrix numbers XAX 841 and 874

gieseking, piano	lp: WCX 1417/C 90531
	other lp issues: angel 35352/emi 3C153 52384-52393

33CX 1418/ceremonial music of the synagogue
recorded in 1956/published in march 1957/ lp matrix numbers XPTX 247-248

kacmann	*other lp issue:* angel 35295

33CX 1419/schumann symphonies nos 1 and 4
recorded in tel aviv on 21-24 february 1956 and 6-8 may 1956 respectively/producer lawrance collingwood/published in april 1957/ lp matrix numbers XTVX 9-10

kletzki	*other lp issue:* angel 35372
israel philharmonic	

33CX 1420/orchestral works by tchaikovsky and balakirev
recorded in kingsway hall london on 11-13 january 1956 and 18 december 1954 (balakirev)/ producer walter jellinek/published in april 1957/lp matrix numbers XAX 911-912

matacic philharmonia
tchaikovsky hamlet fantasy overture
other lp issue: angel 35398
cd: emi CZS 568 7392/CHS 764 8552/testament SBT 1331
tchaikovsky the storm overture
other lp issues: angel 35398/hmv CLP 1843
cd: emi CZS 568 7392/CHS 764 8552/testament SBT 1330
balakirev overture on russian themes
other lp issues: angel 35398/emi XLP 30107
cd: testament SBT 1331

33CX 1421/mussorgsky-ravel pictures at an exhibition
recorded in kingsway hall london on 11-12 october 1955/producer walter legge/published in april 1957/lp matrix numbers XAX 977-978

karajan philharmonia
lp: SAX 2261/FCX 518/SAXF 131/QCX 10266/SAXQ 7271/ WCX 1421/C 90532/SAXW 2261/STC 90532
other lp issues: angel 35430/emi SLS 5019/SXLP 30445/ 1C037 01390/2C053 01169/1C181 25307-25311
cd: emi CDZ 762 8602/562 8692/laserlight 16206
recording completed on 18 june 1956

33CX 1422/works for violin and orchestra
recorded in town hall hornsey on 11-12 june 1956/producers walter legge and walter jellinek/published in april 1957/lp matrix numbers XAX 979-980

galliera philharmonia rabin, violin
tchaikovsky violin concerto
lp: WCX 1422/C 90533
other lp issues: angel 35388/emi MFP 2002
cd: emi CDF 300 0212/CMS 764 1232
saint-saens introduction and rondo capriccioso
lp: WCX 1422/C 90533
other lp issues: angel 35388/emi MFP 2002

33CX 1423/schubert octet
recorded in abbey road studios london on 27 october 1955/producer walter jellinek/ published in april 1957/lp matrix numbers XAX 919-920

oistrakh	lp: FCX 30246
bondarenko	*other lp issues:* angel 35362/hmv LALP 349/melodiya
terian	D04926-04927/D18661-18662
knushevitsky	cd: testament SBT 1113
sorokin	
gertovich	
stidel, shapiro	

33CX 1424/mozart string quartets k421 and k428
recorded in abbey road studios london on 8-12 october 1956/producer walter jellinek/ published in april 1957/lp matrix numbers XAX 1039-1040

smetana   lp: WCX 1424/C 90534/C 80541
string quartet

33CX 1425/prokofiev cello concerto; milhaud cello concerto
recorded in kingsway hall london on 16-17 july 1956/producers walter legge and william mann/published in july 1957/lp matrix numbers XAX 1055-1056

susskind	*other lp issue:* angel 35418
philharmonia	cd: emi CZS 568 7452/CZS 568 4852
starker, cello	

33CX 1426/catalogue number allocated to a recital of chopin piano music by manoru yanagawa recorded in abbey road studios but published only in japan

33CX 1427/beethoven piano sonatas nos 7 op 10/3 and 28 op 101
recorded in abbey road studios london on 13-14 june 1958/producers walter legge and walter jellinek/lp matrix numbers XAX 987-988

anda, piano   cd: testament SBT 1070

33CX 1428/mozart piano sonatas no 7 k309 and no 10 k330; rondo k485; capriccio k395
recorded in abbey road studios london between 3 and 20 august 1953/producers walter legge and geraint jones/published in april 1957/lp matrix numbers XAX 418-419

gieseking, piano	lp: FCX 320/WCX 1428/C 90535
	other lp issues: angel 35077/3511/emi 1C197 03133-03137M/ 3C153 00997-01007M
	cd: emi CHS 763 6882

33CX 1429/works by liszt and brahms
recorded in abbey road studios london on 17-18 december 1955, 13 may 1956 and 10 november 1956 respectively/producer lawrance collingwood/published in april 1957/ lp matrix numbers XAX 1019 and 1066

beecham	**liszt psalm 13**
royal	*other lp issues:* angel 35400/world records T 909/ST 909
philharmonic	cd: emi CDM 763 2992
beecham	
choral society	
midgley	
sung in english	

beecham	**brahms schicksalslied**
royal	*other lp issue:* angel 35400
philharmonic	cd: emi CDM 763 2212
beecham	*recording completed on 30 november 1956*
choral society	
sung in english	

beecham	**brahms academic festival overture**
royal	*other lp issues:* angel 35400/angel seraphim 60083/emi HQS
philharmonic	1143/SXLP 30158/1C047 01489/1C053 00649
	cd: emi CDM 763 2212/CDM 764 4462
	recording completed on 29 november 1956

33CX 1430/works for string quartet by gabrieli, marini, neri, vitali, scarlatti and vivaldi
recorded in milan in 1956-1957/published in april 1957/lp matrix numbers XBX 406-407

quartetto	lp: QCX 10236
italiano	*works by vitali and vivaldi only*
	cd: testament SBT 1124

33CX 1431-1433/mendelssohn elijah
recorded in town hall huddersfield on 30 april-3 may 1956/producer lawrance collingwood/ published in april 1957/lp matrix numbers XAX 1027-1032

sargent	*other lp issue:* angel 3558
liverpool	cd: emi CDCFPSD 4802/568 9382
philharmonic	*excerpts*
huddersfield	lp: emi HQM 1115
choral society	*recording completed in abbey road studios london on 6 may and 17*
morison	*june 1956 using pro arte orchestra in place of liverpool philharmonic*
thomas	
lewis	
cameron	

33CX 1434-1436/cimarosa il matrimonio segreto
recorded in basilica santa eufemia milan on 7-15 february 1956/producers walter legge and edward fowler/published in may 1957/lp matrix numbers XBX 45-50

sanzogno   lp: QCX 10224-10226/WCX 1434-1436/C 90536-90538
la scala   *other lp issue:* angel 3549
orchestra
and chorus
sciutti
ratti
stignani
alva
badioli
calabrese

33CX 1437/stravinsky le rossignol
recorded in maison de la murualité paris on 25-29 march 1955/producer rené challan/ published in may 1957/lp matrix numbers XLX 350-351

cluytens   lp: FCX 439/WCX 1437/C 90539
orchestre   *other lp issue:* angel 35204
national   cd: testament SBT 1135
and chorus   *recording completed in april and may 1955*
micheau
moizan
giraudeau
roux

33CX 1438/orchestral works by mozart and beethoven
recorded in abbey road studios london on 25-27 march 1956/producer walter legge/ published in may 1957/lp matrix numbers XAX 943-944

klemperer   adagio and fugue in c minor
philharmonia   45: ESLQ 1010
                 lp: 33CX 1948/WCX 1438/C 90540/SAX 2587
                 other lp issues: angel 35401/36289/32099/34470/emi SLS 5048/
                      EX 29 04823/SME 80933/1C147 01842-01847/
                      1C153 01842-01847/1C197 53714-53738/2C061 00602/
                      100 6024/2C147 50298-50318/769 4081
                 cd: emi CDM 763 6202

33CX 1438/orchestral works by mozart and beethoven/concluded
klemperer   **serenade no 6 "serenata notturna"**
philharmonia   lp: WCX 1438/WC 514/C 90540/C 70102/C 70366/HC 116
other lp issues: angel 35401/hmv LALP 320/
    emi 1C197 53714-53738
cd: emi CDM 764 1462
grosse fuge in b flat, arranged for orchestra
lp: WCX 1438/C 90540
other lp issues: angel 35401/emi SLS 873/ED 29 02711/
    EX 29 03799/1C147 53400-53419/1C197 53400-53419/
    2C147 50298-50318
cd: emi CDC 747 1862/CDM 763 3562/CDZ 568 0572/
    CZS 573 8952

33CX 1439/berlioz symphonie fantastique
recorded in maison de la murualité paris between 13 and 24 october 1956/producer rené challan/published in july 1957/lp matrix numbers XLX 408-409
cluytens   lp: FCX 459
orchestre   *other lp issue:* angel 35448
national   cd: testament SBT 1234

33CX 1440/orchestral works by prokofiev and shostakovich
recorded in maison de la mutualité paris 23-24 may 1955 and 4-5 january 1955 respectively/producer rené challan/published in may 1957/lp matrix numbers XLX 464-465
markevitch   **prokofiev scythian suite**
orchestre   lp: FCX 541/WCX 1440/C 90541
national   *other lp issue:* angel 35361
cd: emi CZS 762 6472
shostakovich symphony no 1
lp: FCX 541/WCX 1440/C 90541
other lp issue: angel 35361
cd: emi CZS 569 2122

33CX 1441/catalogue number appears not to have been allocated

33CX 1442/beethoven string quartet op 131
recorded in studio magellan paris on 2-6 october 1953/producer norbert gamsohn/published in may 1957/lp matrix numbers XAX 519-520

hungarian   lp: FCX 248/WCX 1442/C 90542
string quartet   *other lp issue:* angel 35114
                cd: emi CZS 767 2362

33CX 1443-1444/chopin works for solo piano
recorded in abbey road studios london between 17 and 29 june 1956/producer walter jellinek/published in may 1957/lp matrix numbers XAX 997-1000

arrau, piano   **études op 10 and op 25; trois nouvelles études**
                lp: WCX 1443-1444/C 90543-90544
                other lp issue: angel 35413-35414
                cd: emi CDH 761 0162
                recordings completed on 5 september 1956
                allegro de concert
                lp: WCX 1443-1444/C 90543-90544
                other lp issue: angel 35413-35414

33CX 1445/schubert impromptus d935; piano sonata no 13 d664
recorded in abbey road studios london on 21-22 june 1955/producer walter jellinek/published in may 1957/lp matrix numbers XAX 894-895

siki, piano

33CX 1446-1447/orff die kluge
recorded in abbey road studios london on 22-26 may 1956/producer walter legge/published in june 1957/lp matrix numbers XAX 955-958

sawallisch   lp: SAX 2257-2258/WSX 510-511/C 90284-90285/
philharmonia   STC 90284-90285
schwarzkopf   *other lp issues:* angel 3551/emi 1C137 43291-43293/
christ   arabesque 8021-8022
kuen   cd: emi CMS 763 7122
frick   *excerpts*
cordes   lp: 33CX 1810/SAX 2456
prey   *other lp excerpts:* emi 1C063 00719
kusche   cd: emi CZS 767 1872
neidlinger

33CX 1448/brahms lieder recital
recorded in abbey road studios london on 19-21 may 1956/producers walter legge and walter jellinek/published in november 1957/lp matrix numbers XAX 1017-1018
hotter lp: WCX 1448/C 90545
moore, piano *other lp issues:* angel 35497
selections from the recital
lp: emi HQM 1072/angel seraphim 60044/60065
cd: emi 562 8072/testament SBT 1198-1199
recordings completed on 31 may 1956

33CX 1449/schumann symphony no 2; overture, scherzo and finale
recorded in tel aviv on 26-29 february 1956 and in march 1956 respectively/producer lawrance collingwood/published in june 1957/lp matrix numbers XTVX 11-12
kletzki lp: WCX 1449/C 90546
israel *other lp issue:* angel 35373
philharmonic

33CX 1450/balakirev symphony no 1
recorded in abbey road studios london between 26 november and 15 december 1955/ producer lawrance collingwood/published in june 1957/lp matrix numbers XAX 935-936
beecham *other lp issues:* angel 35399/angel seraphim 60062/emi
royal XLP 30002/SXLP 30002/SXLP 30171/1C047 01567
philharmonic

33CX 1451/orchestral works by salieri, vivaldi and durante
recorded in july 1955/published in june 1957/lp matrix numbers XBX 352-353
schippers lp: QCX 10179
alessandro *other lp issue:* angel 35335
scarlatti *recordings completed in november 1955*
orchestra

33CX 1452/catalogue number allocated to a recital of piano music by debussy and ravel by manoru yanagawa recorded in abbey road studios but published only in japan

33CX 1453/mozart allegro k400; allegro and minuet k498a; 8 minuets k315a; 6 deutsche tänze k509
recorded in abbey road studios london on 1 august 1953 (allegro and minuet) and 31 march 1954/producers walter jellinek and geraint jones/published in june 1957/lp matrix numbers XAX 545-546

gieseking,   lp: FCX 321/WCX 1453/C 90547
piano   *other lp issues:* angel 35078/3511/emi 1C197 03133-03137M/ 3C153 00997-01007M
                 cd: emi CHS 763 6882

33CX 1454-1455/catalogue numbers appear not to have been allocated

33CX 1456/catalogue number allocated to a recording of bartok bluebeard's conducted by janos ferencsik but published only on the hungaroton label

33CX 1457/symphonies by mozart
recorded in kingsway hall london on 21-25 july 1956/producer walter legge/published in september 1957/lp matrix numbers XAX 991-992

klemperer   **symphony no 25**
philharmonia   45: SEL 1594/ESL 6254
                 lp: SAX 2278/33CX 5252/SAX 5252/QCX 10274/ WCX 1457/SAXW 2278/C 90548/C 91148/C 70736
                 other lp issues: angel 35407/34470/emi SLS 5048/ EX 29 04823/1C147 01842-01847/1C153 01842-01847/ 1C197 53714-53738
                 cd: emi CMS 763 2722
                 symphony no 40
                 lp: SAX 2278/FC 25104/QCX 10274/WCX 1457/WC 521/ SAXW 2278/SBOW 8504/C 90548/C 70376/ STC 90548/STC 70376
                 other lp issues: angel 35407/emi SLS 5048/1C147 01842- 01847/1C153 01842-01847/1C197 53714-53738/ 2C059 01847
                 cd: emi CDC 747 8522/CMS 763 2722

33CX 1458/haydn symphonies nos 101 "clock" and 102
recorded in théatre des champs elysées paris on 3 may 1955 and 26-27 may 1955 respectively/ producer rené challan/published in september 1957/lp matrix numbers XLX 376-377

markevitch   lp: FCX 437/WCX 1458/C 90549
orchestre   *other lp issue:* angel 35312
national   cd: emi CZS 569 2122

33CX 1459/piano music by chopin
recorded in abbey road studios london on 15-22 may 1956/producers walter legge and walter jellinek/published in september 1957/lp matrix numbers XAX 989-990

anda, piano   **études op 25**
     lp: C 60733
     other lp issue: angel 35420
     cd: testament SBT 1066
     ballade no 1
     other lp issue: angel 35420
     cd: testament SBT 1066

33CX 1460/beethoven string quartet no 15 op 132
recorded in studio magellan paris on 6-13 october 1953/producer norbert gamsohn/published in september 1957/lp matrix numbers XAX 521-522

hungarian   lp: FCX 249/WCX 1460/C 90550
string quartet   *other lp issue:* angel 35115
     cd: emi CZS 767 2362

33CX 1461/catalogue number appears not to have been allocated

33CX 1462-1463/mozart die entführung aus dem serail
recorded in kingsway hall london between 9 and 25 may 1956/producer lawrance collingwood/published in september 1957/lp matrix numbers XAX 1035-1038

beecham   lp: FCX 700-701/SAXF 700-702/WCX 1462-1463/
royal   C 90551-90552
philharmonic   *other lp issues:* angel 3555/emi SLS 773/SLS 5153/1C153
beecham   01541-01542/2C167 01541-01542
choral society   cd: emi CHS 763 7152
marshall   *excerpts*
hollweg   lp: hmv ALP 1912/ASD 480/world records T 837/ST 837/
simoneau   emi SEOM 2/1C147 30636-30637/CCPM 130566
unger   *rehearsal extracts*
frick   lp: hmv ALP 1874/world records SH 147
     cd: emi CDM 764 4652

33CX 1464-1465/puccini la boheme
recorded in teatro alla scala milan on 20-25 august 1956/producers walter legge and walter jellinek/published in march 1958/lp matrix numbers XBX 70-73

votto	lp: FCX 773-774/QCX 10272-10273/WCX 1464-1465/
la scala	C 90553-90554
orchestra	*other lp issues:* angel 3560/emi SLS 5029/EX 29 09233/
and chorus	1C153 18182-18183/2C163 18182-18183/
callas	3C163 18182-18183
moffo	cd: emi CDS 747 4758/CDS 556 2952/CMS 252 9432/
di stefano	*excerpts*
panerai	45: SCD 2182/SEBQ 159/SCBQ 3037/SELW 1546/C 50154
zaccaria	lp: 33CX 1725/FCX 802/FCX 929/FCX 30149/QCX 10108/
	QCX 10403/QCX 10437/QCX 10441/QCX 10477/
	WSX 547/WSX 622/WC 610/C 80530/C 80689/C 70400

other lp excerpts: angel 35939/35940/3814/emi SLS 856/
SLS 5104/1C187 28985-28966M/1C191 01433-01434M/
1C191 01593-01594M/3C063 01018/3C065 01480/
SHZE 110
cd: emi CDM 769 5432/CDC 555 2162/CDS 754 1032/
CMS 565 5342/CMS 565 7462/CZS 252 6142'
562 7942/566 6882
recording completed on 3-4 september 1956

33CX 1466/music for violin and piano by suk, kodaly, wieniawski, zarzycki, debussy, falla, tchaikovsky and ysaye
recorded in abbey road studios london between 18 and 28 february 1956/producer walter legge/published in september 1957/lp matrix numbers XAX 915-916

oistrakh,	lp: SAX 2253/SAXF 149/WSX 604
violin	*other lp issues:* angel 35354/angel seraphim 60259/
yampolsky,	emi SHZE 160
piano	cd: emi 562 9142

selections from the recital
45: SEL 1577/ESL 6252/SEB 2515/ESLQ 1007/SEBQ 219
cd: emi CDM 769 3672/testament SBT 1115

33CX 1467-1468/grieg lyric pieces
recorded in abbey road studios london on 22-23 september 1956/producer walter jellinek/published in september 1957/lp matrix numbers XAX 1041-1044

gieseking,	*other lp issues:* angel 35450-35451/3C053 01309-01310/
piano	3C153 52331-52340M

selections from the recording
45: SEL 1693
lp: 33CX 1761/C 90913
other lp selections: angel 35488/emi HQM 1225/RLS 143 6203
grieg lyric pieces were published on cd in japan by toshiba

33CXS 1469-33CX 1471/bellini la sonnambula
recorded in basilica santa eufemia milan on 3-9 march 1957/producer walter legge/
published in september 1957/lp matrix numbers XBX 82-86

votto	lp: FCX 811-813/QCX 10278-10280/WCX 1469-1471/
la scala	C 90555-90557
orchestra	*other lp issues:* angel 3568/angel seraphim 6108/emi SLS 5134/
and chorus	EX 29 00433/2C163 17648-17650/2C163 18359-18360/
callas	2C163 52780-52787/3C163 17648-17650
ratti	cd: emi CDS 747 3788/CDS 556 2782/CMS 252 9432
cossotto	*excerpts*
monti	45: SCBQ 3041
zaccaria	lp: 33CX 1540/QCX 10302/QCX 10425/QCX 10444/
	WSX 523/WSX 566/C 80448/C 80602
	other lp excerpts: angel 35304/36929/3814/emi SLS 5057/
	SLS 5104/1C063 03253/2C065 00741/3C063 00741/
	3C063 01016/3C063 17920
	cd: emi CDC 749 5022/CMS 763 2442/CMS 565 5342/
	CZS 252 1642

33CX 1472-1474/verdi un ballo in maschera
recorded in teatro alla scala milan on 4-12 september 1956/producer walter jellinek/
published in october 1957/lp matrix numbers XBX 74-79

votto	lp: QCX 10263-10265/WCX 1472-1474/
la scala	C 90558-90560
orchestra	*other lp issues:* angel 3557/angel seraphim 6087/emi RLS 736/
and chorus	EX 29 09253/1C153 17651-17653/2C163 17651-17653/
callas	3C163 17651-17653
ratti	cd: emi CDS 747 4988/CDS 556 3202/CMS 252 9432/
barbieri	*excerpts*
di stefano	lp: 33CX 1681/WSX 622/C 80621/C 80689
gobbi	*other lp excerpts:* angel 36929/36940/emi SLS 856/1C053
	18065M/1C191 01433-01434M/1C191 01593-01594M/
	3C063 17919/3C065 17902
	cd: CDM 769 5432/CMS 763 2442/CMS 565 5342/
	CZS 252 6142

33CX 1475/schumann symphony no 3 "rhenish"; manfred overture
recorded in tel aviv on 29 february-5 march 1956/producer lawrance collingwood/published in october 1957/lp matrix numbers XTVX 13-14
kletzki   *other lp issue:* angel 35374
israel
philharmonic

33CX 1476/boccherini symphonies in a and c minor
recorded in june 1955/published in october 1957/lp matrix numbers XBX 360-361
caracciolo   lp: QCX 10161
alessandro   *other lp issue:* angel 35384
scarlatti
orchestra

33CX 1477/dvorak cello concerto; fauré élégie
recorded in kingsway hall london between 11 and 17 july 1956/producer walter legge/ published in october 1957/lp matrix numbers XAX 1003-1004
susskind   lp: SAX 2263/FCX 725/WCX 1477/C 91018/SAXW 2263/
philharmonia   STC 91018
starker, cello   *other lp issues:* angel 35417/world records T 751/ST 751/
                           emi CFP 40070
                    cd: emi CZS 568 7452/CZS 568 4852

33CX 1478/bach toccata and fugue bwv 565; fantasias bwv 542 and 562; chorale preludes bwv 615 and 645; 3 preludes
recorded in cathédrale de saint jean lyon/published in october 1957/lp matrix numbers XLX 399-400
commette,   *other lp issue:* angel 35368
organ

33CX 1479/mendelssohn lieder ohne worte, selection
recorded in abbey road studios london on 21-22 september 1956/producer walter jellinek/ published in october 1957/lp matrix numbers XAX 1045-1046
gieseking,   lp: FCX 605
piano   *other lp issues:* angel 35428/emi 1C047 00451/3C053 00451/
                           3C153 52434-52441M
                    selections from the recording
                    lp: 33CX 1761
                    other lp selections: angel 35488/emi RLS 143 6203
                    also issued on cd in japan by toshiba

33CX 1480/orff carmina burana
recorded in sartorysaal cologne on 15-20 june 1956/producer fritz ganss/published in october 1957/lp matrix numbers XRX 27-28

sawallisch   lp: WCX 1480/C 90283
wdr orchestra   *other lp issue:* angel 35415
and chorus   cd: emi CDM 764 2372
giebel
kuen
cordes

33CX 1481/tchaikovsky piano concerto no 1
recorded in maison de la mutualité paris on 17-21 december 1956/producer norbert gamsohn/published in october 1957/lp matrix numbers XLX 561-562

malko   lp: FC 1062/QCX 10308
orchestre   *other lp issue:* angel 35543
national
malcuzynski,
piano

33CX 1482/christmas carols, arranged by mackerras
recorded in abbey road studios london between 25 may and 1 june 1957/producer walter legge/published in november 1957/lp matrix numbers XAX 1248-1249

mackerras   *other lp issues:* angel 35530/36750/emi ASD 3798/
philharmonia   100 4531
and chorus   cd: emi CDM 763 5742
schwarzkopf   *recordings completed on 30 june-1 july 1957*
this lp was originally given the title "more songs you love"

33CXS 1483-33CX 1485/verdi il trovatore
recorded in teatro alla scala milan on 3-9 august 1956/producer walter legge/published in november 1957/lp matrix numbers XBX 65-69

karajan	lp: FCX 763-765/QCX 10267-10269/WCX 1483-1485/
la scala	C 90561-90563
orchestra	*other lp issues:* angel 3554/emi SLS 869/1C153 00454-00456/
and chorus	2C163 00454-00456/3C165 00454-00456
callas	cd: emi CDS 749 3472/CDS 556 3332
barbieri	*excerpts*
di stefano	45: SEL 1627/SEL 1641/SEL 1645/SEL 1653/SEL 1671/
panerai	SEL 1678/SEL 1789/ESBF 17099/SEBQ 223/
zaccaria	SEBQ 232/SCBQ 3045/SCBQ 3047
	lp: 33CX 1682/FCX 30181/QCX 10441/QCX 10444/
	WSX 530/WC 610/C 80492/C 70400
	other lp excerpts: angel 36966/3743/3814/emi SLS 856/
	SLS 5057/SLS 5104/1C053 01677M/1C063 03253/
	1C065 00741/1C027 03903M/1C191 01433-01434/
	1C191 01593-01594/1C187 28985-28986M/
	2C161 01433-01434/3C165 01433-01434
	cd: emi CDM 763 5572/CDM 566 6692/CMS 557 0622/
	562 5642/566 6882

33CX 1486/symphonies by mozart
recorded in kingsway hall london on 20-24 july 1956/producer walter legge/published in november 1957/lp matrix numbers XAX 993-994

klemperer	**symphony no 38 "prague"**
philharmonia	lp: FC 25102/QCX 10284/WCX 1486/C 90916
	other lp issue: angel 35408
	cd: testament SBT 1094
	symphony no 39
	lp: FC 25103/QCX 10284/WCX 1486/C 90916
	other lp issue: angel 35408
	cd: testament SBT 1094

33CX 1487/orchestral works by brahms
recorded in kingsway hall london on 29 february-3 march 1956 and 5 november 1956 respectively/producer walter legge/published in november 1957/lp matrix numbers XAX 1047-1048

galliera	**double concerto for violin and cello**
philharmonia	lp: SAX 2264/FC 1048/SAXF 143/QCX 10378/SAXQ 7264/
oistrakh,	WCX 1487/C 90564/WC 520/C 70383/SBOW 8501/
violin	STC 70383
fournier, cello	*other lp issues:* angel 35353/hmv LALP 498/emi XLP 30185/ SXLP 30185/EMX 2035/1C037 01974/2C181 52289-52290/SHZE 706
	cd: emi CZS 569 3312/CDZ 762 8542

galliera	**tragic overture**
philharmonia	lp: SAX 2264/FC 1048/SAXF 143/QCX 10378/SAXQ 7264/ WCX 1487/C 90564
	other lp issues: angel 35353/emi XLP 30185/SXLP 30185

33CX 1488/beethoven piano sonatas
recorded in abbey road studios london between 17 september and 20 october 1956/producer walter jellinek/published in november 1957/lp matrix numbers XAX 1091 and 1094

gieseking,	**piano sonata no 8 "pathétique"**
piano	lp: FCX 520/FCX 852-853/QCX 10309/WCX 1488/C 91004
	other lp issues: angel 3600/emi XLP 30129/SXLP 30129/ 3C153 52384-52393
	cd: emi CDZ 762 8572/CDZ 767 8342/CDU 650 502
	piano sonatas nos 1, 19 and 20
	lp: FCX 852-853/QCX 10309/WCX 1488/C 91004
	other lp issues: angel 3600/3C153 52384-52393

33CX 1489/see 33CX 1179-1181

33CX 1490/beethoven piano concerto no 5 "emperor"
recorded in abbey road studios london on 30 april-1 may 1957/producer walter legge/ published in november 1957/lp matrix numbers XAX 1145-1146

ludwig	lp: SAX 2252/FCX 674/FCX 30255/SAXF 113/QCX 10386/
philharmonia	SAXQ 7277/SAXW 2264/STC 91015
gilels, piano	*other lp issues:* angel 35476/emi 1C053 00666
	cd: emi 483 4182/testament SBT 1095

33CX 1491/strauss the two horn concerti
recorded in abbey road studios london on 21-23 september 1956/producer walter jellinek/ published in november 1957/lp matrix numbers XAX 1105-1106

sawallisch **horn concerto no 1**
philharmonia lp: WCX 1491/C 90565
brain, horn *other lp issues:* angel 35496/emi HLS 7001
cd: emi CDC 747 8342/CDM 567 7822/CDM 567 7832
horn concerto no 2
lp: WCX 1491/C 90565
other lp issues: angel 35496/emi HLS 7001/RLS 7701/
1C141 43327-43329M
cd: emi CDC 747 8342/CDM 567 7822/CDM 567 7832

33CX 1492-1495/strauss der rosenkavalier
recorded in kingsway hall london on 10-22 december 1956/producer walter legge/ published in december 1957/lp matrix numbers XAX 1159-1166

karajan lp: SAX 2269-2272/FCX 750-753/CVB 750-753/
philharmonia   WCX 1492-1495/C 90566-90569/SAXW 2269-2272/
chorus   STC 90566-90569
schwarzkopf *other lp issues:* angel 3563/emi SLS 810/EX 29 00453/
ludwig   1C191 00459-00462/2C165 00459-00462/
stich-randall   3C165 00459-00462
welitsch cd: emi CDS 749 3542/CDS 566 2422/CDS 556 1132/
gedda   CDS 567 6052
edelmann *excerpts*
wächter lp: 33CX 1777/SAX 2423/WCX 1777/SAXW 2433/
  C 80661/STC 80661
other lp excerpts: angel 35645/3754/emi 1C063 00720
cd: emi CDM 769 3382/CDM 763 6572/CDM 763 4522/
  CDM 565 5712/CMS 763 7902/CZS 252 1592/
  CMS 567 6342/585 1052/CDM 565 5772
CDS 556 1132 is a re-mastered edition of the mono tapes

33CX 1496/wagner meistersinger overture; tannhäuser overture; tristan und isolde prelude and liebestod
recorded in grünewaldkirche berlin on 7-8 january 1957 and 18-19 february 1957 (meistersinger)/producer walter legge/published in february 1958/lp matrix numbers XRX 217-218

karajan lp: FCX 689/QCX 10321/WSX 512/C 90286
berlin *other lp issues:* angel 35482/emi 1C037 54360-54363/
philharmonic 2C069 02604
cd: emi CMS 763 3212

33CX 1497/mendelssohn violin concerto; beethoven violin romances nos 1 and 2
recorded in kingsway hall london on 20-23 december 1955/producers walter legge and walter jellinek/published in january 1958/lp matrix numbers XAX 898-899

kletzki *other lp issue:* angel 35236
philharmonia *also issued on cd in japan by toshiba*
martzy, violin

33CX 1498/beethoven piano sonatas nos 7 and 11
recorded in abbey road studios london on 20-21 september 1956 and 19-20 october 1956 respectively/producers walter legge and walter jellinek/published in february 1958/ lp matrix numbers XAX 1089-1090

gieseking, *other lp issues:* angel 35653/emi 3C153 52384-52393
piano

33CX 1499-1500/chopin 13 valses; bach partita no 1 bwv 825; mozart sonata no 8 k310; schubert impromptus d899 nos 2 and 3
recorded at lipatti's final recital in salle du parlament besancon on 16 september 1950/ published in february 1958/lp matrix numbers XLX 543-546

lipatti, piano *other lp issues:* angel 3556/emi RLS 761/1C147 00463-00464M
cd: emi CDH 565 1662/562 8192
selections from the recital
lp: angel 35438/emi 2C051 01696
cd: emi CZS 767 1632

135

33CX 1501/tito gobbi at la scala
excerpts from the complete opera recordings on 33CX 1094-1095, 33CXS 1211-33CX 1212, 33CXS 1324-33CX 1326, 33CX 1370-1371 and 33CX 1472-1474

33CX 1502/see 33CX 1258-1260

33CX 1503/rousseau le devin du village
recorded in maison de la mutualité paris on 17-19 april 1956/producer rené challan/ published in february 1958/lp matrix numbers XPTX 394-395
de froment	lp: discophiles francais DF 730.067
de froment	*other lp issue:* angel 35421
chamber	*excerpts*
orchestra	lp: C 70411
micheau	
gedda	
roux	

33CX 1504/brahms symphony no 1
recorded in kingsway hall london on 29 october-1 november 1956/producer walter legge/ published in february 1958/lp matrix numbers XAX 1117-1118
klemperer	lp: SAX 2262/FCX 692/SAXF 201/QCX 10310/
philharmonia	SAXQ 7262/WCX 1504/C 90570/SAXW 2262/
	STC 90570
	other lp issues: angel 35481/3614/emi SLS 804/ASD 2705/
	SXLP 30217/1C053 00466/1C163 50034-50037/
	2C197 50034-50037
	cd: emi CDM 769 6512/CZS 479 8852/562 7422

33CX 1505/délibes ballet music from coppélia and sylvia
recorded in maison de la mutualité paris on 13-16 june 1956/producer rené challan/ published in january 1958/lp matrix numbers XLX 490-491
cluytens	lp: FCX 544/C 90639
paris opéra	*other lp issues:* angel 35416/emi MFP 2022
orchestra	*excerpts*
	45: SCD 2150

33CX 1506/brahms violin concerto
recorded in maison de la mutualité paris on 5-6 march 1955/producer rené challan/published in february 1958/lp matrix numbers XLX 338-339
bruck	lp: FCX 404
conservatoire	*other lp issue:* angel 35412
orchestra	cd: testament SBT 1225/SBT6 1248
kogan, violin	

33CX 1507-1509/rossini il barbiere di siviglia
recorded in kingsway hall london on 7-14 february 1957/producer walter legge/published in february 1958/lp matrix numbers XAX 1230-1235

galliera	lp: SAX 2266-2268/FCX 760-762/SAXF 120-122/
philharmonia	QCX 10297-10299/WCX 1507-1509/C 91030-91032/
chorus	SAXW 2266-2268/STC 91030-91032
callas	*other lp issues:* angel 3559/emi SLS 853/EX 29 10933/
carturan	1C165 00467-00469/2C167 00467-00469/
alva	1C197 00467-00469
gobbi	cd: emi CDS 747 6348/CDS 556 3102/CMS 252 7022
zaccaria	*excerpts*
	45: SEL 1658/SEL 1662/SEL 1687/ESBF 17110/SEBQ 222/
	SEBQ 120/SEBQ 222/SEBQ 226/SCBQ 3065
	lp: 33CX 1790/SAX 2438/FCX 30195/QCX 10443/
	SAXQ 7343/WSX 582/C 80634/SAXW 2438/STC 80634
	other lp excerpts: angel 35936/36293/3696/3699/3841/
	emi SLS 5057/SXLP 30166/SHZE 101/1C063 00735/
	1C187 01398-01399/2C059 43263/2C061 00552/
	2C069 43284/3C065 00552/CVT 3195/EMX 2123/
	143 2631
	cd: emi CDC 749 5022/CDC 555 5022/CDC 252 9382/
	CDS 749 6002/CDCFP 9013/CMS 565 5342/
	CMS 565 7462/CZS 252 6142/557 0622

33CX 1510/catalogue number appears not to have been allocated

33CX 1511/orchestral works by mozart
recorded in abbey road studios london on 6 november 1954 and 28-29 may 1955 respectively/producers walter legge and walter jellinek/published in march 1958/ lp matrix numbers XAX 1204-1205

karajan	**symphony no 35 "haffner"**
philharmonia	lp: C 91304
	other lp issues: angel 35562/toshiba EAC 37001-37019
	cd: emi CMS 763 4562
	recording completed in may 1955
	diverimento no 15 k287
	lp: FCX 735
	other lp issues: angel 35562/toshiba EAC 37001-37019
	cd: emi CMS 763 4562

33CX 1512/hindemith symphony in b flat; concert music for brass and strings
recorded in kingsway hall london on 22-24 november 1956/producer walter legge/published in march 1958/lp matrix numbers XAX 1109-1110

hindemith lp: WCX 1512/C 90903
philharmonia *other lp issues:* angel 35489/angel seraphim 60005/ emi EH 29 11731
  cd: emi CDH 763 3732

33CX 1513/piano sonatas by beethoven
recorded in abbey road studios london in 30 november-1 december 1956/producer walter jellinek/published in march 1958/lp matrix numbers XAX 1067-1068

arrau, piano **piano sonata no 21 "waldstein"**
  lp: C 70491
  cd: emi CZS 767 3792
  recording completed on 19 may 1957
  piano sonata no 28
  cd: emi CZS 767 3792

33CX 1514/beethoven violin concerto
recorded in town hall walthamstow on 18-19 march 1957/producer walter jellinek/published in march 1958/lp matrix numbers XAX 1149-1150

schüchter *other lp issue:* emi TRI 6105
pro arte
orchestra
i.oistrakh, violin

33CX 1515/bach cello suites nos 2 and 5
recorded in abbey road studios london on 20 march 1957 and 29-30 august 1957 respectively/producer walter jellinek/published in march 1958/lp matrix numbers XAX 1308-1309

starker, cello lp: WCX 1515/C 90911
  cd: emi CZS 568 4852
  recording of suite no 5 completed on 3 october 1957

33CX 1516/see 33CX 1309-1310

33CX 1517/orchestral works by brahms
recorded in kingsway hall london on 29-30 october 1956 and 29 march 1957 respectively/ producer walter legge/published in april 1958/lp matrix numbers XAX 1119 and 1175

klemperer   **symphony no 2**
philharmonia   lp: SAX 2362/FCX 693/SAXF 202/QCX 10322/SAXQ 7311/WCX 1517/C 90920/SAXW 2362/STC 90920/ SMC 91632
other lp issues: angel 35532/3614/32049/34413/emi SLS 804/ ASD 2706/SXLP 30238/1C053 00470/1C163 50034-50037/1C197 50034-50037
cd: emi CDM 769 6502/562 7422

tragic overture
lp: SAX 2362/FCX 693/SAXF 202/QCX 10322/SAXQ 7311/WCX 1517/C 90920/SAXW 2362/STC 90920/ SMC 91632/STC 91224-91225
other lp issues: angel 35532/3614/32049/emi SLS 804/ SLS 821/SXLP 30238/1C053 00470/1C153 01295-01296/1C163 50034-50037/1C197 50034-50037
cd: emi CDM 769 6512/CZS 479 8852/562 7422

33CX 1518/orchestral works by stravinsky, bizet and ravel
recorded in kingsway hall london between 1 and 10 october 1956/producer walter jellinek/ published in april 1958/lp matrix numbers XAX 1075-1076

giulini   **firebird suite**
philharmonia   lp: SAX 2279/QCX 10305/SAXQ 7278
other lp issues: angel 35462/emi XLP 30067/SXLP 30067
cd: emi CZS 575 4622
excerpts
45: SEL 1635/ESL 6262/SEBQ 208/ESLQ 1002

jeux d'enfants
lp: SAX 2279/QCX 10305/SAXQ 7278
other lp issues: angel 35462/emi XLP 30067/SXLP 30067
cd: emi CZS 575 4622

ma mere l'oye
lp: SAX 2279/QCX 10305/SAXQ 7278
other lp issues: angel 35462/emi XLP 30067/SXLP 30067

33CX 1519/piano sonatas by beethoven
recorded in abbey road studios london on 19-22 october 1956/producer walter legge/
published in april 1958/lp matrix numbers XAX 1092-1093

gieseking, **piano sonatas nos 9, 10 and 13**
piano lp: SAX 2259/SAXW 2259/STC 91017
　　　other lp issues: angel 35652/emi 3C153 52384-52393
　　　cd: emi CDZ 762 8572
　　　piano sonata no 14 "moonlight"
　　　45: SEL 1583/ESL 6253/SELW 1583/C 50499
　　　lp: SAX 2259/FCX 520/FCX 30104/FC 25079/QCX 10080/
　　　　QCX 10296/QIMX 7000/SAXW 2259/STC 91017/
　　　　WC 513/C 70365
　　　other lp issues: angel 35652/emi SXLP 30129/
　　　　3C153 52384-52393
　　　cd: emi CDZ 762 8572/CDZ 767 8342/CDU 650 502

33CX 1520-1521/gluck orphée et euridice
recorded in maison de la mutualité paris on 20-27 march 1957/priducer rené challan/
published in april 1958/lp matrix numbers XPTX 489-492

de froment lp: DTX 243-244
conservatoire *other lp issue:* angel 3659
orchestra cd: emi CMS 769 8612
aix festival *excerpts*
chorus lp: C 70411
berton *other lp excerpts:* emi 1C137 78233-78236
micheau
gedda

33CX 1522/operatic arias by verdi and wagner
recorded in kingsway hall london on 14-16 may 1957/producer walter legge/published in
april 1958/lp matrix numbers XAX 1216-1217

ludwig lp: C 90571
philharmonia *other lp issues:* angel 35540/emi 1C187 00786-00787
and chorus *selections from the recordings*
nilsson 45: SEL 1584/SEL 1606
　　　cd: testament SBT 1200

33CX 1523/orchestral works by tchaikovsky and mussorgsky
recorded in kingsway hall london on 27-29 september 1956/producer walter jellinek/
published in may 1958/lp matrix numbers XAX 1073-1074

giulini **symphony no 2 "little russian"**
philharmonia lp: SAX 2416/QCX 10314/WCX 1523/C 90905
　　　other lp issues: angel 35463/world records T 816/ST 816/
　　　　emi SXLP 30506
　　　cd: emi CZS 767 7232
　　　night on bare mountain, arranged by rimsky-korsakov
　　　lp: SAX 2416/QCX 10314/WCX 1523/C 90905
　　　other lp issues: angel 35463/world records T 816/ST 816
　　　recording completed on 8 october 1956

33CX 1524/berlioz overtures le carnaval romain; le corsaire; benvenuto cellini; le roi lear; béatrice et bénédict
recorded in maison de la mutualité paris on 4-6 september 1956/producer rené challan/ published in may 1958/lp matrix numbers XLX 500-501

cluytens	lp: FCX 558/C 90640
paris opéra	*other lp issue:* angel 35435
orchestra	*carnaval romain only*
	45: SEBQ 200

33CX 1525/tchaikovsky piano concerto no 1
recorded in paris in 1957/published in may 1958/lp matrix numbers XLX 595-596

iturbi	lp: FCX 646/QCX 10288
colonne	*other lp issue:* angel 35477
orchestra	
iturbi, piano	

33CX 1526/works by mozart and chopin
recorded in kingsway hall london on 25 august 1953 and in abbey road studios london on 18 october 1956 respectively/producer walter jellinek/published in may 1958/lp matrix numbers XAX 1053-1054

karajan	**piano concerto no 24 k491**
philharmonia	lp: FCX 201/FCX 30004/FC 25117/QCX 10323/
gieseking,	WCX 1526/C 91396
piano	*other lp issues:* angel 35501/toshiba EAC 37001-37019/
	emi 3C153 52425-52431M
	cd: emi CHS 763 7092/bramante BBBCD 9024/
	philips 456 8112
gieseking,	**barcarolle in f sharp minor**
piano	lp: FCX 201/QCX 10323/WCX 1526/C 91396
	other lp issues: angel 35501/emi 3C153 52434-52441M

33CX 1527/haydn string quartets op 64 no 5 and op 76 no 2
recorded in paris on 30 november 1954 and 15 december 1954 respectively/producer norbert gamsohn/published in june 1958/lp matrix numbers XLX 436-437

hungarian	lp: FCX 465
string quartet	

33CX 1528/mozart operatic arias from cosi fan tutte, don giovanni, die entführung aus dem serail, idomeneo, la clemenza di tito and die zauberflöte; concert aria k420
recorded in maison de la mutualité paris on 24-26 june 1957/producer rené challam/ published in may 1958/lp matrix numbers XLX 625-626

cluytens
conservatoire
orchestra
gedda

lp: FCX 686/WCX 1528
other lp issue: angel 35510
selections from the recordings
lp: C 70411
other lp selections: emi SLS 5250/1C137 78233-78236
cd: emi 173 1352/CMS 565 6852/CMS 567 4452

33CX 1529-1530/catalogue numbers allocated to a jazz compilation entitled the playboy jazz all stars

33CX 1531/grieg and schumann piano concerti
recorded in abbey road studios london on 19-20 april 1957 and in town hall walthamstow between 24 and 31 may 1957 respectively/producers walter legge and lawrance collingwood/ published in may 1958/lp matrix numbers XAX 1198-1199

galliera
philharmonia
arrau, piano

lp: FCX 745/WCX 1531/C 90904
other lp issue: angel 35561

33CX 1532/beethoven symphony no 6 "pastoral"
recorded in kingsway hall london on 7-8 october 1957/producer walter legge/published in may 1958/lp matrix numbers XAX 1332-1333

klemperer
philharmonia

lp: SAX 2260/FCX 784/SAXF 104/QCX 10317/SAXQ 7265/
WCX 1532/C 90915/SAXW 2260/STC 90915
other lp issues: angel 35711/34426/3619/emi SLS 788/
ASD 2565/ED 29 02531/EX 29 03793/1C053 00472/
1C137 50187-50194/1C147 53400-53419/1C181 50187-
50194/1C197 53400-53419/2C069 00799/2C147 50298-
50318/100 4721
cd: emi CDC 747 1882/CDM 763 3582/CDZ 568 0572/
CZS 573 8952

33CX 1533/orchestral works by hindemith
recorded in kingsway hall london on 21-22 november 1956/producer walter legge/published in may 1958/lp matrix numbers XAX 1111-1112

hindemith **clarinet concerto**
philharmonia lp: WCX 1533/C 90909
cahuzac, *other lp issue:* angel 35490
clarinet

hindemith **nobilissima visione**
philharmonia lp: WCX 1533/C 90909
other lp issue: angel 35490/emi EH 29 11731
cd: emi CDH 763 3732

33CX 1534-1535/orff der mond
recorded in abbey road studios london on 16-20 march 1957/producer walter legge/ published in june 1958/lp matrix numbers XAX 1178-1181

sawallisch lp: WCX 514-515/WSX 564-565/C 90288-90289/
philharmonia SMC 90288-90289
and chorus *other lp issues:* angel 3567/emi 1C137 43291-54293
christ cd: emi CMS 763 7122
kuen *excerpts*
schmitt-walter lp: 33CX 1811/SAX 2457
hotter *other lp excerpts:* emi 1C063 01136

33CX 1536/orchestral works by brahms
recorded in kingsway hall london on 26-29 march 1957/producer walter legge/published in june 1958/lp matrix numbers XAX 1176-1177

klemperer	**symphony no 3**
philharmonia	lp: SAX 2351/FCX 694/SAXF 203/QCX 10402/SAXQ 7314/ WCX 1536/C 90933/SAXW 2351/STC 90933/SMC 91633
	other lp issues: angel 35545/32050/3614/emi SLS 804/ ASD 2707/SXLP 30255/1C053 00473/1C063 00473/ 1C197 50034-50037/2C065 00473/2C197 50034-50037
	cd: emi CDM 769 6492/562 7422
	academic festival overture
	lp: SAX 2351/FCX 694/SAXF 203/QCX 10402/SAXQ 7314/ WCX 1536/C 90933/SAXW 2351/STC 90933/SMC 91633
	other lp issues: angel 35545/32050/3614/emi SLS 804/ ASD 2707/SXLP 30255/1C053 00473/1C063 00473/ 1C197 50034-50037/2C065 00473/2C197 50034-50037
	cd: emi CDM 769 6492/CZS 479 8852/562 7422

33CX 1537/beethoven piano sonatas nos 2 and 3
recorded in abbey road studios london on 17 september 1956/producer walter jellinek/ lp matrix numbers XAX 1085-1086

gieseking, piano	*other lp issues:* angel 35654/emi 3C153 52384-52393

33CX 1538/wieniawski violin concerto no 1; bruch scottish fantasy
recorded in town hall walthamstow on 3-4 january 1957/producer alec robertson/ published in june 1958/lp matrix numbers XAX 1128-1129

boult	lp: WCX 1538/C 90964
philharmonia rabin, violin	*other lp issue:* angel 35484

33CX 1539/orchestral works by boccherini and haydn
recorded in kingsway hall london on 4-7 october 1956/producer walter jellinek/published in september 1958/lp matrix numbers XAX 1071-1072

giulini	**boccherini symphony in c minor; overture in d**
philharmonia	*other lp issues:* angel 35712/32094
	cd: testament SBT 1155
	haydn symphony no 94 "surprise"
	other lp issues: angel 35712/32094

33CX 1540/operatic scenes by bellini, cherubini and spontini
recorded in teatro alla scala milan on 9-12 june 1955 (cherubini and spontini items only)/ producer walter jellinek/published in june 1958/ lp matrix numbers XBX 99-100

serafin   arias from la sonnambula and i puritani
votto   see 33CX 1058-1060 and 33CX 1469-1471
la scala   **dei tuoi figli/medea**
orchestra   lp: WSX 523/C 80448
callas   *other lp issues::* angel 35304/emi 2C165 54178-54188/
     ASD 3535/1C053 01016M/3C065 01016
     cd: emi CDC 747 2822/CDS 749 4532/CDS 749 6002/
     CDS 754 1032/CMS 565 5342/CZS 252 1642/
     566 6182/rodolphe RPC 32484-32487

o nume tutelar/la vestale
lp: WSX 523/C 80448
other lp issues: angel 35304/emi 2C165 54178-54188/
   ASD 3535/1C053 01016M/3C065 01016
cd: emi CDC 747 2822/CDC 555 0162/CDS 749 4532/
   CMS 565 7462/CMS 565 9522/881 2992/566 6182/
   CMS 557 0622

caro oggetto/la vestale
lp: WSX 523/C 80448
other lp issues: angel 35304/emi 2C165 54178-54188/
   ASD 3535/1C053 01016M/3C065 01016
cd: emi CDC 747 2822/CDS 749 4532/566 6182

tu che invoco/la vestale
lp: WSX 523/C 80448
other lp issues: angel 35304/emi 2C165 54178-54188/
   ASD 3535/1C053 01016M/3C065 01016
cd: emi CDC 747 2822/CDS 749 4532/CMS 763 2442/
   CMS 565 5342/CZS 252 1642/566 6182

33CX 1541/mahler symphony no 4
recorded in kingsway hall london on 2-5 april 1957/producer victor olof/published in july 1958/ lp matrix numbers XAX 1202-1203

kletzki   lp: SAX 2345/WCX 1541/C 90965
philharmonia   *other lp issues:* angel 35570/angel seraphim 60105/
loose   emi XLP 30054/SXLP 30054/SQIM 6394/
     1C027 01033
   cd: emi CZS 767 7262
   recording completed on 17 june 1957

33CX 1542/scenes from wagner operas
recorded in abbey road studios london on 16-19 november 1957/producer walter legge/ published in october 1958/lp matrix numbers XAX 1326-1327

ludwig	wie aus der ferne/der fliegende holländer
philharmonia	lp: SAX 2296
nilsson	*other lp issues:* angel 35585/emi SXLP 30557/SREG 2068
hotter	cd: emi CMS 764 0082
	war es so schmählich.....to end/die walküre
	lp: SAX 2296
	other lp issues: angel 35585/emi SXLP 30557/SREG 2068
	cd: emi CMS 565 2122

33CX 1543/menotti the unicorn, the gorgon and the manticore
recorded in new york in 1957-1958/published in july 1958/lp matrix numbers USC 217-218

schippers	*other lp issue:* angel 35437
new york	cd: testament SBT 1179
city ballet	
orchestra	

33CX 1544/orchestral music by berlioz
recorded in maison de la mutualité paris on 10-13 september 1956/producer rené challan/ published in august 1958/lp matrix numbers XLX 502-503

cluytens	la damnation de faust suite
paris opéra	lp: FCX 559
orchestra	*other lp issue:* angel 35431
	roméo et juliette suite
	lp: FCX 559
	other lp issue: angel 35431
	cd: testament SBT 1234/SBT6 7247

33CX 1545/italian opera intermezzi by catalani, mascagni, pick-mangiagalli and wolf-ferrari
recorded in town hall hornsey in june 1956 (wolf-ferrari) and in kingsway hall london on 5-6 november 1956 and 24-25 january 1957/producers walter legge and walter jellinek/ published in july 1958/lp matrix numbers XAX 1226-1227

galliera	lp: QCX 10330
philharmonia	*other lp issues:* angel 35483/emi 3C053 01573
	selections from the recordings
	45: SEL 1596/SEL 1618/ESL 6256/SEBQ 189/ SEDQ 204/SEDQ 689
	lp: emi 100 7691

33CX 1546/works by tchaikovsky, vivaldi and locatelli
recorded in théatre apollo paris on 3-11 june 1956/producers norbert gamsohn and jean-pierre marty/published in august 1958/lp matrix numbers XLX 496-497

vandernoot	**tchaikovsky violin concerto**
conservatoire	lp: WC 522/C 70377
orchestra	*other lp issue:* angel 35444
kogan, violin	cd: testament SBT 1224/SBT6 1248
	vivaldi concerto in g minor, arranged for violin and orchestra by barshai
	other lp issue: angel 35444
	cd: testament SBT 1224/SBT6 1248
kogan, violin	**locatelli sonata in f minor, arranged by ysaye**
mitnik, piano	*other lp issue:* angel 35444
	cd: testament SBT 1224/SBT6 1248

33CX 1547/bartok mikrokosmos, selection; suite for piano; rumanian folk dances; for children, selection
recorded in paris in 1957-1958/published in august 1958/lp matrix numbers XLX 484-485

solchany,
piano

33CX 1548/orchestral works by respighi, berlioz and liszt
recorded in kingsway hall london between 9 and 17 january 1958/producer walter legge/ published in july 1958/lp matrix numbers XAX 1363-1364

karajan   **pini di roma**
philharmonia   lp: QCX 10328/WCX 1548/C 90985
other lp issues: angel 35613/emi SLS 5019/SXLP 30450/
   1C053 03929/1C181 25307-25311
cd: emi CDM 769 4662/CZS 252 1592/disky HR 700 062/
   royal classics ROY 6474
le carnaval romain overture
lp: QCX 10328/WCX 1548/C 90985
other lp issues: angel 35613/emi SLS 5019/SXLP 30450/
   1C053 03929/1C181 25307-25311/2C053 00703/
   CVD 2073/143 5643
cd: emi CDM 769 4662/CZS 252 1592/CDM 566 5982/
   disky HR 700 062/royal classics ROY 6474
les préludes
45: SELW 1813/C 50545
lp: QCX 10328/WCX 1548/WC 529/C 90985/C 70426
other lp issues: angel 35613/emi CVD 2075/1C063 00737/
   2C053 01414/2C059 43355
cd: emi CDM 769 2282/CDZ 762 8602/laserlight 16206

33CX 1549-1550/orff music for children
recorded in abbey road studios london in 1957-1958/producer walter jellinek/published in august 1958/lp matric numbers XAX 1220-1223
orff lp: C 80107-80108
instrumental *other lp issue:* emi CSD 3708-3709
ensemble
and choirs

33CX 1551/falla el sombrero de 3 picos
recorded in maison de la mutualité paris on 8-12 november 1956/producer rené challan/ published in july 1958/lp matrix numbers XLX 565-566
toldra lp: FCX 30119
orchestre *other lp issue:* angel 35553
national
rubio

33CX 1552/lieder by schubert, brahms, wolf, strauss and mahler
recorded in abbey road studios on 11-18 november 1957/producer walter legge/published in august 1959/lp matrix numbers XAX 1339-1340
ludwig *other lp issues:* angel 35592/angel seraphim 60034
moore, piano cd: emi CMS 764 0742
 selections from the recordings
 lp: C 70408
 other lp selection: angel seraphim 6072

33CX 1553/american song recital
recorded in abbey road studios london on 22-23 september 1957/producer walter legge/ published in september 1958/lp matrix numbers XAX 1310-1311
farrell *other lp issue:* angel 35608
trovillo, piano *selection from the recordings*
 cd: testament SBT 1073

33CX 1554/beethoven symphonies nos 1 and 8
recorded in kingsway hall london on 28-30 october 1957/producer walter legge/published in september 1958/lp matrix numbers XAX 1367-1368
klemperer lp: SAX 2318/FCX 776/SAXF 189/QCX 10379/SAXQ
philharmonia 7269/WCX 1554/C 90967/SAXW 2318/STC 90967
 other lp issues: angel 35657/34423/34469/3619/emi SLS 788/
 ASD 2560/EX 29 03793/1C053 00476/1C063 00476/
 1C181 50187-50194/1C197 53400-53419/
 2C147 50298-50318/2C069 00794
 cd: emi CDC 747 1842/CDM 763 3542/
 CDZ 568 0572/CZS 573 8952

33CX 1555-1557 / puccini turandot
recorded in teatro alla scala milan on 9-15 july 1957 / producer walter legge / published in september 1958 / lp matrix numbers XBX 91-96

serafin	lp: FCX 766-768/QCX 10291-10293/WCX 1555-1557/
la scala	C 90934-90936
orchestra	*other lp issues:* angel 3571/emi RLS 741/EX 29 12673/
and chorus	2C153 00969-00971/3C163 00969-00971
callas	cd: emi CDS 747 9718/CDS 556 3072/CMS 252 9432
schwarzkopf	*excerpts*
fernandi	45: SEBQ 127/SEBQ 215/SCBQ 3028/SCBQ 3036/
nessi	SELW 1533/C 50151
zaccaria	lp: 33CX 1792/FCX 30148/QCX 10108/QCX 10466/
	WSX 559/C 80578
	other lp excerps: angel 3814/emi SLS 5104/3C063 01019/
	1C187 28985-28986M
	cd: emi CDC 749 5022/CMS 565 5342/CZS 252 6142

33CX 1558 / see 33CX 1007-1009

33CX 1559 / works by leopold mozart and prokofiev
recorded in abbey road studios london on 28 april 1957 and in kingsway hall london on 22 december 1956 respectively / producer walter legge / published in october 1958 / lp matrix numbers XAX 1334-1335

karajan	cassation in g "toy symphony"
philharmonia	45: ESBF 17079
	lp: SAX 2375/FCX 30531/SAXF 130531/QCX 10339/
	WC 537/C 70391/SBOW 8504/STC 70461/SMC 50600/
	SMC 80975
	other lp issues: angel 35638/emi SLS 839/SXLP 30161/
	SHZE 243/1C047 02350/1C063 00737/1C063 01361/
	1C177 02348-02352/2C053 00723/3C063 00868/
	143 5643
	cd: emi CDM 769 2392/CDZ 252 1522/laserlight 24426

karajan	peter and the wolf
philharmonia	lp: SAX 2375/FCX 30531/FC 25108/SAXF 130531/
ustinov,	QCX 10339/WC 506/C 70081
narrator	*other lp issues:* angel 35638/emi SHZE 243/emi 1C063 01361/
	2C053 01169/3C053 00868
	cd: emi CDM 769 2392/CDZ 252 2012
	recording completed in abbey road studios london on 28 april 1957; narrators for european versions include hirsch (french), schneider (german), rothenberger (german) and carraro (italian)

149

33CX 1560/rossini overtures
recorded in maison de la mutualité paris on 1-4 aptil 1957/producer rené challam/published in september 1958/lp matrix numbers XLX 677-678

markevitch	**guillaume tell**
orcheste	45: SEL 1607
national	lp: FCX 657/FCX 30266
	other lp issues: angel 35548/emi TRI 33125
	cd: emi CZS 569 2122
	la cenerentola; l'italiana in algeri
	45: SEL 1626
	lp: FCX 657/FCX 30266
	other lp issues: angel 35548/emi TRI 33125
	cd: emi CZS 569 2122
	il barbiere di siviglia; la gazza ladra; la scala di seta
	lp: FCX 657/FCX 30266
	other lp issues: angel 35548/emi TRI 33125
	cd: emi CZS 569 2122

33CX 1561/prokofiev symphony no 5
recorded in kingsway hall london on 11-14 may 1957/producer walter legge/published in september 1958/lp matrix numbers XAX 1186-1187

schippers	lp: QCX 10311/WCX 1561/C 90986
philharmonia	*other lp issue:* angel 35527

33CX 1562/works by paganini
recorded in maison de la mutualité paris on 22-24 february 1955/producer rené challan/published in september 1958/lp matrix numbers XLX 336-337

bruck	**violin concerto no 1**
conservatoire	lp: FCX 402/FCX 30081/QCX 10300
orchestra	*other lp issue:* angel 35502
kogan, violin	cd: testament SBT 1226/SBT6 1248
kogan, violin	**cantabile for violin and piano**
mitnik, piano	lp: FCX 402/FCX 30081/QCX 10300
	other lp issue: angel 35502
	cd: testament SBT 1227/SBT6 1248

33CX 1563/works by chopin
recorded in warsaw in march 1955/published in september 1958/lp matrix numbers XPTX 1229-1300

gorzynski   **piano concerto no 2**
warsaw
philharmonic
ashkenazy,
piano
other lp issues: angel 35403/muza L 0017
cd: testament SBT 1045

ashkenazy,   **ballade no 2; étude op 10 no 1; 4 mazurkas; scherzo no 4**
piano
other lp issues: angel 35403/muza L 0017
selections from these solo pieces
cd: testament SBT 1045/SBT 1046

33CX 1564/beethoven piano sonatas nos 4, 5 and 6
recorded in abbey road studios on 18-20 september 1956/producer walter jellinek/published in september 1958/lp matrix numbers XAX 1087-1088
gieseking,   lp: QCX 10325
piano   *other lp issues:* angel 35655/emi 3C153 52384-52393

33CX 1565/tchaikovsky francesca da rimini; marche slave; 1812 overture
recorded in kingsway hall london on 2-3 december 1957/producer victor olof/published in september 1958/lp matrix numbers XAX 1330-1331
kletzki   lp: QCX 10320
royal   *other lp issue* angel 35621:
philharmonic

33CX 1566/schubert string quartet d887
recorded in paris on 25 july 1955/producer norbert gamsohn/published in september 1958/lp matrix numbers XLX 434-435
hungarian
string quartet

33CX 1567/motets and madrigals by palestrina and monteverdi
recorded in bussum on 21-23 march 1957/producer walter legge/published in september 1958/ lp matrix numbers XFX 5-6

de nobel   *other lp issue:* angel 35667
netherlands   *selection from the recordings*
chamber choir   45: SEG 8216

33CX 1568/wagner scenes from der fliegende holländer, lohengrin, tannhäuser, die walküre and parsifal
recorded in kingsway hall london on 3-5 july 1957/producer walter legge/published in september 1958/lp matrix numbers XAX 1298-1299

ackermann   *other lp issue:* angel 35571
philharmonia
edelmann

33CX 1569/piano works by schubert
recorded in abbey road studios london on 22-25 october 1957 and 2-3 september 1956 respectively/producer william mann/published in may 1959/lp matrix numbers XAX 1399-1400

arrau, piano   **wanderer fantasy**
                 other lp issues: angel 35637/desmar GHP 4001-4002
                 cd: emi CDH 761 0192
                 3 klavierstücke d946
                 other lp issues: angel 35637/emi RLS 7712/143 5321
                 cd: emi CDH 761 0192

33CX 1570/operetta arias by lehar, sieczynsky, johann strauss, zeller, heuberger, suppé and millöcker
recorded in kingsway hall london on 2-5 july 1957/producer walter legge/published in february 1959/lp matrix numbers XAX 1403-1404

ackermann   lp: SAX 2283/SAXF 158/CCPM 130 600
philharmonia   *other lp issues:* angel 35696/emi ASD 2807/2C053 00478/
and chorus   SVP 1180
schwarzkopf   cd: emi CDC 747 2842
                 selections from the recordings
                 45: SEL 1642/SEL 1648/SEL 1652/ESL 6263/ESL 6267/
                       ESL 6270/SCD 2128
                 lp: angel 3754/emi CFP 4277/YKM 5014/SEOM 13
                 cd: emi CDM 565 5772/585 1052

33CX 1571/works by tchaikovsky, berlioz, liszt, sibelius and weber
*recorded in kingsway hall london between 9 and 18 january 1958/producer walter legge/
published in september 1959/ lp matrix numbers XAX 1365-1366*

karajan
philharmonia

1812 ouverture solennelle
lp: SAX 2302/FCX 824/SAXF 160/QCX 10359/SAXQ 7260/
C 70486/STC 70486/SBOW 8518
other lp issues: angel 35614/37232/emi SLS 839/SXDW 3048/
CVD 2071/SHZE 150/1C177 02348-02352/
1C053 01413
cd: emi CDM 769 4662/CZS 252 1592/royal classics
ROY 6474/disky DCL 705 872/HR 700 062

marche hongroise/la damnation de faust
lp: SAX 2302/FCX 824/SAXF 160/QCX 10359/SAXQ 7260/
other lp issues: angel 35614/37231/emi SLS 5019/CVD 2072/
SHZE 150/1C137 03059-03060/2C053 00724/
1C181 25307-25311/143 5643
cd: emi CDM 769 4672/CZS 252 1592/CDM 566 5982/
royal classics ROY 6475/disky HR 700 062

hungarian rhapsody no 2, arranged by müller-berghaus
45: SCBQ 3054
lp: SAX 2302/FCX 824/SAXF 160/QCX 10359/SAXQ 7260/
C 70486/STC 70486/SBOW 8518
other lp issues: angel 35614/37231/emi SLS 5019/SXDW 3048/
CVD 2075/SHZE 150/1C137 03059-03060/143 5643/
1C181 25307-25311/2C053 01414
cd: emi CDZ 762 8602/562 8692/laserlight 16206/24426

valse triste
lp: SAX 2302/FCX 824/SAXF 160/QCX 10359/SAXQ 7260
other lp issues: angel 35614/emi SLS 5019/CVD 2074/
SHZE 150/1C137 03059-03060/2C053 00726/143 5643/
1C181 25307-25311
cd: emi CDM 769 4672/CZS 252 1592/522 0492/royal
classics ROY 6475/disky HR 700 062

aufforderung zum tanz, arranged by berlioz
lp: SAX2302/FCX 824/SAXF 160/QCX 10359/SAXQ 7260/
WC 573/C 70497/SBOW 8525/STC 70497
other lp issues: angel 35614/37550/emi SLS 5019/CVD 2075/
SHZE 150/1C137 03059-03060/2C053 00724/143 5643/
1C181 25307-23511/2C059 43355
cd: emi CDM 769 4652/CDZ 252 1342/CZS 252 1592/
royal classics ROY 6473/disky DCL 703 262/HR 700 062

33CX 1572/see 33CX 1013-1015

33CX 1573/brahms symphony no 1
recorded in abbey road studios london on 5-6 december 1957/producer victor olof/published in january 1959/lp matrix numbers XAX 1353-1354
kletzki
royal
philharmonic

33CX 1574-1575/works by beethoven
recorded in kingsway hall london on 30-31 october 1957 (symphony no 9), 21 october 1957 (egmont overture) and 21-25 november 1957 (egmont incidental music)/producer walter legge/ published in october 1958/lp matrix numbers XAX 1409 and 1412-1414

klemperer	**symphony no 9 "choral"**
philharmonia	lp: SAX 2276-2277/FCX 873-874/SAXF 167-168/
orchestra	QCX 10331-10332/SAXQ 7266-7267/WCX 1574-1575/
and chorus	SAXW 2276-2277/C 90981-90982/STC 91047-91048/
nordmo-lövberg	SMC 91629-91630
ludwig	*other lp issues:* angel 3577/3619/emi SLS 788/SLS 790/
kmentt	SXDW 3051/ED 29 02721/EX 29 03793/100 3811/
hotter	1C153 00801-00802/1C153 00949-00950/1C177 00794-
	00802/1C181 50187-50194/1C197 53400-53419/
	2C147 50298-50318
	cd: emi CDC 747 1892/CDM 763 3592/CDZ 568 0572/
	CZS 573 8952
	recording completed on 21-23 november 1957

klemperer	**egmont overture**
philharmonia	45: SEL 1609/SEBQ 227
	lp: 33CX 1930/SAX 2570/FCX 874/QCX 10332/
	WCX 1575/C 90982/STC 90982/SMC 80995
	other lp issues: angel 3577/34469/SLS 788/ED 29 02531/
	EX 29 03793/SXDW 3032/1C177 00794-00802/
	1C153 03103-03104/1C197 53400-53419/
	2C147 50298-50318/ASD 2563
	cd: emi CDC 747 1882/CDM 763 3582/CDZ 568 0572
	klärchens tod/egmont incidental music
	lp: FCX 874/QCX 10332/WCX 1575/C 90982/SMC 80995
	other lp issues: angel 3577/SLS 788/ED 29 02531/
	EX 29 03793/1C177 00794-00802/1C197 53400-53419/
	2C147 50298-50318
	cd: emi CDC 747 1882/CDM 763 3582/CDZ 568 0572

33CX 1574-1575/works by beethoven/concluded
klemperer   **die trommel gerührt; freudvoll und leidvoll/egmont**
philharmonia   **incidental music**
nilsson
                45: SEL 1609/SEBQ 227
                lp: FCX 874/QCX 10332/WCX 1575/C 90982/SMC 80995
                other lp issues: angel 3577/SLS 788/ED 29 02531/
                    EX 29 03793/1C177 00794-00794-00802/
                    1C197 53400-53419/2C147 50298-50318
                cd: emi CDC 747 1882/CDM 763 3582/CDZ 568 0572

33CX 1576/catalogue number appears not to have been allocated

33CX 1577/fauré dolly suite; masques et bergamasques; pelléas et mélisande
recorded in paris/published in february 1959/lp matrix numbers XLX 388-389
tzipine   lp: FCX 463
opéra-comique   *other lp issue:* angel 35311
orchestra

33CX 1578/works by mozart
recorded in paris/published in november 1958/lp matrix numbers XLX 80-81
iturbi   **piano concerto no 22 k482**
colonne   lp: FCX 669/QCX 10319
orchestra   *other lp issue:* angel 35539
iturbi, piano

iturbi, piano   **piano sonata k332**
                 lp: FCX 669/QCX 10319
                 other lp issue: angel 35539

33CX 1579/schumann cello concerto; saint-saens cello concerto no 1
recorded in kingsway hall london on 16-17 september 1957/producer walter legge/published in february 1959/lp matrix numbers XAX 1314-1315
giulini   lp: FCX 323
philharmonia   *other lp issues:* angel 35598/angel seraphim 60266/world
starker, cello   records T 529/ST 529/emi 2M155 53430-53431
                 cd: emi CZS 568 4852

33CX 1580/violin sonatas by beethoven and brahms
recorded in salle colonialle brussels on 19 may 1955/producers walter legge and walter jellinek/published in october 1958/lp matrix numbers XLBX 1-2

oistrakh,	**beethoven sonata op 12 no 3**
violin	lp: FCX 581/FCX 30269/QCX 10324
yampolsky,	*other lp issues:* angel 35331/hmv LALP 365/colosseum
piano	CRLP 148
	cd: testament SBT 1115
	brahms sonata no 3
	lp: FCX 581/FCX 30269/QCX 10324
	other lp issues: angel 35331/hmv LALP 365/colosseum
	CRLP 148

33CX 1581/borodin string quartet no 2; tchaikovsky string quartet no 1
recorded in paris on 22-24 november 1954 and 2-10 december 1954 respectively/producer norbert gamsohn/published in february 1959/lp matrix numbers XLX 442-443
hungarian
string quartet

33CX 1582/see 33CXS 1324-33CX 1326

33CX 1583-1585/puccini manon lescaut
recorded in teatro alla scala milan on 18-27 july 1957/producer walter legge/published in november 1959/lp matrix numbers XBX 9004-9009

serafin	lp: FCX 833-835/QCX 10362-10364/WCX 1583-1585/
la scala	C 91033-91035
orchestra	*other lp issues:* angel 3564/angel seraphim 6089/emi RLS 737/
and chorus	EX 29 00413/2C163 00484-00486/3C163 00484-00486
callas	cd: emi CDS 747 3938/CDS 556 3012/CMS 252 9432
cossotto	*excerpts*
di stefano	45: SEBQ 159/SCBQ 3027/SCBQ 3046/SELW 1546/C 50154
calabrese	lp: QCX 10108/QCX 10441
fioravanti	*other lp excerpts:* angel 3814/36966/emi SLS 856/SLS 5104/
	1C161 01433-01434M/1C191 01433-01434M/
	1C191 01593-01594M/2C187 28985-28986/
	3C065 01480
	cd: emi CDC 555 0162/CDM 769 5432/CDS 754 1032/
	CMS 565 5342/CMS 565 7462/CMS 565 9522/
	CZS 252 6142/566 6882

33CX 1586-1587/bruckner symphony no 8
recorded in grünewaldkirche berlin on 23-25 may 1957/producers walter legge and fritz ganss/published in november 1958/lp matrix numbers XRX 229-232

karajan lp: WCX 1585-1586/C 90972-90973/SAXW 9501-9502/
berlin STC 90972-90973
philharmonic *other lp issues:* angel 3576/world records T 772-773/ST 772-773/
  SXDW 3024/CFP 41 44343/1C187 00763-00764
cd: emi CMS 763 4692/CES 569 0922/CMS 566 1092

33CX 1588/ballet music by offenbach, rossini and gounod
recorded in kingsway hall london between 13 and 18 january 1958/producer walter legge/ published in november 1958/lp matrix numbers XAX 1361-1362

karajan gaité parisienne, suite arranged by rosenthal
philharmonia lp: SAX 2274/FCX 789/SAXF 134/QCX 10325/SAXQ 7286
  other lp issues: angel 35607/world records T 1084/ST 1084/
    emi SLS 5019/SXLP 30224/2C059 03054/
    1C181 25307-25311
  cd: emi CDM 769 0412
  excerpts
  45: SEL 1634/ESL 6261/SEDQ 681/SEGW 7909/C 41132
  passo a 3 e coro tirolese/guillaume tell
  lp: SAX 2274/FCX 789/SAXF 134/QCX 10326/SAXQ 7286
  other lp issues: angel 35607/37231/world records T 1084/
    ST 1084
  cd: emi CDM 763 1132
  ballet music/faust
  lp: SAX 2274/FCX 789/SAXF 134/QCX 10326/SAXQ 7286/
    C 70484/STC 70484
  other lp issues: angel 35607/world records T 1044/ST 1044/
    emi SLS 839/SXLP 30224/SHZE 216/2C053 00724/
    1C177 02348-02352/1C137 03059-03060/3C065 00996/
    2C059 03054
  cd: emi CDM 769 0412

33CX 1589/franck symphony in d minor; psyché et éros
recorded in kingsway hall london on 29-30 july 1957 and in abbey road studios london on 31 may 1958 respectively/producer walter jellinek/published in february 1959/lp matrix numbers XAX 1499-1500
giulini   *other lp issues:* angel 35641/emi XLP 30055/SXLP 30055
philharmonia   cd: emi CZS 767 7232

33CX 1590/bach das musikalische opfer, arranged by markevitch
recorded in masison de la mutualité paris between 18 and 29 june 1956/producer rené challan/published in november 1958/lp matrix numbers XLX 516-517
markevitch   lp: FCX 567
orchestre   *other lp issue:*
national   cd: emi CZS 569 2122

33CX 1591/brahms symphony no 4
recorded in kingsway hall london on 1 november 1956/producer walter legge/published in november 1958/lp matrix numbers XAX 1121-1122
klemperer   lp: SAX 2350/FCX 695/SAXF 204/QCX 10393/SAXQ 7289/
philharmonia   WCX 1591/C 90968/STC 90968/SMC 91634
                     other lp issues: angel 35546/34413/3614/emi SLS 804/
                     ASD 2705/SXLP 30214/1C163 50034-50037/
                     1C053 00487/1C197 50034-50037
                     cd: emi CDM 769 6492/562 7422
                     recording completed on 27-28 march 1957

33CX 1592/allocated to a recording of haydn string quartets by the amadeus quartet which was subsequently published by his master's voice

33CX 1593/beethoven piano sonatas nos 8 and 21 "waldstein"
recorded in abbey road studios london on 3-4 june 1957 and 2 june 1958 respectively/producer walter legge/published in november 1958/lp matrix numbers XAX 1244-1245
a.fischer,   lp: QCX 10333/C 80646
piano   *other lp issue:* angel 35569

33CX 1594/tchaikovsky violin concerto; saint-saens introduction and rondo capriccioso
recorded in town hall walthamstow on 20-22 march 1957/producer walter jellinek/published in november 1958/lp matrix numbers XAX 1151-1152
schüchter   lp: QCX 10341
pro arte   :
orchestra
i.oistrakh, violin

33CX 1595/works by dohnanyi and kodaly
recorded in kingsway hall london on 12-13 july 1956 and on 4 october 1957 respectively/ producers walter legge and william mann/published in november 1958/lp matrix numbers XAX 1355-1356

susskind	**dohnanyi konzertstück for cello and orchestra**
philharmonia	*other lp issues:* angel 35627/world records T 783/ST 783
starker, cello	cd: emi CZS 568 7352/CZS 568 4852
starker, cello	**kodaly sonata for solo cello**
	other lp issues: angel 35627/world records T 783/ST 783
	cd: emi CZS 568 4852

33CX 1596/operatic arias by gluck, weber, verdi, ponchielli, tchaikovsky, massenet, debussy and menotti
recorded in kingsway hall london on 21-25 september 1957/producer walter legge/ published in november 1958/lp matrix numbers XAX 1304-1305

schippers	*other lp issue:* angel 35589
philharmonia	cd: testament SBT 1073
farrell	

33CX 1597/works for violin and orchestra
recorded in town hall walthamstow on 2-5 january 1957 and town hall hornsey on 12-13 june 1956 (saint-saens)/producer walter jellinek/published in november 1958/ lp matrix numbers XAX 1127 and 1130

boult	**mendelssohn violin concerto; ravel tzigane for violin and orchestra**
philharmonia	
rabin, violin	*other lp issue:* angel 35572
	cd: emi CMS 764 1232
galliera	**saint-saens havanaise for violin and orchestra**
philharmonia	*other lp issue:* angel 35572
rabin, violin	cd: emi CMS 764 1232

33CX 1598/operatic duets by verdi, mascagni, bizet and gounod
recorded in milan in june 1957/published in december 1958/lp matrix numbers XBX 434-435

tonini	lp: QCX 10271
milan	*other lp issues:* angel 35601/emi 3C053 17658
symphony	
carteri	
di stefano	

33CX 1599/mozart string quartets k428 and k464
recorded in paris on 26 november 1954 and on 3-12 december 1954 respectively/producer norbert gamsohn/published in april 1959/lp matrix numbers XLX 438-439
hungarian   *recording of quartet k428 completed on 18-27 july 1955*
string quartet

33CX 1600-1602/strauss capriccio
recorded in kingsway hall london on 2-11 september 1957/producer walter legge/published in march 1959/lp matrix numbers XAX 1371-1376
sawallisch   lp: WCX 1600-1602/C 90997-90999
philharmonia   *other lp issues:* angel 3580/world records OC 230-232/
schwarzkopf   emi 143 5243
ludwig   cd: emi CDS 749 0148/CMS 567 3942
moffo   *excerpts*
gedda   lp: C 80695
hotter   *other lp excerpts:* world records OH 233
fischer-dieskau   cd: emi CDM 763 6572/CMS 763 7902
wächter   *orchestral prelude (sextet) recorded on 28 march 1958 with*
schmitt-walter   *producer walter jellinek*

33CX 1603/beethoven piano sonatas nos 12 and 15 "pastoral"
recorded in abbey road studios london on 20-22 october 1956/producer walter legge/published in august 1959/lp matrix numbers XAX 1095-1096
gieseking,   lp: FCX 852-853/QCX 10374
piano   *other lp issues:* angel 3600/emi 3C153 52384-52393
              due to the pianist's death shortly after these sessions the incomplete final movement of sonata no 15 is omitted from the recording

33CX 1604-33CXS 1605/shostakovich symphony no 11
recorded in salle wagram paris on 19-23 may 1958/producer rené challan/published in november 1958/lp matrix numbers XLX 719-720
cluytens   lp: FCX 758-759
orchestre   *other lp issue:* angel 3586
national   cd: testament SBT 1099
recording made in prescence of the composer

33CX 1606/works for cello and piano by bach, haydn, weber, schumann, mendelssohn, chopin, rimsky-korsakov, fauré, saint-saens, granados and kreisler
recorded in abbey road studios london in 1957/producer william mann/published in november 1958/lp matric numbers XAX 1322-1323
fournier, cello   *other lp issue:* angel 35599
moore, piano   *selection from the recital*
               cd: testament SBT 1016

33CX 1607/chopin 17 polish songs
recorded in paris in 1957/published in october 1958/lp matrix numbers XLX 406-407
zareska
favaretto,   :
piano

33CX 1608/orchestral music by bizet
recorded in kingsway hall london on 14-16 january 1958/producer walter legge/published in march 1959/lp matrix numbers XAX 1349-1350

karajan　　**l'arlésienne suites nos 1 and 2**
philharmonia　lp: SAX 2289/FCX 775/SAXF 133/WCX 1608/C 91094/
　　　　　　　　　WC 554/C 70477/SAXW 2289/STC 91094
　　　　　　　other lp issues: angel 35618/world records T 1044/ST 1044/
　　　　　　　　　emi SLS 5019/EMX 2028/1C181 25307-25311/
　　　　　　　　　1C137 03059-03060/1C053 00995/2C059 00995/
　　　　　　　　　3C053 00995/SHZE 216/769 3961
　　　　　　　cd: emi CDZ 762 8532
　　　　　　　excerpts
　　　　　　　45: SEL 1632/SEL 1639/ESL 6257/ESL 6264
　　　　　　　lp: 33SX 1394
　　　　　　　carmen suite
　　　　　　　lp: SAX 2289/FCX 775/SAXF 133/WCX 1608/C 91094/
　　　　　　　　　SAXW 2289/STC 91094
　　　　　　　other lp issues: angel 35618/world records T 1044/ST 1044/
　　　　　　　　　emi SLS 839/SXDW 3048/EMX 2028/1C053 00995/
　　　　　　　　　1C177 02348-02352/2C053 00724/2C059 00995/
　　　　　　　　　3C053 00995/769 3961
　　　　　　　cd: emi CDM 769 4672/CZS 252 1592/CDZ 762 8532/
　　　　　　　　　royal classics ROY 6475/disky HR 700 062

33CX 1609/tchaikovsky symphony no 4
recorded in kingsway hall london on 27-28 may 1957/producer walter legge/published in december 1958/lp matrix numbers XAX 1200-1201
schippers　　*other lp issues:* angel 35443/emi MFP 2073
philharmonia

33CX 1610/piano sonatas by beethoven
recorded in abbey road studios london on 18-23 may 1957/producers walter legge and william mann/published in december 1958/lp matrix numbers XAX 1195-1196
arrau, piano   **sonata no 31**
                    cd: emi CZS 767 3792/testament SBT2 1351
                    sonata no 32
                    cd: emi CZS 767 3792

33CX 1611-1612/schubert 8 impromptus and 3 klavierstücke
recorded in abbey road studios london on 2-6 september 1955 and 17 october 1956 respectively/producers walter legge and walter jellinek/published in december 1958/lp matrix numbers XAX 1049-1052
gieseking,   lp: FCX 870-871/QCX 10335 and 10340
piano   *other lp issues:* angel 35533-35534/emi 3C153 52434-52441M

33CX 1613/see 33CX 1146-1148

33CX 1614/kodaly string quartet no 2; villa-lobos string quartet no 6
recorded in paris on 17 december 1954 and 22-27 july 1955 respectively/producer norbert gamsohn/published in december 1958/lp matrix numbers XLX 440-441
hungarian
string quartet

33CX 1615/orchestral works by beethoven
recorded in kingsway hall london on 4-5 october 1957, 21 october 1957 and 25 november 1957 respectively/producer walter legge/published in january 1959/lp matrix numbers XAX 1367-1368
klemperer   **symphony no 2**
philharmonia   lp: SAX 2331/FCX 880/SAXF 197/QCX 10342/SAXQ 7336/
                    WCX 1615/SAXW 2331/C 91000/STC 91000/SMC 91623
                other lp issues: angel 35658/34425/3619/emi ASD 2561/
                    SLS 788/ED 29 02521/EX 29 03793/1C053 00488/
                    1C181 50187-50194/1C197 53400-53419/2C069 00795/
                    2C147 50298-50318
                cd: emi CDC 747 1852/CDM 763 3552/CDZ 568 0572/
                    CZS 573 8952
                coriolan overture
                lp: 33CX 1930/SAX 2331/SAX 2570/FCX 880/SAXF 197/
                    QCX 10342/SAXQ 7336/WCX 1615/SAXW 2331/
                    C 91000/STC 91000/SMC 91623/SMC 80944/SMC 80995
                other lp issues: angel 35658/34426/34469/3800/emi ASD 2561/
                    SLS 788/ SXDW 3032/ED 29 02701/EX 29 03793/
                    1C053 00488/1C153 03103-03104/1C177 00794-00802/
                    1C181 50187-50194/1C197 53400-53419/2C069 00798/
                    2C147 50298-50318
                cd: emi CDC 747 1902/CDM 763 6112/CDZ 568 0572/
                    CZS 573 8952

33CX 1615/orchestral works by beethoven/concluded
klemperer   **die geschöpfe des prometheus overture**
philharmonia   lp: 33CX 1930/SAX 2331/SAX 2570/FCX 880/SAXF 197/
QCX 10342/SAXQ 7336/WCX 1615/SAXW 2331/
C 91000/STC 91000/SMC 80995/SMC 91623
other lp issues: angel 35658/emi ASD 2561/SLS 788/
ED 29 13411/1C053 00488/1C177 00794-00802/
2C069 00795/2C147 50298-50318
cd: emi CDM 769 1832/CDM 763 3582/CDZ 568 0572/
CZS 573 8952

33CX 1616/works by beethoven
recorded in abbey road studios london on 20 april 1957 and 6 november 1957 respectively/ producers walter legge and william mann/published in january 1959/lp matrix numbers XAX 1192-1193

galliera   **piano concerto no 3**
philharmonia   *other lp issues:* angel 35724/quintessence PMC 7073
arrau, piano   cd: emi CZS 767 3792/pantheon D 15070
recording completed on 19-22 june 1958

arrau, piano   **piano sonata no 26 "les adieux"**
other lp issue: angel 35724
cd: emi CZS 767 3792
recording completed on 4 april 1958

33CX 1617/hoffnung interplanetary music festival
recorded in royal festival hall london on 21-22 november 1958/producer peter andry/ published in january 1959/lp matrix numbers XAX 1569-1570

del mar   *other lp issues:* emi SLS 5069/1C153 52125-52127
hoffnung
amis
hoffnung
symphony
orchestra and
festival chorus

33CX 1618-1620/cherubini medea/american mercury
recorded in teatro alla scala milan between 3 and 19 september 1957/producers wilma cozart and harold lawrence/published in february 1959/lp matrix numbers XBX 9016-9021

serafin	lp: SAX 2290-2292/FCX 825-827/SAXF 155-157
la scala	*american mercury issues*
orchestra	lp: OL3-104/SR3-9000
and chorus	*other lp issues:* ricordi OS 101-103/AOCL 316001/
callas	everest 327/S-437/cetra DOC 101
scotto	cd: emi CMS 763 6252
pirazzini	*excerpts*
picchi	lp: american mercury MG 50233/SR 90233/
modesti	everest SDBR 7437/SDBR 3293/SDBR 3364/
	elite special RLP 2/rodolphe RP 12376
	cd: emi CMS 763 2442

33CX 1621/chopin piano sonata no 3; barcarolle; group of valses and mazurkas
recorded in grünewaldkirche berlin between 25 october and 2 november 1957/producer fritz ganss/published in february 1959/lp matrix numbers XRX 237-238

ashkenazy,	*other lp issue:* angel 35648
piano	*selections from the recital*
	cd: testament SBT 1045/SBT 1046

33CX 1622/works by bach
recorded in paris in 1958/published in february 1959/producer norbert gamsohn/ lp matrix numbers XLX 557-558

vandernoot   **piano concerti bwv 1052 and bwv 1056**
conservatoire
orchestra
j.casadesus, piano

j.casadesus, piano **toccata and fugue bwv 911**

33CX 1623/tchaikovsky ballet suites from casse-noisette and swan lake
recorded in kingsway hall london on 11-12 september 1957 and 28 february 1958 respectively/producer walter legge/published in april 1959/lp matrix numbers XAX 1379-1380

sawallisch	lp: SAX 2285/FCX 955/SAXF 955
philharmonia	*other lp issues:* angel 35644/emi CFP 40002/100 4891
	excerpts
	45: SEL 1628

163

33CX 1624/brahms piano sonata no 3; intermezzi from op 117
recorded in abbey road studios london on 16-18 december 1957/producers walter legge and william mann/published in march 1959/lp matrix numbers XAX 1359-1360
anda, piano   *other lp issue:* angel 35626
                 cd: testament SBT 1068

33CX 1625/works by beethoven
recorded in abbey road studios london on 1-3 may 1958 and on 8-9 april 1958 respectively/producers walter legge and walter jellinek/published in march 1959/lp matrix numbers XAX 1549-1550

galliera   **piano concerto no 1**
philharmonia   *other lp issues:* angel 35723/quintessence PMC 7071
arrau, piano   cd: emi CZS 767 3792/pantheon D 15070
                 recording completed on 7 october 1958

arrau, piano   **piano sonata no 24**
                 other lp issue: angel 35723
                 cd: testament SBT2 1351

33CX 1626/lieder by loewe, schubert, schumann and wolf
recorded in abbey road studios london on 3-5 october and 13-18 november 1957/ producers walter legge and walter jellinek/published in march 1959/lp matrix numbers XAX 1316-1317
hotter   lp: 33CX 1661
moore, piano   *other lp issue:* angel 35583
                 selections from the recital
                 45: SEL 1674
                 lp: C 70410
                 other lp selections: angel seraphim 60025/6072/
                     emi 1C147 01633-01634
                 cd: testament SBT 1197/SBT 1198

33CX 1627/schubert piano trio no 1
recorded in abbey road studios london on 13-16 may 1958/producer walter legge/ published in april 1959/lp matrix numbers XAX 1453-1454
oborin, piano   lp: SAX 2281/FCX 889/SAXF 161/WSX 553/C 80543/
oistrakh, violin   SCXW 7519/STC 80543
knushevitsky,   *other lp issues:* angel 35713/world records CM 88/
cello   emi 1C047 01490/CFP 40037
                 cd: emi CZS 569 3672

33CX 1628/verdi arias from macbeth, nabucco, ernani and don carlos
recorded in abbey road studios london on 19-24 september 1958/producer walter legge/ published in march 1959/lp matrix numbers XAX 1541-1542

rescigno	lp: SAX 2293/FCX 30204/SAXF 140/QCX 10334/
philharmonia	SAXQ 7261
callas	*other lp issues:* angel 35763/world records T 633/ST 633/
	emi ASD 3817/1C053 00865/2C165 54178-54188/
	2C181 53452-53453/3C065 01020
	cd: emi CDC 747 7302/CDS 749 4532/566 6182/
	557 7600
	selections from the recital
	45: SEL 1633/ESL 6280
	lp: WC 610/C 70400
	other selections
	lp: angel 36135/3699/3841/emi ALP 2008/ASD 558/
	QALP 10378/SXLP 30166/EMX 2123/SLS 5057/
	SLS 5104/1C147 30636-30637M/1C181 01398-01399
	cd: emi CDEMX 2123/CDC 555 0162/CMS 565 5342/
	CMS 565 7462/CMS 565 9522/CMS 763 2442/
	CZS 252 6142

33CX 1629/arias by beethoven, weber and mozart
recorded in abbey road studios london on 12-14 may 1958/producers walter legge and walter jellinek/published in july 1959/lp matrix numbers XAX 1423-1424

wallberg	lp: SAX 2282/FCX 822
philharmonia	*other lp issues:* angel 35719/angel seraphim 60353/
nilsson	emi 1C187 00786-00787
	cd: emi CDM 763 1082/testament SBT 1200
	selections from the recital
	lp: emi ASD 3915
	cd: emi CDCFP 4561

33CX 1630/mozart piano concerti nos 21 k467 and 22 k482
recorded in abbey road studios london on 28 february-2 march 1958/producers walter legge and walter jellinek/published in march 1959/lp matrix numbers XAX 1377-1378

sawallisch	lp: WCX 1630/C 90996
philharmonia	*other lp issues:* emi SXLP 30124/1C053 00773/
a.fischer,	2C053 12123
piano	cd: emi CDZ 767 0022/CES 568 5292/562 7502
	recordings completed on 10 march 1958

33CX 1631-1633/puccini la fanciulla del west
recorded in teatro alla scala milan on 16-23 july 1958/producer walter legge/published in april 1959/lp matrix numbers XBX 9012-9017

matacic
la scala
orchestra
and chorus
nilsson
carturan
gibin
ercolani
sordello
zaccaria

lp: SAX 2286-2288/WCX 1631-1633/SAXW 2286-2288/
QCX 10343-10345/SAXQ 7251-7253/C 91036-91038/
STC 91036-91038
other lp issues: angel 3593/angel seraphim 6074/emi SLS 5079
cd: emi CMS 763 9702

33CX 1634-1635/beethoven missa solemnis
recorded in musikvereinssaal vienna on 12-16 september 1958/producer walter legge/published in october 1959/lp matrix numbers XHAX 70-73

karajan
philharmonia
wiener
singverein
schwarzkopf
ludwig
gedda
zaccaria

lp: FCX 828-829/SAXF 177-178/QCX 10369-10370/
SAXQ 7317-7318/WCX 1634-1635/C 91019-91020/
STC 91019-91020
other lp issues: angel 3595/eterna 820 558-820 559/world records T 914-915/emi SLS 5198/CFPD 4420-4421/
1C137 00627-00628/1C191 00627-00628/
2C181 00627-00628/3C153 00627-00628
cd: testament SBT 2126
testament re-issue also includes rehearsal extracts

33CX 1636/rimsky-korsakov scheherazade
recorded in kingsway hall london on 1-2 september 1958/producer walter legge/published in october 1959/lp matrix numbers XAX 1595-1596

matacic
philharmonia

other lp issues: angel 35767/emi MFP 2013/SIT 60042
cd: emi CZS 568 0982/CZS 568 7392/testament SBT 1329

33CX 1637/brahms piano concerto no 2
recorded in grünewaldkirche berlin on 25-30 october 1957/producer fritz ganss/published in april 1959

ludwig
staatskapelle
berlin
ashkenazy,
piano

other lp issue: angel 35649

33CX 1638/operatic arias by verdi, bellini, donizetti, rossini, puccini and boito
recorded in abbey road studios london on 1-6 march 1958/producer walter legge/published in april 1959/lp matrix numbers XAX 1405-1406

wolf-ferrari	lp: QCX 10336
philharmonia	*other lp issues:* angel 35635/emi ASD 4022/101 7411
scotto	*selections from the recital*
	45: SEL 1643

33CX 1639/chopin piano sonata no 2 "funeral march"; grande valse brillante; 2 nocturnes; scherzo no 3
recorded in paris in may 1958/published in july 1959/lp matrix numbers XLX 731-732

malcuzynski,   lp: FCX 785
piano

33CX 1640/catalogue number appears not to have been allocated

33CX 1641/victoria missa pro defunctis
recorded in bussum on 21-22 march 1957/producer walter legge/published in may 1959/lp matrix numbers XFX 7-8

de nobel   *other lp issue:* angel 35668
netherlands
chamber choir

33CX 1642/orchestral works by dvorak and smetana
recorded in grünewaldkirche berlin on 18-20 may 1958/producer walter legge/published in may 1959/lp matrix numbers XRX 246-247

karajan	symphony no 9 "from the new world"
berlin	lp: SAX 2272/FCX 814/SAXF 144/QCX 10348/SAXQ 7263/
philharmonic	WCX 1642/SAXW 2272/C 91003/C 91255/
	STC 91003/STC 91255
	other lp issues: angel 35615/emi SLS 839/ASD 2863/
	SVB 814/100 4911/1C063 02348/1C177 02348-02352/
	2C059 02348/2C065 02348/3C063 00491/
	1C037 02940/SHZE 160
	cd: emi CDZ 252 1342

33CX 1642/orchestral works by dvorak and smetana/concluded
karajan vltava/ma vlast
berlin 45: SELW 1816/C 50546/SEDQ 686
philharmonic lp: SAX 2275/FCX 824/SAXF 160/QCX 10348/SAXQ 7263/
WCX 1642/WC 529/SAXW 2275/C 91003/C 70426/
STC 91003
other lp issues: angel 35615/37232/emi SLS 839/ASD 2863/
SXDW 3048/CVB 814/CVD 2075/1C177 02348-02352/
100 4911/1C053 01414/1C063 00737/1C063 02348/
143 5643/2C059 02348/2C069 02348/3C065 02348
cd: emi CDM 769 4652/CDZ 252 1522/CZS 252 1592/
CZS 569 4582/laserlight 24426/disky DCL 705 872/
HR 700 062

33CX 1643/beethoven piano trio no 6 "archduke"
recorded in abbey road studios london on 9-12 may 1958/producers walter legge and walter jellinek/published in may 1959/lp matrix numbers XAX 1455-1456
oborin, piano lp: SAX 2352/FCX 30526/SAXF 130526/QCX 10337/
oistrakh, SAXQ 7300/WSX 552/C 80542/SCXW 7518/STC 80542
violin *other lp issues:* angel 35704/emi MFP 2117/1C047 00866/
knushevitzky, 2C037 01974/melodiya S10 5735-5736
cello cd: emi CZS 569 3672

33CX 1644/works for cello and piano by boccherini, bach, ravel and fauré
recorded in abbey road studios london in 1958/published in may 1959/producer walter jellinek/lp matrix numbers XAX 1324-1325
fournier, cello
moore, piano

33CX 1645/operatic mad scenes by donizetti, thomas and bellini
recorded in abbey road studios london on 24-25 september 1958/producer walter legge/
published in may 1959/lp matrix numbers XAX 1543-1544

rescigno	**piangete voi? a dolce guidami/anna bolena**
philharmonia	lp: SAX 2320/FCX 806/SAXF 129/QCX 10338/SAXQ 7285/
callas	C 70423
sinclair	*other lp issues:* angel 35764/36930/world records T 591/ST 591/
lanigan	emi ASD 3801/1C053 00784/2C069 00784/3C065 00784/
robertson	2C165 54178-54188
rouleau	cd: emi CDC 747 2832/CDS 749 4532/CMS 763 2442/
	CMS 557 0622/566 6182

rescigno	**a vos jeux mes amis/hamlet**
philharmonia	lp: SAX 2320/FCX 806/SAXF 129/QCX 10228/SAXQ 7285
and chorus	*other lp issues:* angel 35764/3743/world records T 591/ST 591/
callas	emi ASD 3801/1C053 00784/2C069 00784/3C065 00784/
	2C165 54178-54188
	cd: emi CDC 747 2832/CDS 749 4532/CDS 754 1032/
	CMS 565 5342/CZS 252 6142/566 6182

rescigno	**col sorriso d'innocenza/il pirata**
philharmonia	lp: SAX 2320/FCX 806/SAXF 129/QCX 10338/SAXQ 7285
callas	*other lp issues:* angel 35764/36930/world records T 591/ST 591/
	emi ASD 3801/1C053 00784/2C069 00784/3C065 00784/
	2C165 54178-54188
	cd: emi CDC 747 2832/CDS 749 4532/CMS 763 2442/
	566 6182

33CX 1646/catalogue number appears not to have been allocated

33CX 1647/orchestral music by richard strauss
recorded in abbey road studios london on 22-23 february 1958/producer walter legge/
published in june 1959/lp matrix numbers XAX 1385-1386

sawallisch	**der bürger als edelmann suite**
philharmonia	*other lp issue:* angel 35646
	cd: testament SBT 1112
	waltz scene/intermezzo
	other lp issue: angel 35646
	recordings completed on 4 march 1958

33CX 1648/villa-lobos bachianas brasilieras nos 4 and 7
recorded in paris in 1958/producer rené challan.published in june 1959/lp matrix numbers XLX 662-663

villa-lobos	*other lp issue:* angel 35674
orchestre	cd: emi CZS 767 2292
national	

33CX 1649-1650/donizetti l'elisir d'amore
recorded in teatro alla scala milan on 21-27 august 1958/producer walter legge/published in september 1959/lp matrix numbers XBX 9035-9036

serafin	lp: SAX 2298-2299/QCX 10360-10361/SAXQ 7257-7258/
la scala	C 91042-91043/STC 91042-91043
orchestra	*other lp issues:* angel 3594/angel seraphim 6001/
and chorus	3C163 00863-00864
carteri	cd: testament SBT 2150
alva	
panerai	
taddei	

33CX 1651/operatic arias by wagner and verdi
recorded in kingsway hall london on 22-24 april 1958/producer walter legge/published in june 1959/lp matrix numbers XAX 1677-1678

susskind	dich teure halle; allmächt'ge jungfrau/tannhäuser
philharmonia	einsam in trüben tagen; euch lüften/lohengrin
nordmo-lövberg	du bist der lenz/die walküre
	lp: SAX 2353
	other lp issue: angel 35713

braithwaite	tu che la vanita/don carlo
philharmonia	lp: SAX 2353
nordmo-lövberg	*other lp issue:* angel 35713

braithwaite	piangea cantando; ave maria/otello
philharmonia	lp: SAX 2353
nordmo-lövberg	*other lp issue:* angel 35713
sinclair	

33CX 1652/weber overtures: abu hassan; beherrscher der geister; euryanthe; der freischütz; jubel; oberon; preciosa
recorded in kingsway hall london on 24-28 february 1958/producers walter legge and walter jellinek/published in july 1959/lp matrix numbers XAX 1526-1527
sawallisch   lp: SAX 2343
philharmonia   *other lp issues:* angel 35754/emi XLP 30038/SXLP 30038/
        SMVP 8062/1C047 01497
    cd: emi CDM 769 5722

33CX 1653/beethoven piano concerto no 5 "emperor"
recorded in abbey road studios london on 21-22 june 1958/producer walter legge/published in august 1959/lp matrix numbers XAX 1613-1614
galliera   lp: SAX 2297/QCX 10505/SAXQ 7372
philharmonia   *other lp issues:* angel 35722/world records T 645/ST 645/
arrau, piano   quintessence PMC 7075
    cd: emi CZS 767 3792/pantheon D 15070

33CX 1654/russian orchestral music by mussorgsky, borodin and rimsky-korsakov
recorded in kingsway hall london on 4-5 september 1958/producer walter legge/published in july 1959/lp matrix numbers XAX 1537-1538
matacic   mussorgsky night on bare mountain; borodin prince
philharmonia   igor: overture, march and polovtsian dances
    lp: SAX 2327/FCX 819/SAXF 227
    other lp issues: angel 35768/emi XLP 30070/SXLP 30070
    polovtsian dances only
    cd: emi CZS 568 5501
    rimsky-korsakov russian easter festival overture
    lp: SAX 2327/FCX 819/SAXF 227
    other lp issues: angel 35768/emi XLP 30070/SXLP 30070
    cd: emi CZS 568 0982

33CX 1655/orchestral music by wagner
recorded in kingsway hall london on 25-26 february 1958 (götterdämmerung) and 28-29 july 1958 (tannhäuser and meistersinger)/producers walter legge and walter jellinek/published in october 1959/lp matrix numbers XAX 1539-1540
sawallisch   rhine journey and funeral march/götterdämmerung
philharmonia   *other lp issue:* angel 35755
    cd: emi CMS 565 2122/testament SBT 1112
    tannhäuser overture; die meistersinger von nürnberg overture
    other lp issue: angel 35755
    cd: testament SBT 1112

33CX 1656/bach cello suites nos 1 and 3
recorded in abbey road studios london on 23 may 1958 and on 20 march 1957 respectively/ producer walter jellinek/published in august 1959/ lp matrix numbers XAX 1545-1546
starker, cello   lp: C 91028
                cd: emi CZS 568 4852
                recording of suite no 1 completed on 1 february 1959

33CX 1657/wolf selection from the goethe-lieder
recorded in abbey road studios london on 3-8 april 1956, 8-10 june 1957 and 11 january 1958/producer walter legge/published in march 1960/ lp matrix numbers XAX 1693-1694
schwarzkopf   lp: SAX 2333/FCX 837/SAXF 256
moore, piano   *other lp issues:* angel 35909/emi SLS 5197/1C037 03725
                selections from the recordings
                lp: angel 3754/emi 154 6133
                cd: emi CDM 763 6532/CMS 763 7902/CHS 565 8602/
                     585 1052/notablu 935 0911

33CX 1658/operatic scenes by wagner and weber
recorded in abbey road studios london on 25 may 1958 (euch lüften) and in kingsway hall london on 27-28 april 1956/producer walter legge/published in september 1959/ lp matrix numbers XAX 1464-1465
wallberg   **euch lüften....entweihte götter!/lohengrin**
philharmonia   lp: SAX 2300/FCX 821
schwarzkopf   *other lp issues:* angel 35806/world records T 520/ST 520/
ludwig   emi SXDW 3049/1C181 52291-52292
                cd: emi CDM 769 5012/CMS 567 6342

susskind   **allmächt'ge jungfrau/tannhäuser; und ob die wolke/**
philharmonia   **der freischütz**
schwarzkopf   lp: SAX 2300/FCX 821
                other lp issues: angel 35806/world records T 520/ST 520/
                     emi SXDW 3049/1C181 52291-52292
                cd: emi CDM 769 5012
                einsam in trüben tagen/lohengrin
                lp: SAX 2300/FCX 821
                other lp issues: angel 35806/world records T 520/ST 520/
                     emi SXDW 3049/1C181 52291-52292
                cd: emi CDM 769 5012/CDM 565 5772/585 1052

33CX 1658/operatic scenes by wagner and weber/concluded
susskind   **dich teure halle!/tannhäuser**
philharmonia   lp: SAX 2300/FCX 821
schwarzkopf   *other lp issues:* angel 35806/world records T 520/ST 520/
         emi SXDW 3049/1C181 52291-52292
       cd: emi CDM 769 5012/585 1052
       leise leise/der freischütz
       lp: SAX 2300/FCX 821
       other lp issues: angel 35806/world records T 520/ST 520/
         emi SXDW 3049/1C181 52291-52292
       cd: emi CDM 769 5012/CMS 567 6342/585 1052/
         CDM 565 5772

33CX 1659/catalogue number appears not to have been allocated

33CX 1660/violin concerti by prokofiev and mozart
recorded in abbey road studios london between 14 and 22 may 1958/producers walter legge and walter jellinek/published in september 1959/lp matrix numbers XAX 1512-1513
galliera   **prokofiev violin concerto no 2**
philharmonia   lp: SAX 2304/FCX 30249/QCX 10355/SAXQ 7315
oistrakh,   *other lp issues:* angel 35714/angel seraphim 60223/
violin   emi SLS 5004/SXLP 30155
       cd: emi CZS 569 3312/562 8882

oistrakh   **mozart violin concerto no 3 k216**
philharmonia   lp: SAX 2304/FC 25125/QCX 10355/SAXQ 7315
oistrakh,   *other lp issues:* angel 35714/angel seraphim 60223/emi
violin   SXLP 30086/1C047 50510/SREG 1090/SHZE 152
       cd: emi CZS 569 3312

33CX 1661/see 33CX 1626

33CX 1662/orchestral works by schumann
recorded in kingsway hall london on 2-4 june 1958/producers walter legge and walter jellinek/published in september 1959/lp matrix numbers XAX 1709-1710
giulini   **symphony no 3 "rhenish", orchestrated by mahler**
philharmonia   lp: QCX 10368
       other lp issue: angel 35753
       cd: emi CZS 575 4622
       manfred overture
       lp: QCX 10368
       other lp issue: angel 35753
       cd: emi CZS 767 7232

174

33CX 1663/ravel daphnis et chloé second suite; bizet carmen suite no 1; respighi pini di roma
recorded in kingsway hall london on 6 november 1956 and 24 january 1957/producer walter jellinek/published in september 1959/lp matrix numbers XAX 1206-1207
galliera   lp: SAX 2303
philharmonia   *other lp issue:* emi CFP 120

33CX 1664/schumann fantasia in c; carnaval
recorded in abbey road studios london on 29 may-3 june 1957/producer walter legge/published in october 1959/lp matrix numbers XAX 1242-1243
a.fischer,   lp: C 80648
piano

33CX 1665/cello concerti by haydn and boccherini
recorded in abbey road studios london on 29-30 may 1958/producer walter legge/published in october 1959/lp matrix numbers XAX 1460-1461
giulini   **haydn cello concerto in d**
philharmonia   lp: QCX 10356/WCX 1665/C 91046
starker, cello   *other lp issues:* angel 35725/emi 2M155 53430-53431/ 1C047 50806
                         cd: emi CZS 568 4852
                         boccherini cello concerto in b flat, arranged by grützmacher
                         lp: QCX 10356/WCX 1665/C 91046
                         other lp issues: angel 35725/emi 2M155 53430-53431/ 1C047 50806
                         cd: emi CZS 568 4852/CZS 568 7452

33CX 1666/beethoven piano sonatas nos 31 and 32
recorded in abbey road studios london on 7-8 april 1959/producers walter legge and walter jellinek/published in october 1959/lp matrix numbers XAX 1697-1698
richter-haaser,
piano

33CX 1667/beethoven piano concerti
recorded in salle wagram paris on 22 june 1957/producer norbert gamsohn/published in october 1959/lp matrix numbers XLX 82-83

vandernoot	**piano concerto no 1**
conservatoire	lp: FCX 671
orchestra	*other lp issue:* angel 35672
gilels, piano	cd: emi 483 4182
	piano concerto no 2
	lp: FCX 673/FC 25033
	other lp issue: angel 35672
	cd: emi 483 4182

33CX 1668-1670/handel messiah
recorded in town hall huddersfield on 15-19 june 1959/producer victor olof/published in october 1959

sargent	lp: SAX 2308-2310
liverpool	cd: emi CFPD 4718
philharmonic	*excerpts*
huddersfield	lp: 33CX 1713/SAX 2365
choral society	*other lp excerpts:* emi CFP 40020
morison	*recording completed in abbey road studios london on 24 august 1959*
thomas	*using pro arte orchestra in place of liverpool philharmonic*
lewis	
milligan	

33CX 1671/song cycles by mahler
recorded in abbey road studios london on 18-19 october 1958/producer walter legge/ published in october 1959/lp matrix numbers XAX 1589-1590

boult	**lieder eines fahrenden gesellen**
philharmonia	lp: SAX 2321/FCX 872/SAXF 191
ludwig	*other lp issues:* angel 35776/angel seraphim 60026/
	world records T 703/ST 703/emi 143 6521
	cd: emi CDM 769 4992
vandernoot	**kindertotenlieder**
philharmonia	lp: SAX 2321/FCX 872/SAXF 191
ludwig	*other lp issues:* angel 35776/angel seraphim 60026/
	world records T 703/ST 703/emi 143 6521
	cd: emi CDM 769 4992

33CX 1672/beethoven violin concerto
recorded in salle wagram paris on 8-10 november 1958/producer walter legge/published in april 1960/lp matrix numbers XLX 84-85
cluytens
orchestre national
oistrakh, violin
    lp: SAX 2315/FCX 817/SAXF 119/QCX 10384/SAXQ 7275/WCX 1672/C 91051/SAXW 2315/STC 91051
    other lp issues: angel 35780/34457/emi SLS 5004/XLP 30168/SXLP 30168/1C037 90905/1C063 90905/SHZE 143 melodiya D 033639-033640
    cd: emi CDM 769 2612/483 4182

33CX 1673/berlioz symphonie fantastique
recorded in kingsway hall london on 4-5 november 1958/producer walter legge/published in november 1959/lp matrix numbers XAX 1615-1616
cluytens
philharmonia
    lp: FCX 858/SAXF 123
    other lp issue: emi CFP 168
    cd: emi CDZ 762 6052

33CX 1674/tchaikovsky francesca da rimini; marche slave; romeo and juliet fantasy overture
recorded in kingsway hall london on 20-21 november 1958/producer walter jellinek/published in november 1959/lp matrix numbers XAX 1617-1618
wallberg
philharmonia

33CX 1675/piano sonatas by beethoven
recorded in abbey road studios london in 1959/producer walter jellinek/published in november 1959/lp matrix numbers XAX 1611-1612
a.fischer, piano   **sonata no 14 "moonlight"**
                    lp: C 80646
                    other lp issue: angel 35791
                    cd: emi CZS 569 2172
                    sonatas nos 24 and 30
                    other lp issue: angel 35791
                    cd: emi CZS 569 2172

33CX 1676/works by hindemith
recorded in kingsway hall london on 19-21 november 1956/producer walter legge/published in november 1959/lp matrix numbers 1639-1640

hindemith   **horn concerto**
philharmonia   lp: WCX 1676/C 91080
brain, horn   *other lp issues:* angel 35491/emi HLS 7001/RLS 7701/
                    1C141 43327-43329M/EH 29 11731
                cd: emi CDC 747 8342/CDH 763 3732

hindemith   **sinfonia serena**
philharmonia   lp: WCX 1676/C 91080
                other lp issue: angel 35491

33CX 1677/dvorak symphony no 9 "from the new world"; carnival overture
recorded in kingsway hall london on 21-24 february 1958/producer walter legge/published in january 1960/lp matrix numbers XAX 1383-1384
sawallisch   lp: SAX 2322
philharmonia   *other lp issues:* emi CFP 104/1C037 00650/1C051 00650/
                  29 11641

33CX 1678/operatic arias by verdi, borodin and tchaikovsky
recorded in abbey road studios london on 11-13 december 1958/producer walter legge/published in november 1959/lp matrix numbers XAX 1591-1592
fistoulari   *selections from the recital*
philharmonia   45: SEL 1649/SEL 1664/ESL 6269/ESL 6276
ladysz

177

33CX 1679/works by walton
recorded in kingsway hall london on 2-6 february 1959/producer walter jellinek/published in december 1959/lp matrix numbers XAX 1699-1700

walton	**belshazzar's feast**
philharmonia	lp: SAX 2319
orchestra	*other lp issues:* angel 35681/emi SXLP 30236/SLS 5246
and chorus	cd: emi CHS 565 0032
bell	

walton	**partita for orchestra**
philharmonia	lp: SAX 2319
	other lp issues: angel 35681/emi SXLP 30236/SLS 5246
	cd: emi CHS 565 0032
	recording completed on 16 february 1959

33CX 1680/brahms piano concerto no 2
recorded in grünewaldkirche berlin on 30 november-1 december 1958/producer walter legge/published in february 1960/lp matrix numbers XRX 1507-1508

karajan	lp: SAX 2328/QCX 10492/SAXQ 7369/WCX 1680/
berlin	C 91052/SAXW 2328/STC 91052
philharmonic	*other lp issues:* angel 35796/world records T 1090/ST 1090/
richter-haaser,	eterna 825 433/emi 1C053 01973
piano	cd: emi CDM 566 0932/disky DCL 705 732/EH 701 542

33CX 1681/callas sings verdi at la scala
excerpts from the complete opera recordings on 33CX 1258-1260, 33CX 1318-1320, 33CXS 1324-33CX 1326 and 33CX 1472-1474

33CX 1682/see 33CX 1483-1485

33CX 1683/works for violin and orchestra by lalo and tchaikovsky
recorded in abbey road studios london on 25-27 february 1959/producers walter legge and walter jellinek/published in february 1960/lp matrix numbers XAX 1669-1670

kondrashin	**symphonie espagnole**
philharmonia	lp: SAX 2329/FCX 845/SAXF 169/C 70384/STC 70432/
kogan, violin	SBO 8202
	other lp issues: angel 35721/world records T 562/ST 562/ emi CFP 40040
	sérénade mélancolique
	lp: SAX 2329/FCX 845/SAXF 169
	other lp issues: angel 35721/world records T 562/ST 562/ emi CFP 40040
	cd: testament SBT 1224/SBT6 1248

33CX 1684/operatic overtures by verdi
recorded in kingsway hall london on 19 february 1959 (royal philharmonic) and 27 february 1959 (philharmonia)/producers walter legge and walter jellinek/published in february 1960/ lp matrix numbers XAX 1665-1666

serafin	**la traviata acts 1 and 3 and vespri siciliani**
royal	lp: SAX 2324
philharmonic	*other lp issues:* angel 35676/hmv QALP 10335/ASDQ 5316/ emi 1C053 00867/29 00867
	cd: emi CDZ 762 6092
	la forza del destino
	45: SEL 1536
	lp: SAX 2324
	other lp issues: angel 35676/hmv QALP 10335/ASDQ 5316/ emi 1C053 00867/29 00867
	cd: emi CDZ 762 6092
serafin	**nabucco, giovanna d'arco and aida**
philharmonia	lp: SAX 2324
	other lp issues: angel 35676/hmv QALP 10335/ASDQ 5316/ emi 1C053 00867/29 00867

33CX 1685/chopin the 14 valses
recorded in paris in 1959/published in march 1960/lp matrix numbers XLX 830-831

malcuzynski,	lp: SAX 2332/FCX 820/SAXF 820
piano	*other lp issue:* angel 35726
	selection from the recital
	45: SEL 1682/ESL 6286

33CX 1686/mozart piano concerti nos 20 k466 and 23 k488
recorded in abbey road studios lomdon on 13-15 february 1959/producer walter jellinek/
published in march 1960/lp matrix numbers XAX 1635-1636

boult	lp: SAX 2335/FCX 851/SAXF 171/WCX 1686/
philharmonia	C 91067/SAXW 2335/STC 91067
a.fischer,	*other lp issues:* emi XLP 30148/SXLP 30148/1C037 00496
piano	cd: emi CDZ 767 0002/CES 568 5292

33CX 1687/instrumental music by mozart, ibert and jacob
recorded in memorial hall studio london on 22 july 1957/published in march 1960/
lp matrix numbers XAX 1561-1562

dennis brain	**mozart divertimento no 14 k270**
chamber	*other lp issues:* emi RLS 7701/1C141 43327-43329M
ensemble	**ibert 3 pieces breves**
	other lp issues: emi RLS 7701/1C141 43327-43329M

dennis brain	**jacob sextet for piano and wind**
chamber	
ensemble	
malcolm, piano	

33CX 1688-1689/j.strauss die fledermaus
recorded in abbey road studios london on 25 june-2 july 1959/producer walter legge/published
in august 1960/lp matrix numbers XAX 1816-1819

ackermann	lp: SAX 2336-2337/WCX 1688-1689/SCXW 7606-7607/
philharmonia	SAXW 2336-2337/STC 80596-80597
orchestra	*other lp issues:* angel 3581/emi 1C147 01652-01653/CFPD 4702
and chorus	cd: emi CDCFPD 4702
scheyrer	*excerpts*
lipp	lp: emi XLP 20091/SXLP 20091/1C037 03193
ludwig	
terkal	
dermota	
kunz	
berry	
wächter	

33CX 1690/chopin the 6 polonaises
recorded in paris on 18-29 may 1958/producer norbert gamsohn/published in april 1960/ lp matrix numbers XLX 828-829
malcuzynski,   lp: SAX 2338/FCX 818/SAXF 127/C 80647
piano   *other lp issue:* angel 35728

33CX 1691/orchestral music by tchaikovsky
recorded in abbey road srudios london on 17-18 february 1959/producer walter jellinek/ published in june 1960/lp matrix numbers XAX 1689-1690
markevitch   **romeo and juliet**
philharmonia   lp: SAX 2339/FCX 847/FC 25086/SAXF 124
                       other lp issues: angel 35680/emi 1M055 12892
                       ballet suite from casse noisette
                       lp: SAX 2339/FCX 847/SAXF 124
                       other lp issues: angel 35680/emi 1M055 12892

33CX 1692/brahms violin concerto
recorded in abbey road studios london on 22-26 february 1959/producers walter legge and walter jellinek/published in may 1960/lp matrix numbers XAX 1667-1668
kondrashin   lp: SAX 2307/FCX 839/SAXF 166/QCX 10385/
philharmonia   SAXQ 7276
kogan, violin   *other lp issues:* angel 35690/emi XLP 30063/SXLP 30063

33CX 1693/brahms lieder; schumann frauenliebe und –leben
recorded in abbey road studios london on 3-6 may 1959/producer walter legge/published in november 1960/lp matrix numbers XAX 1766-1767
ludwig   lp: SAX 2340
moore, piano   cd: emi CMS 764 0742
                       selections from the recital
                       lp: angel seraphim 6072/emi 1C063 00826

33CX 1694/orchestral music by falla and ravel
recorded in kingsway hall london on 25-29 july 1957 (falla) and 4-10 june 1959/producer walter jellinek/published in june 1960/lp matrix numbers XAX 1733-1734
giulini   **el sombrero de 3 picos suite**
philharmonia   lp: SAX 2341/QCX 10383/SAXQ 7284/WCX 1694/
                          C 91071/SAXW 2341/STC 91071
                       other lp issues: angel 35820/emi XLP 30140/SXLP 30140/
                          CFP 4512/2C053 01317
                       cd: emi CDM 769 0372/CDM 764 7462
                       excerpts
                       45: SEL 1635/SEL 1679/ESL 6262/ESL 6284

33CX 1694/orchestral music by falla and ravel/concluded

giulini
philharmonia

alborada del gracioso
45: SEL 1684/ESL 6288
lp: SAX 2341/WCX 1694/C 91071/SAXW 2341/STC 91071/
    QCX 10383/SAXQ 7284
other lp issues: angel 35820/emi SXLP 30198/EMX 412 0761
cd: emi CZS 767 7232/562 7462

daphnis et chloé second suite
lp: SAX 2341/WCX 1694/C 91071/SAXW 2341/STC 91071/
    QCX 10383/SAXQ 7284
other lp issues: angel 35820/emi SXLP 30198/EMX 412 0761
cd: emi CZS 767 7232/562 7462

33CX 1695/works by chopin
recorded in abbey road studios london on 6-7 july 1959 and in paris on 27 july 1959 respectively/producers john hughes and norbert gamsohn/published in november 1960/ lp matrix numbers XAX 1833-1834

susskind
london
symphony
malcuzynski,
piano

piano concerto no 2
lp: SAX 2344
other lp issue: angel 35729/emi 769 3991
cd: emi CZS 568 2262

malcuzynski,
piano

fantasy in f minor
lp: SAX 2344
other lp issues: angel 35729/emi 769 3991

33CX 1696/works by beethoven
recorded in abbey road studios london on 2-3 may 1958 and 6-7 october 1958 respectively/ producers walter legge and walter jellinek/published in september 1960/lp matrix numbers XAX 1593 and 1824

galliera
philharmonia
arrau, piano

piano concerto no 2
lp: SAX 2346
other lp issues: world records T 568/ST 568/quintessence
    PMC 7072
cd: emi CZS 767 3792/pantheon D 15070
recording completed on 7 october 1958

arrau, piano

piano sonata no 7
lp: SAX 2346
other lp issues: world records T 568/ST 568
recording completed in october 1959

33CX 1697-1698/wagner orchestral music from the operas
recorded in kingsway hall london between 23 february and 10 march 1960/producers walter legge and walter jellinek/published in june 1960/lp matrix numbers XAX *1905-1908*

klemperer der fliegende holländer overture; rienzi overture;
philharmonia tannhäuser overture; lohengrin act 1 prelude
lp: SAX 2347-2348/FCX 868-869/SAXF 187-188/
    QCX 10391-10392/SAXQ 7280-7281
other lp issues: angel 36187/32039/34418/3610/emi SLS 5075/
    ASD 2695/SXLP 30436/1C153 50347-50349/
    1C037 03459/1C187 00498-00499/2C069 00498/
    F668 525-533
cd: emi CDC 747 2542/CDM 763 6172/CMS 567 8932
die meistersinger von nürnberg overture;
prelude and liebestod/tristan und isolde
lp: SAX 2347-2348/FCX 868-869/SAXF 187-188/
    QCX 10391-10392/SAXQ 7280-7281
other lp issues: angel 36188/32057/3610/emi SLS 5075/
    ASD 2696/SXLP 30525/1C153 50347-50349/
    1C037 03459/1C053 00499/2C069 01356/
    1C187 00498-00499/F668 525-533
cd: emi CDC 747 2542/CDM 763 6172/CMS 567 8932
lohengrin act 3 prelude
45: SCD 2178/SEBQ 260
lp: SAX 2347-2348/FCX 868-869/SAXF 187-188/
    QCX 10391-10392/SAXQ 7280-7281
other lp issues: angel 36188/32057/3610/emi SLS 5075/
    ASD 2696/SXLP 30525/1C153 50347-50349/
    1C037 03459/1C053 00499/2C069 01356/
    1C187 00498-00499/F668 525-533
cd: emi CDC 747 2542/CDM 763 6172/CMS 567 8932
siegfried's funeral march/götterdämmerung; entry
of the apprentices and entry of the masters/
die meistersinger von nürnberg
45: SEL 1677/ESL 6283/SEBQ 234
lp: SAX 2347-2348/FCX 868-869/SAXF 187-188/
    QCX 10391-10392/SAXQ 7280-7281/C 91281/
    STC 91281
other lp issues: angel 36188/32057/3610/emi SLS 5075/
    ASD 2696/SXLP 30525/1C153 50347-50349/
    1C037 00567/1C053 00499/2C069 01356/
    1C187 00498-00499/F668 525-533
cd: emi CDC 747 2552/CDM 763 6182/CMS 567 8932

33CX 1699/orchestral works by rimsky-korsakov, mussorgsky, borodin and ravel
recorded in kingsway hall london on 5 november 1958 (la valse) and 18-19 november 1958/ producer walter jellinek/published in july 1960/lp matrix numbers XAX 1719-1720

cluytens   **capriccio espagnol**
philharmonia   lp: SAX 2355/FCX 857/SAXF 857
other lp issues: emi XLP 20106/SXLP 20106
cd: emi CDM 769 1102/CDE 574 7632
night on bare mountain
lp: SAX 2355/FCX 857/FC 25509/SAXF 857/ SBOF 125509
other lp issues: emi XLP 20106/SXLP 20106
cd: emi CDM 769 1102/CDE 574 7632
in the steppes of central asia
lp: SAX 2355/FCX 857/FC 25509/SAXF 857/ SBOF 125509
other lp issues: emi XLP 20106/SXLP 20106
cd: emi CDM 769 1102/CDE 574 7632/252 5782
la valse
lp: SAX 2355
other lp issues: emi XLP 20106/SXLP 20106
cd: emi CZS 575 1062

33CX 1700/works for cello and piano by bach, kreisler, saint-saens, debussy, chopin, popper, schubert, mussorgsky, schumann, tcherepnin and paganini
recorded in abbey road studios london on 4-7 june 1958/producers walter legge and walter jellinek/published in june 1960/lp matrix numbers XAX 1451-1452
starker, cello   cd: emi CZS 568 4852
moore, piano

33CX 1701/piano music by chopin
recorded in paris/published in march 1961/lp matrix numbers XLX 790-791
iturbi, piano

33CX 1702/orchestral works by beethoven
recorded in kingsway hall london on 21-22 october 1957 and in abbey road studios london on 28 october 1959 respectively/producer walter legge/published in june 1960/lp matrix numbers XAX 1829-1830

klemperer philharmonia	**symphony no 4** lp: SAX 2354/FCX 881/SAXF 198/QCX 10438/ SAXQ 7339/WCX 1702/C 91070/SAXW 2354/ STC 91070/SMC 91625 *other lp issues:* angel 35661/34423/34469/3619/emi SLS 788/ ASD 2563/ED 29 02701/EX 29 03793/1C053 00500/ 1C177 00794-00802/1C181 50187-50194/2C069 00797/ 1C197 53400-53419/2C147 50298-50318 cd: emi CDC 747 1852/CDM 763 3552/ CDZ 568 0572/CZS 573 8952 **die weihe des hauses overture** lp: SAX 2354/33CX 1930/SAX 2570/FCX 881/SAXF 198/ QCX 10438/SAXQ 7339/WCX 1702/C 91070/ SAXW 2354/STC 91070/SMC 91625 *other lp issues:* angel 35853/34426/34469/emi SLS 788/ SXDW 3032/ED 29 03281/1C177 00794-00802/ 1C147 03103-03194/1C053 00500/1C197 53400-53419/ 2C069 00800/2C147 50298-50318 cd: emi CDC 747 1902/CDM 763 6112/CDZ 568 0572/ CZS 479 5622

33CX 1703/symphonies by mozart
recorded in grünewaldkirche berlin on 29 february-1 march 1960 and in musikvereinssaal vienna on 16-17 september 1958 respectively/producer walter legge/published in august 1960/ lp matrix numbers XRX 1519 and XAX 1747

karajan berlin philharmonic	**symphony no 29** lp: SAX 2356/FCX 810/SAXF 810/QCX 10401/SAXQ 7296/ WSX 523/C 91069/SAXW 2356/STC 91069 *other lp issues:* angel 35739/angel seraphim 6062/world records T 1032/ST 1032/emi RLS 768/F669 711-715/1C037 00653/ 1C137 54095-54099/1C053 00726/2C053 00726 cd: emi CDF 300 0122/CDM 764 3272/CDM 566 0982/ CDZ 252 1462/CMS 769 8822/CMS 566 1132
karajan philharmonia	**symphony no 38 "prague"** lp: SAX 2356/FCX 810/SAXF 810/QCX 10401/SAXQ 7296/ WSX 523/C 91069/SAXW 2356/STC 91069 *other lp issues:* angel 35739/world records T 1032/ST 1032/ emi 1C037 00635/1C137 54095-54099 cd: emi CDZ 252 1462/testament SBT 2126

33CX 1704/tchaikovsky symphony no 4
recorded in grünewaldkirche berlin on 29 february-1 march 1960/producer walter legge/ published in september 1960/lp matrix numbers XRX 1517-1518

karajan
berlin
philharmonic

lp: SAX 2357/QCX 10398/SAXQ 7295/WSX 522/ C 91068/SAXW 9507/STC 91068
other lp issues: angel 35885/world records T 872/ST 872/ emi SXLP 30433/1C037 00648/1C053 00648/ 2C053 01413/3C053 00648
cd: emi CMS 769 8832

33CX 1705/mahler selection from lieder und gesänge aus der jugendzeit, des knaben wunderhorn and rückert-lieder
recorded in abbey road studios london on 3-6 may 1959/producer walter legge/published in september 1960/lp matrix numbers XAX 1768-1769

ludwig
moore, piano

lp: SAX 2358
other lp issue: angel seraphim 60070
cd: emi CMS 764 0742
selections from the recital
45: C 50577
lp: C 70408
other lp selections: angel seraphim 60044/6072/emi HQM 1072/143 6521/XLP 30182/SXLP 30182

33CX 1706-1708/ponchielli la gioconda
recorded in teatro alla scala milan on 4-11 september 1959/producer walter legge/ published in october 1960/lp matrix numbers XBX 9046-9051

votto
la scala
orchestra
and chorus
callas
cossotto
ferraro
cappuccilli
vinco

lp: SAX 2359-2361/FCX 854-856/SAXF 172-174/ QCX 10387-10389/SAXQ 7292-7294
other lp issues: angel 3606/angel seraphim 6031/emi SLS 5176/ 1C163 00881-00883/2C163 00881-00883/ 3C163 00881-00883
cd: emi CDS 749 5182/CDS 556 2912/CMS 252 9432
excerpts
45: SCBQ 3050
lp: 33CX 1848/SAX 2491/FCX 30161/QCX 10433/ QCX 10444/C 80863/SMC 80863
other lp excerpts: angel 35940/36818/3743/world records OH 193/emi SLS 5057/1C065 00741/2C059 43263/ 3C063 00741/3C063 01508/143 2631
cd: emi CDC 754 7022/CMS 763 2442/562 5642 CMS 565 7462/CMS 565 9522

33CX 1709/schubert 6 moments musicaux; allegretto d915; march d606
recorded in abbey road studios london on 3-4 september 1956 (moments musicaux) and 15 october 1959/producer walter jellinek/published in october 1960/lp matrix numbers XAX 1825-1826
arrau, piano   lp: SAX 2363

33CX 1710/beethoven symphony no 3 "eroica"
recorded in abbey road studios london on 29 october 1959/producer walter legge/published in february 1962/lp matrix numbers XAX 1835-1836
klemperer   lp: SAX 2364/FCX 943/SAXF 261/QCX 10435/
philharmonia   SAXQ 7338/WCX 1710/C 90943/SAXW 2364/
                        STC 90943/SMC 91624
                        other lp issues: angel 35853/32052/34424/3619/emi SLS 788/
                                         ASD 2562/SXLP 30310/ED 29 02711/EX 29 03793/
                                         1C053 00796/1C177 00794-00802/1C181 50187-50194/
                                         1C197 53400-53419/100 5011/2C069 00796/
                                         2C147 50298-50318
                        cd: CDC 747 1862/CDM 763 3562/CDZ 568 0572/
                            CZS 573 8952
                        recording completed on 11-13 november 1959

33CX 1711/works for violin and orchestra by tchaikovsky
recorded in salle wagram paris on 10-17 november 1959/producer norbert gamsohn/published in 1960/lp matrix numbers XLX 864-865
silvestri   **violin concerto**
conservatoire   lp: SAX 2323/QCX 10413/SAXQ 7310/C 70436/
orchestra   STC 70436
kogan, violin   cd: emi CZS 767 7322/CDE 574 6912
                      méditation pour violon et orchestre
                      lp: SAX 2323/QCX 10413/SAXQ 7310
                      cd: emi CZS 767 7322/testament SBT 1224/SBT6 1248

33CX 1712/see 33CX 1051-1052 and 33CX 1114-1115

33CX 1713/see 33CX 1668-1670

33CX 1714/wolf aus dem italienischen liederbuch
recorded in abbey road studios london 1-7 april 1958/producer walter legge/published in october 1961/lp matrix numbers XAX 1883-1884
schwarzkopf   lp: SAX 2366
moore, piano   *other lp issue:* angel 35883
                      cd: emi CHS 565 8602
                      recordings completed on 19-23 december 1959

33CX 1715/orchestral works by richard strauss
recorded in kingsway hall london on 5-10 march 1960/producer walter legge/published in january 1961/lp matrix numbers XAX 1917-1918

klemperer   **don juan; dance of the seven veils/salome**
philharmonia   lp: SAX 2367/FCX 809/SAXF 185/QCX 10404/SAXQ 7299
other lp issues: angel 35737/34472/emi SXLP 30298/
1C053 03538/2C181 50557-50558
cd: emi CDM 763 3502

till eulenspiegels lustige streiche
lp: SAX 2367/FCX 809/SAXF 185/QCX 10404/SAXQ 7299
other lp issues: angel 35737/34472/emi SXLP 30298/
1C053 03538/2C181 50557-50558
cd: emi CDM 764 1462

33CX 1716/tchaikovsky symphony no 6 "pathétique"
recorded in kingsway hall london on 2-4 june 1959/producer walter legge/published in march 1961/lp matrix numbers XAX 1750-1751

giulini   lp: SAX 2368/SAXQ 7302
philharmonia   *other lp issues:* angel seraphim 60031/world records T 634/
ST 634/emi SXLP 30208/3C053 01210
cd: emi CDZ 762 6032/CDE 767 7892

33CX 1717-1720/mozart don giovanni
recorded in kingsway hall london on 7-15 october 1959/producer walter legge/published in february 1961/lp matrix numbers XAX 1843-1850

giulini   lp: SAX 2369-2372/FCX 875-878/SAXF 192-195/
philharmonia   QCX 10394-10397/SAXQ 7288-7291/WSX 518-521/
orchestra   C 91059-91062/SAXW 9503-9506/STC 91059-91062
and chorus   *other lp issues:* angel 3605/emi SLS 5083/1C165 00504-00507/
schwarzkopf   2C165 00504-00507
sutherland   cd: emi CDS 747 2608/CDS 556 2322/CMS 567 8692
sciutti   *excerpts*
alva   lp: 33CX 1918/SAX 2559/C 80714/STC 80714
wächter   *other lp excerpts:* angel 36948/3754/emi ASD 2915/
taddei   SXLP 30300/YKM 5002/1C061 02056/1C037 03069/
frick   2C061 02056
cappuccilli   cd: CDM 763 0782/CDM 565 5772/CDM 566 5672/
585 1052
recording completed on 23-24 november 1959

33CX 1721/orchestral works by beethoven
recorded in abbey road studios london on 22-29 october 1959/producer walter legge/ published in december 1960/lp matrix numbers XAX 1831-1832

klemperer symphony no 5
philharmonia lp: SAX 2372/QCX 10410/SAXQ 7306/SAXW 9550/
  STC 91137
  other lp issues: 35843/34425/34469/3619/emi SLS 788/
    ASD 2564/ED 29 02521/EX 29 03793/1C053 00736/
    1C177 00794-00802/1C181 50187-50194/100 7361/
    1C197 53400-53419/2C069 00798/2C147 50298-50318
  cd: emi CDC 747 1872/CDM 763 3572/
    CDZ 568 0572/CZS 573 8952

  könig stefan overture
  lp: SAX 2372/33CX 1930/SAX 2570/QCX 10410/
    SAXQ 7306/SMC 80995
  other lp issues: angel 35843/32032/34441/emi SLS 788/
    SLS 790/SXDW 3032/SXDW 3051/ED 29 04011/
    1C153 00801-00802/1C177 00794-00802/2C069 00800/
    1C197 53400-53419/2C147 50298-50318
  cd: emi CDM 763 6112/CDZ 568 0572/CZS 479 5622

33CX 1722/chamber music by schumann and stravinsky
recorded in milan in 1959/published in october 1960/lp matrix numbers XBX 1001-1002

quartetto schumann string quartet op 41 no 3
italiano lp: QCX 10380
  other lp issue: angel 35733
  stravinsky 3 pieces for string quartet
  lp: QCX 10380
  other lp issue: angel 35733
  cd: testament SBT 1123

33CX 1723-1724/donizetti lucia di lammermoor
recorded in kingsway hall london on 16-21 march 1959/producer walter legge/published in november 1960/lp matrix numbers XAX 1685-1688

serafin lp: SAX 2316-2317/FCX 840-841/SAXF 175-176/
philharmonia QCX 10375-10376/SAXQ 7282-7283/WCX 1723-1724/
orchestra C 91096-91097/SAXW 2316-2317/STC 91096-91097
and chorus *other lp issues:* angel 3601/emi SLS 5056/EX 29 08763/
callas 1C163 00509-00510/2C169 00509-00510/
elkins 3C165 00509-00510
tagliavini cd: emi CDS 747 4408/CDS 556 2842/CMS 252 9432
casellato *excerpts*
cappuccilli lp: C 80724/STC 80724
ladysz *other lp excerpts:* angel 35831/36361/36933/36935/
  36948/3696/emi SHZE 101/143 2631/1C063 00772/
  1C187 01398-01399/2C059 43263
  cd: emi CDC 252 9382/CDC 555 0162/CDM 565 7472/
    CDS 754 1032/CMS 565 7462/CMS 565 9522

33CX 1725/callas and di stefano sing love duets
excerpts from the complete opera recordings on 33CX 1093-1094, 33CXS 1181-33CX 1182 and 33CX 1464-1465

33CX 1726/overtures by verdi and rossini
recorded in kingsway hall london between 31 may and 10 june 1958 and 21-24 november 1959 (scala di seta)/producer walter jellinek/published in december 1961/lp matrix numbers XAX 1731-1732

giulini
philharmonia

la forza del destino; la traviata acts 1 and 3; i vespri siciliani
lp: SAX 2377/QCX 10414/SAXQ 7313
other lp issues: emi XLP 30094/SXLP 30094/2C181 52567-52568

l'italiana in algeri; la scala di seta
45: SEL 1696/ESL 6296/SEBQ 104/SEBQ 250
lp: SAX 2377/QCX 10414/SAXQ 7313
other lp issues: angel seraphim 60138/emi XLP 30094/ SXLP 30094/CFP 40379/1C037 00814/1C053 00814/ 2C053 00814/2C181 52567-52568/3C047 00590
cd: emi CDM 769 0422

il signor bruschino
lp: SAX 2377/QCX 10414/SAXQ 7313
other lp issues: angel seraphim 60138/emi XLP 30094/ SXLP 30094/1C037 00814/1C053 00814/2C053 00814/ 2C181 52567-52568/3C047 00590
cd: emi CDM 769 0422

il barbiere di siviglia
45: SEL 1696/ESL 6296/SEBQ 120/SEBQ 250/SCDQ 2004
lp: SAX 2377/QCX 10414/SAXQ 7313
other lp issues: angel seraphim 60138/emi XLP 30094/ SXLP 30094/CFP 40379/1C037 00814/1C053 00814/ 2C053 00814/2C181 52567-52568/3C047 00590
cd: emi CDM 769 0422

33CX 1727/string quartets by ravel and mozart
recorded in milan in 1959/published in december 1960/lp matrix numbers XBX 486-487

quartetto
italiano

ravel quartet in f
lp: QCX 10381/SAXQ 7274/C 60698
cd: emi CDZ 574 7922

mozart quartet k156
lp: QCX 10381/SAXQ 7274
cd: testament SBT 1125

33CX 1728/operatic arias by donizetti, rossini, bellini and verdi
recorded in abbey road studios london on 2-6 december 1959/producer walter jellinek/ published in june 1961/lp matrix numbers XAX 1875-1876
davis lp: SAX 2376
philharmonia *other lp issues:* angel 35861/emi SREG 2064
moffo *selections from the recital*
45: SEL 1692/SEL 1698/ESL 6294/ESL 6297/SEBQ 237

33CX 1729/rossini overtures
recorded in abbey road studios london on 26-30 march 1960/producer walter legge/published in february 1961/lp matrix numbers XAX 1937-1938
karajan **guillaume tell**
philharmonia lp: SAX 2378/FCX 798/FC 25507/SAXF 132/SBOF 125507/
QCX 10412/SAXQ 7309/WC 548/C 70467/SMC 80850
other lp issues: angel 35890/37321/emi SLS 839/SXLP 30203/
1C053 00512/1C177 02348-02352/2C053 00512/
2C059 00512/769 4121
cd: emi CDM 763 1132
il barbiere di siviglia
45: SEGW 7964/C 41336/ESLW 7508/STC 41336
lp: SAX 2378/FCX 798/FC 25507/SAXF 132/SBOF 125507/
QCX 10412/SAXQ 7309/SMC 80850
other lp issues: angel 35890/emi SLS 5019/SXDW 3048/
SXLP 30203/1C181 25307-25311/1C063 00512/
1C187 03059-03060/2C053 00512/2C059 00512/769 4121
cd: emi CDM 763 1132/CDM 763 5572
semiramide
lp: SAX 2378/FCX 798/SAXF 132/QCX 10412/SAXQ 7309/
SMC 80850
other lp issues: angel 35890/emi SXLP 30203/1C053 00512/
2C053 00512/2C069 00512/769 4121
cd: emi CDM 763 1132
l'italiana in algeri
lp: SAX 2378/FCX 798/SAXF 132/QCX 10412/SAXQ 7309/
WC 549/C 70467/SMC 80850
other lp issues: angel 35890/emi SXLP 30203/1C053 00512/
2C053 00512/2C069 00512/769 4121
la scala di seta
45: SEGW 7964/C 41336/ESLW 7508/STC 41336
lp: SAX 2378/FCX 798/SAXF 132/QCX 10412/SAXQ 7309/
WC 548/C 70467/SMC 80850
other lp issues: angel 35890/emi SXLP 30203/1C053 00512/
2C053 00512/2C069 00512/769 4121
cd: emi CDM 763 1132

33CX 1729/rossini overtures/concluded
karajan **la gazza ladra**
philharmonia lp: SAX 2378/FCX 798/FC 25507/SAXF 132/SBOF 125507/
QCX 10412/SAXQ 7309/WC 548/C 70467/SMC 80850
other lp issues: angel 35890/emi SLS 5019/SXLP 30203/
1C181 25307-25311/1C053 00512/2C053 00512/
2C059 00512/769 4121
cd: emi CDM 763 1132

33CX 1730/sibelius symphony no 2
recorded in kingsway hall london on 28-29 march 1960/producer walter legge/published in january 1961/lp matrix numbers XAX 1939-1940
karajan lp: SAX 2379/QCX 10409/SAXQ 7305/WCX 1730/
philharmonia C 91093/SAXW 2379/STC 91093
other lp issues: angel 35981/emi SXLP 30414
cd: emi CDM 566 5992

33CX 1731/works for piano and orchestra by tchaikovsky and weber
recorded in abbey road studios london on 18-19 april 1960/producer walter legge/published in april 1961/lp matrix numbers XAX 1943-1944
galliera **piano concerto no 1**
philharmonia lp: SAX 2380/SAXW 9540/STC 91133
arrau, piano *other lp issues:* angel seraphim 60020/world records T 581/
ST 581/emi SHZE 161/1C037 01697/1C051 01697
konzertstück
lp: SAX 2380/C 70514
other lp issues: angel seraphim 60020/world records T 581/
ST 581/emi RLS 7712/1C037 01697/1C051 01697
cd: emi CDM 562 8842

33CX 1732-1735/mozart le nozze di figaro
recorded in kingsway hall london on 16-27 september 1959/producer walter legge/published in june 1961/lp matrix numbers XAX 1863-1870
giulini lp: SAX 2381-2384/FCX 862-865/SAXF 114-117/
philharmonia QCX 10419-10422/SAXQ 7320-7323/C 91184-91186/
orchestra STC 91184-91186
and chorus *other lp issues:* angel 3608/emi SLS 5152/1C165 00514-
schwarzkopf 00517/1C147 01751-01753/1C191 03464-03466/
moffo 2C165 00514-00517/3C165 00514-00517
fusco cd: emi CMS 763 2662
cossotto *excerpts*
gatta lp: 33CX 1934/SAX 2573/C 80859/SMC 80859
ercolani *other lp excerpts:* angel 35640/3754/emi CVT 3558/YKM 5002/
wächter SXLP 30303/1C061 01392/1C063 00839/2C061 01392/
taddei 1C147 30636-30637
vinco cd: emi CDM 566 0492/CDM 565 5772/585 1052

33CX 1736 / orchestral works by mendelssohn
recorded in abbey road studios london on 22-28 january 1960 and 15 february 1960 respectively / producer walter legge / published in july 1961 / lp matrix numbers XAX 1909-1910

klemperer	**symphony no 3 "scotch"**
philharmonia	lp: SAX 2342/FCX 838/SAXF 190/QCX 10427/SAXQ 7327/ WSX 524/C 91131/SAXW 9541/STC 91131
	other lp issues: angel 35880/32072/emi 1C037 00518/ 1C051 00518
	cd: emi CDM 763 8532/CZS 479 8852
	hebrides overture
	lp: SAX 2342/FCX 838/SAXF 190/QCX 10427/SAXQ 7327/ WSX 524/C 91131/SAXW 9541/STC 91131
	other lp issues: angel 35880/32072/emi 1A137 53562-53563/ 1C037 00518/1C051 00518

33CX 1737 / beethoven piano sonatas no 17 "tempest" and no 30
recorded in abbey road studios in 1960 / producer walter jellinek / published in february 1961 / lp matrix numbers XAX 1752-1753
richter-haaser, piano   lp: SAX 2385/C 80654/STC 80654

33CX 1738 / beethoven violin concerto
recorded in salle wagram paris on 16-28 november 1959 / producer norbert gamsohn / published in february 1961 / lp matrix numbers XLX 858-859
silvestri
conservatoire
orchestra
kogan, violin   lp: SAX 2386/FCX 850/SAXF 162/QCX 10411/ SAXQ 7308/SMC 91333

33CX 1739 / brahms piano concerto no 1
recorded in abbey road studios london on 21-23 april 1960 / producers walter legge and walter jellinek / published in may 1961 / lp matrix numbers XAX 1945-1946

giulini	lp: SAX 2387/FCX 950/SAXF 950/WCX 1739/C 91260/ SAXW 2387/STC 91260
philharmonia	
arrau, piano	*other lp issues:* angel 35892/angel seraphim 60264/ emi CFP 40028/1C037 00519/1C051 00519/ 1C063 00519/1C187 50266-50267/2C069 00519/ 3C065 00519
	cd: emi CDM 769 1772/CZS 567 0132

33CX 1740/brahms violin sonatas nos 1 and 2
recorded in abbey road studios london on 16-17 may 1960/producer walter jellinek/ published in october 1961/lp matrix numbers XAX 1959-1960
i.oistrakh,   lp: SAX 2388
violin
ginzburg,
piano

33CX 1741/works by mozart and handel
recorded in grünewaldkirche berlin on 30-31 december 1959 and 9-11 november 1960 (german dances), and in musikvereinssaal vienna on 28 july 1955 (ave verum corpus)/ producer walter legge/published in june 1961/lp matrix numbers XRX 37-38

karajan	**serenade no 13 "eine kleine nachtmusik"**
berlin	lp: SAX 2389/FCX 887/SAXF 206/QCX 10416/SAXQ 7316/
philharmonic	WC 544/C 70461/SBOW 8504/STC 70461

                other lp issues: angel 35948/emi SLS 839/SXLP 30161/
                     SHZE 303/CVD 2076/1C177 02348-02352/1C047 02350/
                     1C063 00737/2C053 00723/3C053 00520/143 5643
                cd: emi CDM 769 4652/CDZ 252 1522/CMS 769 8822/
                     CZS 252 1592/CZS 569 4582/royal classics ROY 6473/
                     disky DCL 705 872/HR 700 062
                water music suite, arranged by harty
                lp: SAX 2389/FCX 887/SAXF 206/QCX 10416/SAXQ 7316
                other lp issues: angel 35948/emi SLS 839/SXLP 30161/
                     CVD 2076/1C177 02348-02352/1C047 02350/
                     2C053 00723/3C053 00520
                cd: emi CDM 769 4652/CZS 252 1592/royal classics ROY 6473/
                     disky HR 700 062
                german dance k600 no 5; german dance k602 no 3
                lp: SAX 2389/FCX 887/SAXF 206/QCX 10416/SAXQ 7316
                other lp issues: angel 35968/emi CVD 2076/SHZE 303/
                     2C053 00723/3C063 00520
                cd: emi CMS 763 3262

33CX 1741/works by mozart and handel/concluded
karajan **german dance k605 no 3**
berlin lp: SAX 2389/FCX 887/SAXF 206/QCX 10416/SAXQ 7316
philharmonic *other lp issues:* angel 35948/emi SLS 839/SXLP 30161/
    CVD 2076/SHZE 303/1C177 02348-02352/1C047 02350/
    2C053 00723/3C053 00520
    cd: emi CDM 769 4652/CMS 769 8822/CZS 252 1592/
    royal classics ROY 6473/disky HR 700 062

karajan **ave verum corpus**
philharmonia lp: SAX 2389/FCX 887/SAXF 206/QCX 10416/SAXQ 7316
wiener *other lp issues:* angel 35968/emi SLS 839/SXLP 30161/
singverein   YKM 5002/1C177 02348-02352/1C047 02350/
    3C053 00520

33CX 1742/piano sonatas by beethoven
recorded in abbey road studios london on 6 november 1957 and 11-12 april 1960 respectively/ producers walter legge and walter jellinek/published in august 1961/ lp matrix numbers XAX 1941-1942
arrau, piano **piano sonata no 23 "appassionata"**
    lp: SAX 2390
    cd: emi CZS 767 3792/pantheon D 15070
    recording completed on 12 april 1960
    piano sonata no 22
    lp: SAX 2390
    cd: emi CZS 767 3792

33CX 1743/piano music by albeniz and granados
recorded in paris/published in july 1961/lp matrix numbers XLX 794-795
iturbi, piano   lp: SAX 2391/FCX 30214/SAXF 106

33CX 1744/violin concerti by mendelssohn and mozart
recorded in salle wagram paris between 19 and 27 november 1959/producer norbert gamsohn/ published in may 1961/lp matrix numbers XLX 866-867
silvestri **mendelssohn violin concerto**
conservatoire lp: FCX 843/FCX 30127/SAXF 138
orchestra cd: testament SBT 1225/SBT6 1248
kogan, violin **mozart violin concerto no 3 k216**
    lp: FCX 843/SAXF 138
    cd: testament SBT 1223/SBT6 1248

196
33CX 1745/bach cello suites nos 4 and 6
recorded in abbey road studios london on 9-10 june 1959 and 31 january-1 february 1959 respectively/producers walter legge and william mann/published in april 1961/lp matrix numbers XAX 1711-1712
starker, cello   cd: emi CZS 568 4852:

33CX 1746/mendelssohn a midsummer night's dream incidental music
recorded in abbey road studios london on 28-29 january 1960/producers walter legge and walter jellinek/published in july 1961/lp matrix numbers XAX 1901-1902

klemperer	lp: SAX 2347/FCX 897/SAXF 209/QCX 10428/
philharmonia	SAXQ 7329/WCX 1746/C 91180/SAXW 2393/
orchestra	STC 91180
and chorus	*other lp issues:* angel 35881/34445/emi SXLP 30196/CVB 897/
harper	1C053 00521/2C059 00521/1A 137 53562-53563
baker	cd: emi CDC 747 2302/CDM 764 1442
	excerpts
	45: SEL 1708
	lp: emi SLS 5073
	recording completed on 16-19 february 1960

33CX 1747/ravel piano concerto in g; piano concerto for left hand
recorded in salle wagram paris on 2-3 july 1959 and 16 june 1959 respectively/producer rené challan/published in june 1961/lp matrix numbers XLX 846-847

cluytens	lp: SAX 2394/FCX 836/SAXF 136
conservatoire	*other lp issue:* angel 35874/world records T 871/ST 871/
orchestra	emi CFP 40071
francois, piano	cd: emi CDC 747 3682/CDM 566 9052/29 04472

33CX 1748/haydn symphonies nos 98 and 101 "clock"
recorded in abbey road studios london on 18-21 january 1960/producer walter legge/ published in december 1961/lp matrix numbers XAX 1881-1882

klemperer	lp: SAX 2395/FCX 901/SAXF 208/QCX 10454/
philharmonia	WCX 1748/C 91130/C 91409/SAXW 2395/
	STC 91130/STC 91409
	other lp issue: angel 35872
	cd: emi CMS 763 6672

33CX 1749/schubert string quartet no 15 d887
recorded in paris on 28 july 1957/producer norbert gamsohn/published in 1962/ lp matrix numbers XLX 854-855
hungarian
string quartet

33CX 1750/orchestral works by sibelius
recorded in kingsway hall london on 20-23 september 1960 and 5-6 january 1959 respectively/ producer walter legge/published in september 1961/lp matrix numbers XAX 2301-2302
karajan   **symphony no 5**
philharmonia   lp: SAX 2392/SAXQ 7328/WC 558/C 70480/STC 70480
    other lp issues: angel 35922/emi SXLP 30430/1C053 00523/
       1C053 03791
    cd: emi CDM 566 5992
    finlandia
    lp: SAX 2392/SAXQ 7328
    other lp issues: angel 35922/37232/emi SLS 5019/
       1C053 00523/1C181 25307-25311
    cd: emi CDM 769 4672/CZS 252 1592/royal classics
       ROY 6475/disky DCL 705 872/HR 700 062

33CX 1751/symphonies by mendelssohn and schumann
recorded in abbey road studios london on 15-19 february 1960/producer walter legge/ published in august 1961/lp matrix numbers XAX 1969-1970
klemperer   **mendelssohn symphony no 4 "italian"**
philharmonia   lp: SAX 2398/FCX 896/SAXF 218/QCX 10438/SAXQ 7340/
       HC 149/SHC 149/WS 550/C 70437/SBOW 854/
       STC 70437/SMC 91274
    other lp issues: angel 35629/34453/emi SXLP 30178/
       1C047 00524/2C053 00524/ED 29 0643
    cd: emi CDM 763 8532/CZS 479 8852
    schumann symphony no 4
    lp: SAX 2398/FCX 896/SAXF 218/QCX 10438/SAXQ 7340/
       C 70478/STC 70478/SMC 91274
    other lp issues: angel 35629/34453/emi SXLP 30178/
       1C047 00524/2C053 00524/ED 29 0643/
       1C197 52497-52499
    cd: emi CMS 763 6132/CZS 479 8852

33CX 1752-1753/leoncavallo i pagliacci; operatic choruses by verdi
recorded in teatro alla scala milan on 3-7 july 1960/producers walter legge and walter jellinek/ published in june 1961/lp matrix numbers XBX 9058-9060 and 9063

matacic	lp: SAX 2399-2400/FCX 907-908/SAXF 228-229/
la scala	QCX 10407-10408/SAXQ 7303-7304
orchestra	*other lp issues:* angel 3618
and chorus	cd: emi CMS 763 9672
amara	*excerpts*
corelli	lp: 33C 1065/SBO 2756
mercuriali	*other lp excerpts:* emi 1C063 00721
gobbi	
zanasi	

33CX 1754/schubert symphony no 9 "great"
recorded in kingsway hall london on 16-19 november 1960/producer walter legge/published in september 1961/lp matrix numbers XAX 2063-2064

klemperer	lp: SAX 2397/FCX 900/SAXF 212/QCX 10429/
philharmonia	SAXQ 7330
	other lp issues: angel 35946/32001/34463/emi ED 29 0426/ CVB 900/SHZE 381/1C037 00527/2C059 00517
	cd: emi CDM 763 8542/CZS 479 8852

33CX 1755/piano music by chopin
recorded in abbey road studios london on 14 april 1960 and 2 june 1960 respectively/ producer walter jellinek/published in february 1962/lp matrix numbers XAX 2053-2054

arrau, piano	**piano sonata no 3**
	lp: SAX 2401
	cd: arlecchino ARL 160/emi CDM 562 8842
	recording completed on 21 june 1960
	fantasy in f minor
	lp: SAX 2401
	cd: emi CDM 562 8842

33CX 1756/schubert piano sonata no 21 d960; 2 impromptus
recorded in 1960/producer walter jellinek /published in september 1961/lp matrix numbers XAX 2049-2050

a.fischer,	lp: SAX 2402
piano	cd: emi CZS 569 2172

33CX 1757/works by beethoven
recorded in abbey road studios london on 20-23 july 1960/producers walter legge and walter jellinek/published in february 1962/lp matrix numbers XAX 1991-1992

kertesz	**piano concerto no 4**
philharmonia	lp: SAX 2403/SAXQ 7345/SMC 70440
richter-haaser,	*other lp issues:* emi CFP 155/1C037 00528
piano	cd: testament SBT 1299
richter-haaser,	**rondo op 51 no 2**
piano	lp: SAX 2403/SAXQ 7345
	other lp issues: emi CFP 155/1C037 00528

33CX 1758/philharmonia promenade concert
recorded in kingsway hall london on 21-24 september 1960/producer walter legge/published in october 1961/lp matrix numbers XAX 2029-2030

karajan   **waldteufel les patineurs waltz**
philharmonia
lp: SAX 2404/FCX 894/SAXF 216/C 80464/STC 80464
other lp issues: angel 35926/37250/world records T 838/
    ST 838/emi SLS 839/SXDW 3048/CFP 40368/
    1C037 00765/1C137 03059-03060/2C059 03054/
    1C177 02348-02352/CVD 2074
cd: emi CDM 769 4672/CZS 252 1592/562 8692/royal classics
    ROY 6475/disky DCL 705 872/HR 700 062/laserlight
    24426

chabrier espana
lp: SAX 2404/FCX 894/SAXF 216/C 80464/STC 80464
other lp issues: angel 35926/world records T 838/ST 838/
    emi SLS 839/SXDW 3048/CFP 40368/1C037 00765/
    1C137 03059-03060/1C177 02348-02352/2C053 01414/
    143 5643/CVD 2075
cd: emi CDM 769 4672/CZS 252 1592/562 8692/royal classics
    ROY 6475/disky HR 700 062/laserlight 24426

chabrier marche joyeuse
lp: SAX 2404/FCX 894/SAXF 216/C 80464/STC 80464
other lp issues: angel 35926/37250/world records T 838/
    ST 838/SLS 5019/1C037 00765/1C181 25307-25311/
    2C053 00726/CVD 2074
cd: emi CDM 769 4672/CZS 252 1592/562 8692/royal classics
    ROY 6475/disky HR 700 062/laserlight 24426

33CX 1758/philharmonia promenade concert/concluded
karajan j.strauss I radetzky march
philharmonia lp: SAX 2404/FCX 894/SAXF 216/C 80464/STC 80464
  other lp issues: angel 35926/37232/world records T 838/
    ST 838/emi SXDW 3048/CFP 40368/1C037 00765/
    1C137 03059-03060/2C053 00726/143 5643/CVD 2074
  cd: emi CDM 769 4672/CZS 252 1592/royal classics
    ROY 6475/disky HR 700 062/laserlight 24426
  j.strauss tritsch-tratsch polka
  lp: SAX 2404/FCX 894/SAXF 216/C 80464/STC 80464
  other lp issues: angel 35926/world records T 838/ST 838/
    emi CFP 40368/1C037 00765/1C137 03059-03060/
    2C053 00726/CVD 2074
  cd: laserlight 24426
  j.strauss thunder and lightning polka
  lp: SAX 2404/FCX 894/SAXF 216/C 80464/STC 80464
  other lp issues: angel 35926/37231/world records T 838/
    ST 838/emi CFP 40368/1C037 00765/2C053 00726/
    CVD 2074
  cd: laserlight 24426
  offenbach orfée aux enfers overture
  lp: SAX 2404/FCX 894/SAXF 216/C 80464/STC 80464
  other lp issues: angel 35926/world records T 838/ST 838/emi
    CFP 40368/SLS 839/1C037 00765/1C177 02348-02352/
    2C053 00703/CVD 2073
  cd: emi CDM 769 4672/CZS 252 1592/royal classics ROY
    6475/disky DCL 703 332/HR 700 062/laserlight 24426
  weinberger schwanda the bagpiper polka
  lp: SAX 2404/FCX 894/SAXF 216/C 80464/STC 80464
  other lp issues: angel 35926/world records T 838/ST 838/emi
    CFP 40368/SLS 5019/1C037 00765/1C181 25307-25311
  cd: emi CDM 769 4672/CZS 252 1592/562 8692/royal
    classics ROY 6475/disky HR 700 062/laserlight 24426
  suppé light cavalry overture
  45: SEGW 7907/C 41132/SMC 41132
  lp: SAX 2404/FCX 894/SAXF 216/C 80464/STC 80464
  other lp issues: angel 35926/37931/world records T 838/ST 838/
    emi CFP 40368/emi SLS 839/1C177 02348-02352/
    1C037 00765/1C137 03059-03060/2C053 00703/
    143 5643/CVD 2073
  cd: emi CDM 769 4672/CZS 252 1592/royal classics
    ROY 6475/disky HR 700 062

33CX 1759/orchestral works by dvorak
recorded in kingsway hall london between 18 and 27 january 1961/producer walter legge/ published in march 1962/lp matrix numbers XAX 2097-2098

giulini   **symphony no 9 "from the new world"**
philharmonia   lp: SAX 2405
                       other lp issues: angel 34449/angel seraphim 60045/
                         emi XLP 30163/SXLP 30163/1C053 00529/2C053 00529/
                         CVD 2101
                       cd: emi CDZ 762 5142/CDE 767 7712/CZS 568 6282
                       carnival overture
                       lp: SAX 2405
                       other lp issues: angel seraphim 60045/emi XLP 30163/
                         SXLP 30163/1C053 00529/2C053 00529/CVD 2101
                       cd: emi CDE 767 7712/CZS 568 6282

33CX 1760/mozart the 4 horn concerti
recorded in abbey road studios london between 11 and 19 may 1960/producer walter legge/ published in october 1961/lp matrix numbers XAX 1963-1964

klemperer   lp: SAX 2406/FCX 899/SAXF 211/STC 91205
philharmonia   *other lp issues:* angel 35689/32028/34410/emi SXLP 30207/
civil, horn   1C037 00530/1C053 00530/2C061 00530
                       cd: emi CDZ 767 0122/CDM 767 0322/
                         testament SBT 1102

33CX 1761/piano pieces by scriabin, debussy, schumann and chopin
recorded in abbey road studios london on 22 and 28 september 1951 (clair de lune),
1 september 1955 (schlummerlied) and on 17 october 1956/producers geraint jones and
walter jellinek/published in september 1961/lp matrix numbers XAX 1062-1063

gieseking,   **scriabin poeme op 32 no 1; prélude op 15 no 4; schumann**
piano   **vogel als prophet/waldszenen; chopin berceuse**
                       other lp issues: angel 35488/emi 3C153 52434-52441M
                       debussy clair de lune/suite bergamasque
                       78: LX 8899/LFX 1026/LDX 13/LCX 5002
                       45: SEL 1540
                       other lp issues: american columbia ML 4539/3236 0021/
                         angel 35067/35488/angel seraphim 60210/emi HQM 1225/
                         2C061 01029/3C053 01029/3C153 52331-52440M/
                         F667 473-478M
                       schumann schlummerlied/albumblätter
                       45: SCD 2163
                       other lp issues: angel 35488/emi 3C153 52434-52441M

recital also includes pieces by mozart, schumann, mendelssohn, grieg, debussy and ravel taken from the previous lps 33C 1014, 33CX 1098, 33CX 1137, 33CX 1315, 33CX 1352, 33CX 1467-1468 and 33CX 1479

33CX 1762/beethoven piano sonatas no 27 and no 29 "hammerklavier"
recorded in abbey road studios london in 1960/producer walter jellinek/published in october 1961/lp matrix numbers XAX 2015-2016
richter-haaser,   lp: SAX 2407/C 80655/STC 80655
piano

33CX 1763-1764/bach the 6 brandenburg concerti
recorded in abbey road studios london on 30 september-11 october 1960/producer walter legge/ published in november 1961/lp matrix numbers XAX 2019-2022
klemperer   lp: SAX 2408-2409/FCX 910-911/SAXF 224-225/
philharmonia   SAXQ 7341-7342
          other lp issues: angel 3627/34001-34002/1C187 00532-00533/
          1C197 54135-54136/2C181 00532-00533
          cd: emi CMS 763 6192

33CX 1765/brahms violin concerto
recorded in salle wagram paris on 17-19 june 1960/producer walter legge/published in november 1961/lp matrix numbers XLX 872-873
klemperer   lp: SAX 2411/FCX 879/SAXF 196/QCX 10447/SAXQ 7347/
orchestre   WSX 560/C 91134/SAXW 9542/STC 91134
national   *other lp issues:* angel 35836/32031/emi SXLP 30264/SLS 5004/
oistrakh,   CFP 4398/1C053 00534/1C177 05777-05781/
violin   2C059 00534/2C181 52289-52290
          cd: emi CDM 769 0342/CZS 479 8902/CDM 764 6232

33CX 1766-1768/bellini norma
recorded in teatro alla scala milan on 5-12 september 1960/producer walter legge/published in november 1961/lp matrix numbers XBX 9064-9069
serafin   lp: SAX 2412-2414/FCX 891-893/SAXF 213-215/
la scala   QCX 10430-10432/SAXQ 7332-7334/C 91192-91194/
orchestra   STC 91192-91194
and chorus   *other lp issues:* angel 3615/emi SLS 5186/2C165 00535-00537/
callas   3C163 00535-00537/CCA 891-893
ludwig   cd: emi CMS 763 0002/556 2842
corelli   *excerpts*
zaccaria   lp: WSX 622/C 80689/C 80729/SMC 80729/FC 130 550/
          QCX 10444/QCX 10477
          other lp excerpts: angel 35666/36818/3743/3841/emi ASD 3908/
          SHZE 101/1C053 01017/1C063 01342/2C065 01017/
          2C059 43263/2C069 01342/143 2631
          cd: emi CDC 749 5022/CDC 754 7022/CDC 252 9382/
          CMS 565 7462/CMS 565 9522/CMS 557 0622/585 0992

33CX 1769/beethoven symphony no 7
recorded in kingsway hall london on 25 october 1960/producer walter legge/published in january 1962/lp matrix numbers XAX 2079-2080

klemperer   lp: SAX 2315/FCX 895/SAXF 217/QCX 10434/
philharmonia   SAXQ 7337/SMC 91628
other lp issues: angel 35945/34427/3619/emi SLS 788/ ASD 2566/ED 29 03281/EX 29 03793/1C181 50187-50194/1C197 53400-53419/2C147 50298-50318/2C069 00800/100 5381
cd: emi CDC 747 1842/CDM 763 3542/CDZ 568 0572/CZS 573 8952
recording completed on 19 november and 3 december 1960

33CX 1770/overtures by weber, gluck and humperdinck
recorded in kingsway hall london on 5-6 may 1960 (oberon and freischütz) and 27-29 september 1960/producer walter legge/published in march 1962/lp matrix numbers XAX 2059-2060

klemperer   **oberon; der freischütz; euryanthe**
philharmonia   lp: SAX 2417
other lp issues: angel 36175/32079
cd: emi CDM 763 9172

hänsel und gretel
lp: SAX 2417
other lp issues: angel 36175/32079
cd: emi CDM 763 9172/562 6212

hänsel und gretel dream pantomine
45: SCD 2239
lp: SAX 2417
other lp issues: angel 36175/32079
cd: emi CDM 763 9172

iphigenie in aulis, arranged by wagner
lp: SAX 2417
other lp issues: angel 36175/32079
cd: emi CDM 764 1432/562 6212

204

33CX 1771/french opera arias from orphée et euridice, alceste, carmen, samson et dalila, roméo et juliette, mignon, le cid and louise
recorded in salle wagram paris on 28 march-5 april 1961/producer walter legge/published in october 1961/lp matrix numbers XLX 98-99

pretre	lp: SAX 2410/FCX 902/SAXF 219/QCX 10418/SAXQ 7319/
orchestre	C 91155/STC 91155
national	*other lp issues:* angel 35882/3950/emi ASD 4306/1C053 00540/
callas	2C069 00540/3C065 00540/2C165 54178-54188/CVB 902
	cd: emi CDC 749 0592/566 6182
	selections from the recital
	45: SCD 2233/SCD 2253
	lp: angel 36135/36816/3696/emi SXLP 30166/EMX 2123/
	SHZE 101/143 3481
	cd: emi CDC 252 9382/CDC 555 0162/CDC 754 7022/
	CDEMX 2123/CDS 749 4532/CDS 754 1032/
	CMS 557 0622/CMS 565 5342/CMS 565 7462/
	CMS 565 9522/CMS 763 2442/CZS 252 6142

33CX 1772/orchestral music by tchaikovsky
recorded in teatro alla scala milan in september 1960/published in october 1961/lp matrix numbers XBX 9072-9073

matacic	**orchestral suite no 3**
la scala	lp: SAX 2418/QCX 10450/SAXQ 7350
orchestra	*other lp issues:*
	cd: emi CZS 568 7392/testament SBT 1331
	introduction, waltz and polonaise/evgeny onegin
	lp: SAX 2418/QCX 10450/SAXQ 7350
	other lp issues:
	cd: emi CZS 568 7392/testament SBT 1330
	capriccio italien
	lp: SAX 2418/QCX 10450/SAXQ 7350
	other lp issues:
	cd: testament SBT 1330

33CX 1773/brahms symphony no 1
recorded in kingsway hall london on 16-17 january 1961/producer walter legge/published in january 1962/lp matrix numbers XAX 2133-2134

giulini	lp: SAX 2420
philharmonia	*other lp issues:* angel 35835/emi SLS 5241/1C197 53776-
	53779
	cd: emi CZS 252 1682/CDM 252 1322

33CX 1774/ballet music from the operas
recorded in kingsway hall london on 21-23 september 1960/producer walter legge/published in december 1961/lp matrix numbers XAX 2025-2026

karajan	**ponchielli dance of the hours/la gioconda**
philharmonia	lp: SAX 2421/FCX 898/SAXF 210/SAXQ 7344/ C 70484/STC 70484

other lp issues: 35925/37250/emi SLS 5019/SHZE 216/ CVD 2072/1C181 25307-25311/2C053 00724/ 1C137 03059-03060
cd: emi CDM 769 0412
wagner venusberg music/tannhäuser
lp: SAX 2421/FCX 898/SAXF 210/SAXQ 7344
other lp issue: angel 35925
verdi ballet music from act two/aida
lp: SAX 2421/FCX 898/SAXF 210/SAXQ 7344/ C 70484/STC 70484
other lp issues: angel 35925/37250/emi SHZE 216
cd: emi CDM 769 0412
mussorgsky dance of the persian slaves/khovantschina
lp: SAX 2421/FCX 898/SAXF 210/SAXQ 7344
other lp issues: angel 35925/emi SLS 839/EMX 41 26071/ SXLP 30200/SXLP 30445/CVD 2071/1C053 03870/ 1C177 02348-02352/2C053 01413
cd: emi CZS 568 5502
borodin dance of the polovtsian maidens and polovtsian dances/prince igor
lp: SAX 2421/FCX 898/SAXF 210/SAXQ 7344
other lp issues: angel 35925/37232/emi SLS 5019/SXDW 3048/SXLP 30445/CVD 2071/SHZE 216/1C037 01390/ 1C181 25307-25311/2C053 01413/143 5642
cd: emi CDM 769 0412

this compilation was a precise re-make of the earlier lp 33CX 1327

33CX 1775/works by beethoven
recorded in abbey road studios london on 20-23 july 1960/producers walter legge and walter jellinek/published in december 1961/lp matrix numbers XAX 1993-1994

kertesz	**piano concerto no 5 "emperor"**
philharmonia	lp: SAX 2422/SMC 91144
richter-haaser, piano	*other lp issues:* emi 1C037 00542/1C051 00542
	cd: testament SBT 1299
richter-haaser, piano	**rondo op 51 no 1**
	lp: SAX 2422
	other lp issues: emi 1C037 00542/1C051 00542

33CX 1776/rossini-respighi la boutique fantasque; dukas apprenti sorcier
recorded in kingsway hall london on 28-29 may 1959/producers walter legge and walter jellinek/published in november 1961/lp matrix numbers XAX 1989-1990
galliera   lp: SAX 2419
philharmonia   *other lp issues:* world records T 582/ST 582
         recordings completed in may and june 1960

33CX 1777/see 33CX 1492-1495

33CX 1778/orchestral works by schubert and brahms
recorded in kingsway hall london on 25-27 january 1961/producer walter legge/published in january 1962/lp matrix numbers XAX 2183-2184
giulini   **symphony no 8 "unfinished"**
philharmonia   lp: SAX 2424/QCX 10446/SAXQ 7366
         other lp issues: angel seraphim 60335/emi SXLP 30278
         haydn variations
         lp: SAX 2424/QCX 10446/SAXQ 7366
         other lp issues: angel seraphim 60335/emi SXLP 30278/SLS 5241
         cd: emi CZS 252 1682/CDM 253 8382

33CX 1779/catalogue number appears not to have been allocated

33CX 1780/mozart piano concerti nos 17 and 26 "coronation"
recorded in abbey road studios london on 1-3 april 1961/producer walter legge/published in april 1962/lp matrix numbers XAX 2160-2161
kertesz   lp: SAX 2426/QCX 10472/SAXQ 7367/SMC 91136
philharmonia   *other lp issues:* world records T 1072/ST 1072/emi CFP 40310/
richter-haaser,   1C037 00955/769 4071
piano   cd: emi CDZ 767 0032

33CXS 1781-33CX 1782/brahms ein deutsches requiem
recorded in kingsway hall london on 2 january 1961 and between 21 march and 26 april 1961/ producer walter legge/published in february 1962/lp matrix numbers XAX 2151-2153
klemperer   lp: SAX 2430-2431/FCX 915-916/SAXF 233-234/
philharmonia   QCX 10455-10456/SAXQ 7355-7356/C 91224-91225/
orchestra   STC 91224-91225
and chorus   *other lp issues:* angel 3624/emi SLS 821/1C153 01295-01296/
schwarzkopf   2C167 01295-01296/1C161 00545-00546/ED 29 02793
fischer-dieskau   cd: emi CDC 747 2382/566 9032

33CX 1783/orchestral works by bartok and hindemith
recorded in grünewaldkirche berlin on 9-11 november 1960 and 28 october 1957 respectively/ producers walter legge and fritz ganns/published in january 1962/ lp matrix numbers XRX 39-40

karajan	**music for strings, percussion and celesta**
berlin	lp: SAX 2432/FCX 917/SAXF 235/QCX 10502/
philharmonic	WCX 562/C 91179/STC 91179
	other lp issues: angel 35949/emi SXLP 30536/1C063 00547/
	1C137 54360-54363
	cd: emi CDM 769 2422
	mathis der maler symphony
	lp: SAX 2432/FCX 917/SAXF 235/QCX 10502/
	WCX 562/C 91179/STC 91179
	other lp issues: angel 35949/emi SXLP 30536/1C063 00547/
	1C137 54360-54363
	cd: emi CDM 769 2422/CMS 566 1092
	recording completed on 28-29 november 1957

33CX 1784/giuseppe di stefano at la scala
excerpts from the complete opera recordings on 33CX 1094-1095, 33CXS 1182-33CX 1183, 33CXS 1211-33CX 1212, 33CXS 1324-33CX 1326, 33CX 1370-1371, 33CX 1464-1465 and 33CX 1472-1474

33CX 1785/the hoffnung astronautical music festival
recorded in royal festival hall london on 28 november 1961/producer peter andry/published in february 1962/ lp matrix numbers XAX 2260-2261

del mar	lp: SAX 2433
hoffnung	*other lp issues:* emi SLS 5069/1C153 52125-52127
symphony	
orchestra and	
choral society	

33CX 1786/orchestral works by mozart
recorded in abbey road studios london on 22-23 october 1960, in kingsway hall london on 19-20 july 1956 and in kingsway hall london on 29 september 1960 respectively/producer walter legge/published in april 1962/ lp matrix numbers XAX 2057-2058

klemperer	**symphonies nos 35 "haffner" and 36 "linz"**
philharmonia	lp: SAX 2436/FCX 918/SAXF 236/C 91143/STC 91143
	other lp issues: angel 36128/emi SLS 5048/EX 29 04823/
	1C147 01842-01847/1C197 53714-53738/2C061 01190/
	1A137 53556-53557
	cd: emi CMS 763 2722

33CX 1786/orchestral works by mozart/concluded
klemperer   **die entführung aus dem serail overture**
philharmonia   lp: SAX 2436/33CX 1948/SAX 2587/FCX 918/SAXF 236/
C 91136/STC 91136/STC 91332/SME 80933/SMC 80944
other lp issues: angel 36128/36289/32099/34470/emi SLS 5048/
EX 29 04823/1C147 01842-01847/1C197 53714-53738/
1A137 53556-53557/769 4081
cd: emi CMS 763 6192

33CX 1787/see 33CX 1296-1298

33CX 1788/piano music by debussy and ravel
recorded in paris/published in 1962/lp matrix numbers XLX 792-793
iturbi, piano   lp: SAX 2434

33CX 1789/orchestral works by richard strauss
recorded in kingsway hall london between 23 october and 13 november 1961/producer walter legge/published in may 1962/lp matrix numbers XAX 2256-2257
klemperer   **tod und verklärung**
philharmonia   lp: SAX 2437/FCX 939/SAXF 258/QCX 10465/
SAXQ 7363/C 91190/STC 91190
other lp issues: angel 35796/34472/emi ED 29 06161/
2C181 50557-50558
cd: emi CDM 763 3502
metamorphosen
lp: SAX 2437/FCX 939/SAXF 258/QCX 10465/
SAXQ 7363/C 91190/STC 91190
other lp issues: angel 35796/34472/emi ED 29 06161/
2C181 50557-50558
cd: emi CDM 763 3502/CMS 567 0362

33CX 1790/see 33CX 1507-1509

33CX 1791/german romantic overtures by weber, wagner, nicolai and mendelssohn
recorded in grünenwaldkirche berlin on 16-20 september 1960/producer fritz ganss/ published in may 1962/lp matrix numbers XRX 1526-1527

karajan
berlin
philharmonic

der freischütz overture
lp: SAX 2439/WC 573/C 70497/SBOW 8525/
STC 70497/SGHX 10508
other lp issues: angel 35950/world records T 639/ST 639/
emi SXLP 30210/EMX 41 20521/1C053 01143/CVD 2073
cd: emi CZS 569 4582

der fliegende holländer overture; lohengrin act 1 prelude
lp: SAX 2439/WC 572/C 70496/SBOW 8524/
STC 70496/SGHX 10508
other lp issues: angel 35950/world records T 639/ST 639/
emi SXLP 30210/EMX 41 20521/1C053 01143/
1C137 54360-54363/143 5643
cd: emi CMS 763 3212/CZS 569 4582

nicolai die lustigen weiber von windsor overture
lp: SAX 2439/WC 573/C 70497/SBOW 8525/
STC 70497/SGHX 10508
other lp issues: angel 35950/world records T 639/ST 639/
emi SXLP 30210/EMX 41 20521/1C053 01143
cd: emi CZS 569 4582

hebrides overture
lp: SAX 2439/SGHX 10508
other lp issues: angel 35050/world records T 639/ST 639/
emi SXLP 30210/SXDW 3048/EMX 41 20521/
CVD 2073/1C053 01143
cd: emi CDM 769 4662/CDM 764 6292/CZS 252 1592/
CZS 569 4582/royal classics ROY 6474/disky
CDL 705 872/HR 700 062

33CX 1792/see 33CX 1555-1557

33CX 1793/mahler symphony no 4
recorded in kingsway hall london on 6-10 april 1961/producer walter legge/published in june 1962/lp matrix numbers XAX 2154-2155

klemperer
philharmonia
schwarzkopf

lp: SAX 2441/FCX 941/SAXF 259/QCX 10473/
C 91191/STC 91191
other lp issues: angel 35829/angel seraphim 60356/emi ASD
2799/1C063 00553/2C069 00553/100 5534/
CVB 941/2C165 52519-52526
cd: emi CDM 769 6672

33CX 1794/catalogue number appears not to have been allocated

33CX 1795-1796/bizet les pecheurs de perles
recorded in paris in october 1960/published in june 1962/lp matrix numbers XLX 890-893

dervaux	lp: SAX 2442-2443/FCX 866-867/SAXF 182-183
opéra comique	*other lp issues:* emi SLS 877
orchestra	cd: emi CMS 769 7042/CMS 566 0202
and chorus	*excerpts*
micheau	45: SCD 2206
gedda	lp: emi 1C063 29064
blanc	
mars	

33CX 1797/chopin piano sonatas nos 2 "funeral march" and 3
recorded in paris on 5-8 june 1961/producer norbert gamsohn/published in june 1962/lp matrix numbers XLX 922-923

malcuzynski,	lp: SAX 2444/FCX 905/SAXF 222/C 80650/STC 80650
piano	cd: emi CZS 568 2262

33CX 1798/works by poulenc
recorded in paris in 1961/published in june 1962/lp matrix numbers XLX 908-909

pretre	**organ concerto**
orchestre	lp: SAX 2445/FCX 882/SAXF 882
national	cd: emi CDC 747 7232/CMS 566 8372
duruflé, organ	

pretre	**gloria for soprano, chorus and orchestra**
orchestre	lp: SAX 2445/FCX 882/SAXF 882
national	cd: emi CDC 747 7232
and chorus	
carteri	

33CXS 1799-33CX 1803/bach matthäus-passion
recorded in abbey road studios london on 21 november 1960, in kingsway hall london on 25-26 november 1960 and in kingsway hall london on 3-4 january 1961, 14-15 april 1961 and 4-12 may 1961/producer walter legge/published in may 1962/lp matrix numbers XAX 2234-2241

klemperer	lp: SAX 2446-2450/FCX 942-946/SAXF 243-247/
philharmonia	QCX 10458-10462/SAXQ 7358-7362/
orchestra	C 91200-91203/STC 91200-91203
and chorus	*other lp issues:* angel 3699/emi SLS 827/1C191 01312-01315/
hampstead	1C197 54135-54145/2C167 01312-01315
church choir	cd: emi CMS 763 0582/567 5382
schwarzkopf	*excerpts*
ludwig	45: SEL 1707
pears	lp: 33CX 1881/33CX 5253/SAX 2525/SAX 5253/
gedda	SMC 81021/C 80693-80694/STC 80693-80694
fischer-dieskau	*other lp excerpts:* angel 36162/36163/emi 1C037 00580
berry	cd: emi CDEMX 2223
	recording completed on 28 november and 4 december 1961

33CX 1804-1806/beethoven fidelio
recorded in kingsway hall london on 6-19 february 1962/producer walter legge/published in july 1962/lp matrix numbers XAX 2292-2297

klemperer	lp: SAX 2451-2453/FCX 921-923/SAXF 240-242/
philharmonia	QCX 10467-10469/SAXQ 7364-7366/
orchestra	C 91206-91208/STC 91206-91208
and chorus	*other lp issues:* angel 3625/emi SLS 5006/1C153 00559-
ludwig	00561/1C197 53400-53419/2C147 50298-50318
hallstein	cd: emi CMS 769 3242/567 3642
vickers	*excerpts*
unger	lp: 33CX 1902/33CX 1907/SAX 2542/SAX 2547/FCX 1016/
frick	SAXF 1016/C 80775/STC 80775/SMC 80898
berry	*other lp excerpts:* angel 36168/36209/34003/34428/angel
crass	seraphim 60261/emi SXLP 30307/SXLP 30310/SXDW 3032/HQS 1408/1C053 00586/1C053 00796/
	1C063 00831/ASD 2562/ED 29 02721/1C063 00583/
	1C197 03103-03104
	cd: emi CDC 747 1902/CDM 763 6112/CDZ 568 0572/
	CZS 479 5652

33CX 1807/beethoven piano sonatas nos 18 and 32
recorded in abbey road studios london on 13-15 june 1961/producers walter legge and walter jellinek/published in june 1963/lp matrix numbers XAX 2306-2307
a.fischer,   lp: SAX 2435
piano

33CX 1808-1809/orchestral works by bruckner and wagner
recorded in kingsway hall london on 1-5 november 1960 and 25 october 1961 respectively/ producer walter legge/published in november 1962/lp matrix numbers XAX 2244-2247
klemperer   **symphony no 7**
philharmonia   lp: SAX 2454-2455/FCX 945-946/SAXF 945-946/
                   QCX 10475-10476/C 91210-91211/STC 91210-91211
                 other lp issues: angel 3626/34420/emi ED 29 0041/
                     CCA 945-946
                 cd: emi CDM 769 1262
                 siegfried idyll original version
                 lp: SAX 2454-2455/FCX 945-946/SAXF 945-946/
                     QCX 10475-10476/C 91281/STC 91281
                 other lp issues: angel 3626/emi 2C069 01356/F668 525-533
                 cd: emi CMS 763 2772/CMS 567 8932/CMS 567 0362/
                     562 8152

33CX 1810/see 33CX 1446-1447

33CX 1811/see 33CX 1534-1535

33CX 1812/tchaikovsky symphony no 6 "pathétique"
recorded in kingsway hall london on 18-20 october 1961/producer walter legge/published in november 1962/lp matrix numbers XAX 2250-2251
klemperer   lp: SAX 2458/FCX 939/SAXF 248/SAXW 2458
philharmonia   *other lp issues:* angel 35787/3711/emi SLS 5003/SHZE 296/
                     EM 29 02823/1C037 00564
                 cd: emi CDM 763 8382

33CX 1813/piano music by liszt, rachmaninov and prokofiev
recorded in grünewaldkirche berlin 25 october-2 november 1957/producer fritz ganss/ published in july 1962/lp matrix numbers XRX 235-236
ashkenazy,   cd: testament SBT 1046
piano

33CX 1814/works by weill, klemperer and johann strauss
recorded in kingsway hall london between 20 and 31 october 1961/producer walter legge/ published in november 1962/lp matrix numbers XAX 2262-2263

klemperer	**kleine dreigroschenmusik**
philharmonia	lp: SAX 2460/QCX 10480

other lp issues: angel 35927/emi SXLP 30226/ED 29 03321/ 2C069 00565
cd: emi CDM 764 1422

merry waltz and one-step/das ziel
lp: SAX 2460/QCX 10480
other lp issues: angel 35927/emi SXLP 30226/ED 29 03321/ 2C069 00565
cd: emi CDM 763 9172

kaiserwalzer
lp: SAX 2460/QCX 10480
other lp issues: angel 35927/emi SXLP 30226/SLS 5073/ 2C069 00565
cd: emi CDM 764 1462

wiener blut waltz
lp: SAX 2460/QCX 10480
other lp issues: angel 35927/emi SXLP 30226/SLS 5073/ 2C069 00565
cd: emi CDM 764 1422

die fledermaus overture
lp: SAX 2460/QCX 10480
other lp issues: angel 35927/emi SXLP 30226/SLS 5073/ 2C069 00565
recordings completed on 2 december 1961

33CX 1815/orchestral works by dvorak
recorded in kingsway hall london on 17-18 january 1962/producer walter legge/published in november 1962/lp matrix numbers XAX 2326-2327

giulini	**symphony no 8**
philharmonia	lp: SAX 2461

other lp issues: angel 35847/34449/world records T 590/ST 590
cd: emi CZS 568 6282

scherzo capriccioso
lp: SAX 2461
other lp issues: angel 35847/world records T 590/ST 590
cd: emi CDZ 762 5142/CDE 767 7712/CZS 568 6282
recordings completed between 18 and 25 april 1962

33CX 1816/orchestral works by walton/american epic
recorded in severance hall cleveland on 24 february 1961 and 21 january 1959 respectively/ producer howard scott/published in september 1962/lp matrix numbers XAX 2330-2331

szell
cleveland
orchestra

symphony no 2
lp: SAX 2459
american epic issues
lp: LC 3812/BC 1149
other lp issues: american columbia ML 6136/MS 6736/ Y-33519/cbs 61087/78721
cd: sony MPK 46732/SBK 62753
recording completed on 3 march 1961
partita for orchestra
lp: SAX 2459
american epic issues
lp: LC 3568/BC 1024
other lp issues: cbs 61264
cd: sony MPK 46732/SBK 62753

33CX 1817/works by brahms and wagner
recorded in kingsway hall london on 21-23 march 1962/producer walter legge/published in january 1963/lp matrix numbers XAX 2318-2319

klemperer
philharmonia
orchestra
and chorus
ludwig

alto rhapsody
lp: SAX 2462/FCX 935/SAXF 252/WCX 907/SAXW 9587/ SME 91365/STC 91224-91225
other lp issues: angel 35923/emi SLS 821/ASD 2391/1C063 00826/1C153 01295-01296/1C161 00545-00546/ SXLP 27 00001/29 02793
cd: emi CZS 479 8852/562 7422

klemperer
philharmonia
ludwig

wesendonk-lieder
lp: SAX 2462/FCX 935/SAXF 252/WCX 907/SAXW 9587/ SME 91365/QCX 10507
other lp issues: angel 35923/emi ASD 2391/SXLP 27 00001/ 1C063 00826/1C161 00545-00546/F668 525-533/29 02793
cd: emi CMS 764 0742/585 0992
585 0992 contains only three of the wesendonk-lieder
isoldes liebestod/tristan und isolde
lp: SAX 2462/FCX 935/SAXF 252/QCX 10507
other lp issues: angel 35923/emi SXLP 27 00001/1C063 00826/ F668 525-533
cd: emi CMS 764 0742/585 0992

33CX 1818/debussy la mer; trois nocturnes
*recorded in kingsway hall london between 11 and 26 april 1962/producer walter legge/
published in march 1963/lp matrix numbers XAX 2334-2335*
giulini lp: SAX 2463/QCX 10478/C 91232/STC 91232
philharmonia *other lp issues:* angel 35977/32033/emi SXLP 30146/
orchestra 1C047 00566/3C053 00566
and chorus cd: emi CDM 769 1842/562 7462

33CX 1819/see 33CX 1096-1097

33CX 1820/wagner music from the ring, tannhäuser and parsifal
*recorded in kingsway hall london between 3 and 10 march 1960 (tannhäuser and walküre),
24 october 1961 (rheingold and siegfried) and between 14 and 22 november 1961 (parsifal
and götterdämmerung)/producer walter legge/published in april 1963/lp matrix
numbers XAX 2254-2255*
klemperer einzug der götter in walhall/das rheingold; siegfrieds
philharmonia rheinfahrt/götterdämmerung; parsifal prelude;
tannhäuser act 3 prelude
lp: SAX 2464/FCX 937/SAXF 254/QCX 10479/
    WCX 600/C 91281/SAXW 9880/STC 91281
other lp issues: angel 35947/32058/34407/emi ASD 2697/
    SLS 5075/SXLP 30528/1C153 50347-50349/
    1C053 00567/2C069 00567/F668 525-533
cd: emi CDC 747 2552/CMS 763 6182/CMS 567 8932
walkürenritt/die walküre
45: SCD 2178
lp: SAX 2464/FCX 937/SAXF 254/QCX 10479/
    WCX 600/C 91281/SAXW 9880/STC 91281
other lp issues: angel 35947/32058/34407/emi ASD 2697/
    SLS 5075/SXLP 30528/1C153 50347-50349/
    1C053 00567/2C069 00567/F668 525-533
cd: emi CDC 747 2552/CMS 763 6182/CMS 567 8932
waldweben/siegfried
lp: SAX 2464/FCX 937/SAXF 254/QCX 10479/
    WCX 600/C 91281/SAXW 9880/STC 91281
other lp issues: angel 35947/32058/34407/emi ASD 2697/
    SLS 5075/SXLP 30528/1C153 50347-50349/
    1C053 00567/2C069 00567/F668 525-533
cd: emi CDC 747 2552/CMS 763 6182/CMS 567 8932
recording completed on 13 november 1961

33CX 1821/chopin selection of mazurkas
recorded in paris on 9-11 october 1961/published in january 1963/lp matrix numbers XLX 979-980
malcuzynski,   lp: SAX 2465
piano   *other lp issue:* angel 35983
                 cd: emi CZS 568 2262

33CX 1822/brahms piano concerto no 2
recorded in abbey road studios london on 21-22 april 1962/producer walter legge/published in march 1963/lp matrix numbers XAX 2328-2329
giulini   lp: SAX 2466/C 91401/STC 91401
philharmonia   *other lp issues:* angel seraphim 60052/emi CFP 40034/
arrau, piano   1C037 00568/1C187 50266-50267/2C069 00568
                 cd: emi CDM 769 1782/CZS 567 0132

33CX 1823/strauss also sprach zarathustra; till eulenspiegel
recorded in kingsway hall london between 19 and 28 june 1962/producer walter legge/ published in august 1963/lp matrix numbers XAX 2380-2381
maazel   lp: SAX 2467/FCX 969/SAXF 969/QCX 10481/SAXQ 7368
philharmonia   SMC 91402
                 other lp issues: angel 35944/world records T 935/ST 935/
                     emi SXLP 30133/1C037 00781/2C053 00781
                 recordings completed on 23 august 1962

33CX 1824/mozart symphonies no 38 "prague" and no 39
recorded in kingsway hall london on 26-28 march 1962/producer walter legge/published in march 1963/lp matrix numbers XAX 2364-2365
klemperer   lp: SAX 2468/FCX 938/SAXF 255/C 91145/STC 91145
philharmonia   *other lp excerpts:* angel 36129/34470/emi SLS 5048/
                 EX 29 04823/1C147 01842-01847/1C053 00569/
                 1C197 53714-53738/2C061 00569
                 cd: emi CMS 763 2722

33CX 1825/piano music by debussy
recorded in paris in 1962/published in march 1963/lp matrix numbers XLX 957-958
francois,   lp: SAX 2469/FCX 914/SAXF 232
piano

33CX 1826-1828/mozart   the 6 quartets dedicated to haydn/american epic
recorded in columbia studios new york between 1 and 31 may 1962/published in march 1963
juilliard   lp: SAX 2470-2472/FCX 956-958/SAXF 956-958
string quartet   *american epic issue*
                         lp: SC 6043/BSC 143
                         cd: sony (france)

33CX 1829-1830/mahler   symphony no 2 "resurrection"
recorded in kingsway hall london on 22-24 november 1961/producer walter legge/published in july 1963/lp matrix numbers XAX 2320-2323
klemperer   lp: SAX 2473-2474/FCX 948-949/SAXF 948-949/
philharmonia   C 91268-91269/STC 91268-91269
orchestra   *other lp issues:* angel 3634/emi SLS 806/1C163 00570-00571/
and chorus   1C191 00570-00571/CCA 948-949/100 5703/
schwarzkopf   2C165 52519-52526
rössl-majdan   cd: emi CDM 769 6622/567 2352

33CX 1831/symphonies by schumann/american epic
recorded in severance hall cleveland on 24-25 october 1958 and 12 march 1960 respectively/ producer howard scott/published in october 1963
szell   **symphony no 1 "spring"**
cleveland   lp: SAX 2475/FCX 980/SAXF 980/QCX 10486
orchestra   *american epic issues*
                           lp: LC 3612/BC 1039/SC 6039/BSC 110
                           other lp issues: american columbia Y3-30844/cbs 77344/61595
                           cd: sony MH2K 62349
                           symphony no 4
                           lp: SAX 2475/FCX 980/SAXF 980
                           american epic issues
                           lp: LC 3854/BC 1254/SC 6039/BSC 110
                           other lp issues: american columbia Y3-30844/cbs 77344/
                               philips S04602L
                           cd: sony MH2K 62349

33CX 1832/ravel   daphnis et chloé   complete ballet
recorded in salle wagram paris on 1-8 june 1962/producer rené challan/published in april 1963/lp matrix numbers XLX 990-991
cluytens   lp: SAX 2476/FCX 934/FCX 951-952/SAXF 251/
conservatoire   SAXF 951-952
orchestra   *other lp issue:* angel 36109
duclos choir   cd: testament SBT 1128

33CX 1833/ravel boléro; rapsodie espagnole; la valse
recorded in salle wagram paris on 27-30 november 1961/producer rené challan/published in april 1963/lp matrix numbers XLX 994-995

cluytens lp: SAX 2477/FCX 913/FCX 951-952/SAXF 231/
conservatoire SAXF 951-952/SMC 80762
orchestra *other lp issue:* angel 36108
cd: emi CZS 767 8972/CMS 769 1652
selections
lp: emi 769 4111
cd: emi CZS 575 1062/CZS 767 7472

33CX 1834/ravel ma mere l'oye; valses nobles et sentimentales
recorded in salle wagram paris on 20-25 april 1962/producer rené challan/published in april 1963/lp matrix numbers XLX 988-989

cluytens lp: SAX 2478/FCX 933/FCX 953-954/SAXF 250/
conservatoire SAXF 953-954
orchestra *other lp issue:* angel 36110
cd: emi CZS 767 8972/CMS 769 1652

33CX 1835/ravel le tombeau de couperin; menuet antique; alborada del gracioso; une barque sur l'océan; pavane pour une infante défunte
recorded in salle wagram paris on 26 september-3 october 1962/producer rené challan/published in april 1963/lp matrix numbers XLX 1006-1007

cluytens lp: SAX 2479/FCX 930/FCX 953-954/SAXF 947/
conservatoire SAXF 953-954/SMC 80765
orchestra *other lp issue:* angel 36111
cd: emi CZS 767 8972/CMS 769 1652
alborada del gracioso and pavane only
lp: emi 769 4111

33CX 1836/piano music by stravinsky and schoenberg/american epic
recorded in columbia studios new york on 28-30 december 1960/published in april 1963/lp matrix numbers LC 3792A-3792B

rosen, piano lp: SAX 2480/FCX 973/SAXF 973
american epic issues
lp: LC 3792/BC 1140

33CX 1837/arias by adam, berlioz, gounod, lalo, massenet and thomas
recorded in salle wagram paris on 1-9 september 1961/producer michel glotz/published in april 1963/lp matrix numbers XLX 935-936

pretre lp: SAX 2481/FCX 906/SAXF 906
orchestre *other lp issues:* angel 36106/34055/emi 1C063 11272/CVC 906
national *selections from the recital*
gedda lp: angel 3204/emi SLS 5250/1C137 78233-78236/ASD 2574
cd: emi CDM 769 5502/CMS 565 6852/CMS 567 4452

33CX 1838/cherubini scenes from médée
recorded in salle wagram paris between 2 and 16 april 1962/producer rené challan/published in april 1963/lp matrix numbers XPTX 950-951
pretre
paris opéra
orchestra
and chorus
gorr
esposito
chauvet
bianco

lp: SAX 2482/FCX 30502/SAXF 130502
other lp issues:
cd: emi 573 0892

33CX 1839/brahms handel variations; waltzes op 39/american epic
recorded in columbia studios new york on 31 may-1 june 1956 and between 9-17 august 1956 respectively/producer howard scott/published in august 1963/lp matrix numbers LC 3331A-3331B
fleisher, piano   *american epic issue*
               lp: LC 3331

33CX 1840/orchestral works by tchaikovsky
recorded in kingsway hall london on 9-11 april 1962/producer walter legge/published in september 1963/lp matrix numbers XAX 2332-2333
giulini   **francesca da rimini**
philharmonia   lp: SAX 2483/QCX 10485
               other lp issues: angel 35980/angel seraphim 60311/
                  emi SXLP 30509
               romeo and juliet fantasy overture
               lp: SAX 2483/QCX 10485
               other lp issues: angel 35980/angel seraphim 60311
               cd: emi CDC 747 6162/CDE 767 7892

33CX 1841/orchestral works by mussorgsky-ravel and debussy
recorded in kingsway hall london between 20 and 29 june 1962/producer walter legge/published in october 1963/lp matrix numbers XAX 2384-2385
maazel   **pictures from an exhibition**
philharmonia   lp: SAX 2484/FCX 968/SAXF 968/QCX 10483
philharmonia   *other lp issues:* angel 36132/world records T 830/ST 830/
                  emi SXLP 30233/EMX 2008/1C051 03014
               cd: emi CDEMX 2008
               prélude a l'apres-midi d'un faune
               lp: SAX 2484/FCX 968/SAXF 968/QCX 10483
               other lp issues: angel 36132/world records T 830/ST 830/
                  emi SXLP 30233/EMX 2008/1C051 03014

33CX 1842/piano concerti by schumann and liszt
recorded in abbey road studios london on 22-24 may 1960/producer walter legge/published in november 1963/lp matrix numbers XAX 2348-2349

klemperer	**schumann piano concerto**
philharmonia	lp: SAX 2485/FCX 967/SAXF 967/C 91284/STC 91284
a.fischer,	*other lp issue:* emi 1C197 52497-52499
piano	cd: emi CDM 764 1452/priceless C 16442
	recording completed between 9 and 16 august 1962
	liszt piano concerto no 1
	lp: SAX 2485/FCX 967/SAXF 967/C 91284/STC 91284
	cd: emi CDM 764 1442
	recording completed between 10 and 31 may 1962

33CX 1843/symphonies by mozart
recorded in kingsway hall london on 6-8 march 1962/producer walter legge/published in november 1963/lp matrix numbers XAX 2366-2367

klemperer	**symphony no 41 "jupiter"**
philharmonia	lp: SAX 2486/FCX 942/SAXF 942/C 91147/STC 91147
	other lp issues: angel 36183/32098/34405/34470/emi SLS 5048/EX 29 04823/1C147 01842-01847/769 4091/1C053 00574/1C197 53718-53738/1A 137 53556-53557
	cd: emi CDC 747 8522/CMS 763 2722/567 3342
	symphony no 40
	lp: SAX 2486/FCX 942/SAXF 942/C 91147/STC 91147
	other lp issues: angel 36183/32098/34405/34470/emi SLS 5003/EX 29 04823/1C191 52130-52134/769 4091/1C053 00574/1A 137 53556-53557
	cd: emi 567 3322
	recording completed on 28 march 1962

33CX 1844/soviet army ensemble sing folksongs
recorded in abbey road studios london in 1962/producer walter legge/published in 1963/lp matrix numbers XAX 2469-2470

alexandrov	lp: SAX 2487
soviet army	*selections from the recording*
ensemble	45: SEL 1706/SCD 2237

33CX 1845/orchestral works by mahler and strauss/american epic
recorded in severance hall cleveland on 1 november 1958 and in masonic temple cleveland on 29-30 march 1957 respectively/producer howard scott/published in july 1963/ lp matrix numbers XAX 2429-2430

szell
cleveland
orchestra

adagio and purgatorio/symphony no 10
lp: SAX 2488
american epic issues
lp: LC 3568/BC 1024
other lp issues: philips fontana CFL 1071/SCFL 107/ 699 062CL/american columbia M2 31313/cbs 77272
adagio only
cd: sony SBK 53259
tod und verklärung
lp: SAX 2488/FCX 991/SAXF 991
american epic issues
lp: LC 3439/BC 1011
other lp issues: philips fontana 699 505CL/american columbia Y-30313/cbs 61216/77258/5059
cd: sony SBK 53511

33CX 1846/german opera arias by mozart, kreutzer, marschner, lortzing, wagner, nessler, humperdinck and korngold
recorded in berlin in october 1961/published in 1963/lp matrix numbers XRX 1573-1574

stein
berliner
sinfoniker
prey

lp: SAX 2489/WSX 618/C 80675/STC 80675
other lp issue: emi 1C063 28424
selections from the recital
lp: C 70417/STC 70417
other lp selections: emi HZE 123/SHZE 123
cd: emi CDM 769 5072

33CX 1847/works by tchaikovsky, borodin, rimsky-korsakov and mussorgsky/american epic
recorded in severance hall cleveland between 28 february and 14 march 1958 and on 28 may 1958 (tchaikovsky)/producer howard scott/published in october 1963/lp matrix numbers LC 3483A-3483B

szell
cleveland
orchestra

capriccio italien
lp: SAX 2490
american epic issues
lp: LC 3483/BC 1002
other lp issues: philips fontana EFR 2019/664 500ER/699 511CL/ 876 502CY/american columbia M2X-787/Y-30044/cbs 61213
polovtsian dances; khovantschina prelude
lp: SAX 2490
american epic issues
lp: LC 3483/BC 1002
other lp issues: philips fontana 699 511CL/876 502CY/american columbia Y-30044/cbs 61213
cd: sony MBK 44805

33CX 1847/works by tchaikovsky, borodin, rimsky-korsakov and mussorgsky/ concluded

szell **capriccio espagnol**
cleveland lp: SAX 2490
orchestra *american epic issues*
  lp: LC 3483/LC 3891/BC 1002/BC 1291/BC 24146
  45 rpm issue: philips fontana 496 503CE
  other lp issues: philips fontana EFR 2019/664 500ER/american columbia Y-30044/cbs 61213
  cd: sony MBK 44805

this is the last columbia mono lp in the 33CX series which the compiler has sighted with the original blue and gold label: all subsequent mono lps seem to have been produced with red, black and white label which later became standard for both columbia and hmv lps

33CX 1848/see 33CX 1706-1708

33CX 1849/debussy études/american epic
recorded in columbia studios new york on 26-28 february 1962/published in september 1963/ lp matrix numbers LC 3842A-3842B
rosen, piano lp: SAX 2492/FCX 1009/SAXF 1009
  american epic issues
  lp: LC 3842/BC 1242

33CX 1850/symphonies by beethoven and schubert/american epic
recorded in severance hall cleveland on 15 april 1961 and 12 march 1960 respectively/ producers thomas frost (beethoven) and howard scott (schubert)/published in august 1963
szell **beethoven symphony no 8**
cleveland lp: SAX 2493
orchestra *american epic issues*
  lp: LC 3854/BC 1254/SC 6041/BSC 112/BSC 150
  other lp issues: american columbia M7X 20281/ cbs 61155-61156/77704
  cd: sony SB5K 48356/SBK 46328
  schubert symphony no 8 "unfinished"
  lp: SAX 2493
  american epic issues
  lp: LC 3828/BC 1156
  other lp issues: american columbia ML 6375/MS 6975/ MG 30371/cbs 4455/5455
  cd: sony MK 42415/SBK 48268

33CX 1851/tchaikovsky symphony no 4
recorded in kingsway hall london on 23-25 january 1963/producer walter legge/published in november 1963/lp matrix numbers XAX 2451-2452
klemperer   lp: SAX 2494/FCX 976/SAXF 976/C 91241/STC 91241
philharmonia   *other lp issues:* angel 36134/3711/emi EM 29 02823
                 cd: emi CMS 763 8382
                 recording completed on 2 february 1963

33CX 1852/orchestral works by richard strauss/american epic
recorded in masonic temple cleveland on 29-30 march 1957 and in severance hall cleveland on 28-29 october 1960 respectively/producer howard scott/published in september 1963
szell   **don juan**
cleveland   lp: SAX 2495/FCX 991/SAXF 991
orchestra   *american epic issues*
                 lp: LC 3439/BC 1011
                 other lp issues: philips fontana 699 505CL/american columbia
                     Y-30313/cbs 61216/5059/77258/30047/SPM 1/SPS 1
                 cd: sony SBK 48272/MHK 63123

szell   **don quixote**
cleveland   lp: SAX 2495/QCX 10495/FCX 992/SAXF 992
orchestra   *american epic issues*
fournier, cello lp: LC 3786/BC 1135
                 other lp issues: american columbia Y-32224/cbs 61110/
                     4332/5054
                 cd: sony MHK 63123

33CX 1853/schumann symphony no 2/american epic
recorded in severance hall cleveland on 24 october 1960/producer howard scott/published in september 1963/lp matrix numbers LC 3832A-3832B
szell   lp: SAX 2496/QCX 10496/FCX 981/SAXF 981
cleveland   *american epic issues*
orchestra   lp: LC 3832/BC 1159/SC 6039/BSC 110
                 other lp issues: american columbia Y3-30844/cbs 77344
                 cd: sony MH2K 62349

33CX 1854/tchaikovsky symphony no 5
recorded in kingsway hall london on 16-21 january 1963/producer walter legge/published in november 1963/lp matrix numbers XAX 2445-2446
klemperer   lp: SAX 2497/FCX 979/SAXF 979/QCX 10490/
philharmonia   C 91245/STC 91245
                 other lp issues: angel 36141/3711/emi EM 29 02823/
                     1C037 00577
                 cd: emi CMS 763 8382

33CX 1855/brahms symphony no 2
recorded in kingsway hall london on 10-11 october 1962/producer walter legge/published in december 1963/lp matrix numbers XAX 2419-2420
giulini lp: SAX 2498/C 91149/STC 91149
philharmonia *other lp issues:* emi SLS 5241/1C197 53776-53779
  cd: emi CZS 252 1682/CDM 253 6672

33CX 1856/orchestral works by dvorak and strauss/american epic
recorded in severance hall cleveland on 18-19 march 1960 and in masonic temple cleveland on 29-30 march 1957 respectively/producer howard scott/published in december 1963
szell **symphony no 7**
cleveland lp: SAX 2501/FCX 987/SAXF 987
orchestra *american epic issues*
  lp: LC 3748/BC 1111/SC 6038/SC 6055/BSC 109/BSC 155
  other lp issues: american columbia D3S-814/cbs 78304/
    4441/5441
  cd: sony MH2K 63151
  till eulenspiegels lustige streiche
  lp: SAX 2501/FCX 991/SAXF 991
  american epic issues
  lp: LC 3439/BC 1011
  other lp issues: american columbia Y-30313/cbs 77258/
    61216/5059
  cd: sony SBK 48272

33CX 1857/schubert piano sonata no 20 d959; mozart rondo k511/
american epic
recorded in columbia studios new york on 3-6 april 1961/published in october 1963/ lp matrix numbers LC 3855A-3855B
rosen, piano lp: SAX 2502
  american epic issues
  lp: LC 3855/BC 1255
  recording completed on 2 march 1962

33CX 1858/french opera arias from iphigénie en tauride, la damnation de faust, les pecheurs de perles, manon, werther and faust
recorded in salle wagram paris on 3-8 may 1963/producer walter legge/published in september 1963/lp matrix numbers XLX 1018-1019

pretre	lp: SAX 2503/FCX 975/SAXF 975/QCX 10482/
conservatoire	C 91246/STC 91246
orchestra	*other lp issues:* angel 36147/3950/emi 1C053 00578/2C063
callas	00578/2C165 54178-54188/ 3C065 00578/CVB 975
	cd: emi CDC 749 0592/CDS 749 5432/566 8182
	selections from the recital
	45: SEBQ 264
	lp: angel 3699/3743/emi SLS 5057/EMX 2123/
	1C187 01398-01399
	cd: emi CDC 749 5022/CDC 555 0162/CDEMX 2123/
	CDS 754 1032/CDS 749 6002/CMS 565 5342/CMS
	565 7462/CMS 565 9522/CMS 763 2442/CZS 252 6142/
	CMS 557 0622

33CX 1859/beethoven string quartets op 18 nos 3 and 6
recorded in 1962/published in august 1963/lp matrix numbers XRX 1579-1580

drolc string	lp: SAX 2504/C 80558/STC 80558
quartet	

33CX 1860/beethoven lieder recital
recorded in 1962/published in june 1963/lp matrix numbers XRX 1551-1552

prey	lp: SAX 2505/C 80635/STC 80635
moore, piano	*other lp issue:* emi CFP 40025
	selections from the recital
	lp: SMC 80941/SCXW 7679

33CX 1861/schumann symphony no 3 "rhenish"/american epic
recorded in severance hall cleveland on 21 october 1960/producer howard scott/published in november 1963/lp matrix numbers LC 3774A-3774B

szell	lp: SAX 2506/FCX 982/SAXF 982
cleveland	*american epic issues*
orchestra	lp: LC 3774/BC 1130/SC 6039/BSC 110
	other lp issues: american columbia Y3-30844/cbs 77344/61595
	cd: sony MH2K 62349

33CX 1862/lieder by brahms
recorded in 1962/published in december 1963/lp matrix numbers XRX 1542-1543
prey   **vier ernste gesänge**
mälzer, piano   lp: C 60134
                  selection of deutsche volkslieder
                  lp: WS 531/C 60562
                  selections from the recital
                  lp: SMC 80941/SCXW 7679
                  other lp selection: emi 1C037 28507

33CX 1863/beethoven violin concerto/american angel
recorded in abbey road studios london on 23-26 june 1961/published in november 1963/ lp matrix numbers 35783-1 and 35783-2
leinsdorf   lp: SAX 2508/FCX 955/SAXF 955
philharmonia   *other lp issues:* angel 35783/world records T 597/ST 597
milstein,   cd: emi CDM 764 8302/CDM 566 2642
violin

33CX 1864/chopin the 4 ballades
recorded in paris on 10-14 december 1962/published in december 1963/lp matrix numbers XLX 1012-1013
malcuzynski,   lp: SAX 2509/FCX 970/SAXF 970
piano

33CX 1865/prokofiev string quartet no 1; tchaikovsky string quartet no 1/ american epic
recorded in 1962/published in november 1963/lp matrix numbers LC 3691A-3692B
kroll string   lp: SAX 2507
quartet   *american epic issues*
                  lp: LC 3691/BC 1082

33CX 1866/loewe ballads
recorded in 1962/published in december 1963/lp matrix numbers XRX 1611-1612
prey   lp: SAX 2511/C 80733/STC 80733
weissenborn,   *other lp issues:* emi 1C063 28147
piano   *selection from the recital*
                  lp: emi 1C037 28507

33CX 1867-1868/works by beethoven and wagner/american epic
recorded in severance hall cleveland on 15-22 april 1961 and on 26 january 1962 (wagner)/ producers howard scott and thomas frost (wagner)/published in january 1964

szell	**symphony no 9 "choral"**
cleveland	lp: SAX 2512-2513
orchestra	*american epic issues*
and chorus	lp: SC 6041/SC 6050/SC 6063/BSC 112/BSC 150/BSC 163
addison	*other lp issues:* philips fontana 697 305EL/american columbia
hobson	M7X 30287/Y-34625/cbs 61155-61156
lewis	cd: sony SB5K 48396/SBK 46533/SBK 87896/MYK 42532
bell	

szell	**die meistersinger von nürnberg overture**
cleveland	lp: SAX 2512-2513/CX 5277/SAX 5277
orchestra	*american epic issues*
	lp: LC 3845/BC 1245
	other lp issues: ML 6371/MS 6971/MS 7511/SOG 5/MGP 13/ D3M 32317/cbs 61263/30008
	cd: sony MLK 39438/MYK 42597/M2YK 46466/SBK 48175
	tristan und isolde prelude and liebestod
	lp: SAX 2512-2513
	american epic issues
	lp: LC 3845/BC 1245
	other lp issues: american columbia ML 6371/MS 6971/ D3M 32317/cbs 77235
	cd: sony MYK 42597/M2YK 46466/SBK 48175

33CX 1869/works by beethoven and wagner/american epic
recorded in severance hall cleveland on 30-31 october 1959 and on 26 january 1962 respectively/producer howard scott/published in march 1964/lp matrix numbers LC 3658A-3658B

szell	**symphony no 7**
cleveland	lp: SAX 2510
orchestra	*american epic issues*
	lp: LC 3658/BC 1066/SC 6050/BSC 150
	other lp issues: philips fontana 697 303EL/american columbia M7X 30281/Y-34624/cbs 61154
	cd: sony SB5K 48396/SBK 48158

33CX 1869/works by beethoven and wagner/concluded
szell **tannhäuser overture**
cleveland lp: SAX 2510
orchestra *american epic issues*
lp: LC 3845/BC 1245
other lp issues: american columbia ML 6371/MS 6971/D3M 32317
cd: sony MYK 42597/M2YK 46466

33CX 1870/symphonies by schubert
recorded in kingsway hall london on 4-6 february 1963 and 13-16 may 1963 respectively/ producer walter legge/published in april 1964/lp matrix numbers XAX 2512-2513
klemperer **symphony no 8 "unfinished"**
philharmonia lp: SAX 2514/FCX 994/SAXF 994/C 91306/STC 91306
other lp issues: angel 36164/34444/32038/emi SLS 5003/
ED 29 04601/EMX 2135/1C191 52130-52134/1C037
00579/2C069 00579
cd: emi CDM 763 8542/CZS 479 8852
symphony no 5
lp: SAX 2514/FCX 994/SAXF 994/C 91306/STC 91306
other lp issues: angel 36164/34444/32038/emi ED 29 04601/
EMX 2135/1C037 00759/2C069 00759
cd: emi CDM 763 8692

33CX 1871/rachmaninov piano concerto no 3/ars polonia
recorded in warsaw in 1963/published in february 1964/lp matrix numbers XAX 2510-2511
rowicki lp: SAX 2515/FCX 983/SAXF 983/C 91324/STC 91324
warsaw *other lp issues:* angel 36197
philharmonic
malcuzynski,
piano

33CX 1872/orchestral works by brahms
recorded in kingsway hall london on 12 october 1962/producer walter legge/published in june 1963/lp matrix numbers XAX 2425-2426

giulini	**symphony no 3**
philharmonia	lp: SAX 2516/C 91316/STC 91316
	other lp issues: angel seraphim 60101/emi SLS 5241/ 1C197 53776-53779/2C053 43099
	cd: emi CZS 252 1682/CDM 253 6672
	recording completed on 9-11 november 1962
	tragic overture
	lp: SAX 2516/C 91316/STC 91316
	other lp issues: angel seraphim 60101/emi SLS 5241/ 1C197 53776-53779/2C053 43099
	cd: emi CZS 252 1682/CDM 252 1322

33CX 1873/schubert symphony no 9 "great"/american epic
recorded in severance hall cleveland on 1 november 1957/producer howard scott/published in 1963/lp matrix numbers LC 3431A-3431B

szell	lp: SAX 2517
cleveland	*american epic issues*
orchestra	lp: LC 3431/BC 1009
	other lp issues: philips fontana CFL 1017/699 506CL/american columbia Y-30669/cbs 60132/61603/world records T 627/ST 627
	cd: sony MK 42415/MYK 37239/SBK 48268

33CX 1874/vivaldi 4 concerti for violin and orchestra/american angel
recorded in manhattan centre new york on 23-24 january 1962/published in january 1964 lp matrix numbers 36001-1 and 36001-2

milstein	lp: SAX 2518/FCX 990/SAXF 990/QCX 10457/
chamber	SAXQ 7357
orchestra	*other lp issue:* angel 36001
milstein, violin	

33CX 1875/schubert string quartet no 14 d810 "der tod und das mädchen"; haydn string quartet op 64 no 5/american epic
published in august 1964/lp matrix numbers LC 3690A-3690B

kroll string	lp: SAX 2519
quartet	*american epic issues*
	lp: LC 3690/BC 1081

33CX 1876/beethoven string quartet op 95; hindemith string quartet no 3/
american epic
published in february 1964/lp matrix numbers LC 3779A-3779B
kroll string   lp: SAX 2520
quartet   *american epic issues*
    lp: LC 3779/BC 1133

33CX 1877/chopin the 24 préludes
recorded in salle wagram paris in february and may 1959/producer rené challan/published in march 1964/lp matrix numbers XLX 764-765
francois,   lp: SAX 2521/FCX 974 /SAXF 974
piano   *other lp issues:*
    cd: emi CZS 568 1512/CMS 573 3862/CZS 574 4572

33CX 1878/schumann davidsbündlertänze; carnaval/american epic
recorded in columbia studios new york on 4-8 march 1963/producer jane friedman/published in march 1964/lp matrix numbers LC 3689A-3689B
rosen, piano   lp: SAX 2522
    american epic issues
    lp: LC 3689/BC 1269

33CX 1879/beethoven piano sonatas nos 16 and 18
recorded in abbey road studios london on 12-13 december 1962 and 24-25 may 1963 respectively/producers walter legge and suvi raj grubb/published in june 1964/ lp matrix numbers XAX 2545-2546
richter-haaser,   lp: SAX 2523/QCX 10501
piano   *other lp issues:*

33CX 1880/orchestral works by mendelssohn and weber/american epic
recorded in severance hall cleveland on 26 october 1962/producer thomas frost/published in may 1964/lp matrix numbers LC 3859A-3859B

szell	**symphony no 4 "italian"**
cleveland	lp: SAX 2524
orchestra	*american epic issues*
	lp: LC 3859/BC 1259
	other lp issues: american columbia ML 6375/MS 6975/cbs 61019
	cd: sony MYK 42547/SBK 46536
	hebrides overture
	lp: SAX 2524
	american epic issues
	lp: LC 3859/BC 1259
	other lp issue: cbs 61019
	cd: sony SBK 46536
	oberon overture
	lp: SAX 2524
	american epic issues
	lp: LC 3859/BC 1259
	other lp issue: cbs 61019
	recordings completed on 4-5 january 1963

33CX 1881/catalogue number appears not to have been allocated

33CX 1882/brahms piano concerto no 1/american epic
recorded in severance hall cleveland on 21-22 february 1958/producer howard scott/ published in may 1964/lp matrix numbers LC 3484A-3484B

szell	lp: SAX 2526/FCX 1020/SAXF 1020
cleveland	*american epic issues*
orchestra	lp: LC 3484/BC 1003
fleisher,	*other lp issues:* philips fontana 699 507CL/876 501CY/
piano	american columbia Y-31273/cbs 61105/77259
	cd: sony MH2K 63225

33CX 1883/walton incidental music for henry V and richard III; funeral march from hamlet
recorded in abbey road studios london on 15-16 october 1963/producer walter legge/published in may 1964/lp matrix numbers XAX 2587-2588

walton	lp: SAX 2527
philharmonia	*other lp issues:* angel 36198/angel seraphim 60205/emi
	SXLP 30139/world records T 656/ST 656
	cd: emi CHS 565 0032
	henry V suite and richard III prelude only
	lp: emi SLS 5246

33CX 1884/symphonic poems by franck
recorded in palais des beaux-arts brussels on 20-21 december 1962/producer rené challan/ published in may 1964/lp matrix numbers XLX 1014-1015

cluytens	**le chasseur maudit; les eolides; rédemption**
orchestre	lp: SAX 2528/FCX 959/SAXF 959
national	*other lp issue:*
de belgique	cd: emi CDM 565 1532

cluytens	**les djinns**
orchestre	lp: SAX 2528/FCX 959/SAXF 959
national	*other lp issue:*
de belgique	cd: emi CDM 565 1532
ciccolini, piano	

33CX 1885/symphonies by haydn and mozart/american epic
recorded in severance hall cleveland on 20 october 1961 and 8 january 1960 respectively/ producer howard scott/published in july 1964/lp matrix numbers XAX 2443-2444

szell
cleveland
orchestra

    symphony no 92 "oxford"
    lp: SAX 2529
    american epic issues
    lp: LC 3828/BC 1156
    other lp issue: cbs 78236
    cd: sony SBK 46332
    symphony no 35 "haffner"
    lp: SAX 2529
    american epic issues
    lp: LC 3740/BC 1106
    other lp issues: american columbia ML 6258/MS 6858/
        MG 30368/cbs 61023
    cd: sony MBK 45640/SBK 46333/SB3K 62773/SM3K 46515
    recording of haffner symphony completed on 11 march 1960

33CX 1886/beethoven string quartets op 18 nos 4 and 5
recorded in 1963/published in may 1964/lp matrix numbers XRX 1615-1616

drolc string	lp: SAX 2530/C 80751/STC 80751
quartet	

33CX 1887/sonatas for 2 violins by leclair, telemann and ysaye
recorded in salle wagram paris on 25-26 may 1962/producer eric macleod/published in may 1964
kogan and   lp: SAX 2531/FCX 984/SAXF 984
elizaveta   cd: testament SBT 1227/SBT6 1248
gilels, violins   *recordings completed on 14 march 1963*

33CX 1888/ravel le tombeau de couperin; gaspard de la nuit/american epic
recorded in columbia studios new york on 9-13 january 1959/published in june 1964/ lp matrix numbers LC 3589A-3589B
rosen, piano   *american epic issue*
                 lp: LC 3589

33CX 1889/piano concerti by prokofiev
recorded in abbey road studios london on 27 june-3 july 1963/producer eric macleod/ published in june 1964/lp matrix numbers XLX 1069-1070
rowicki   **piano concerto no 3**
philharmonia   lp: SAX 2533/FCX 986/SAXF 986
francois, piano   cd: emi CZS 574 3242
                 piano concerto no 5
                 lp: SAX 2533/FCX 986/SAXF 986
                 cd: emi CZS 574 3242/CZS 762 9512

33CX 1890/brahms piano concerto no 2/american epic
recorded in severance hall cleveland on 19-20 october 1962/producer thomas frost/published in august 1964/lp matrix numbers LC 3853A-3853B
szell   lp: SAX 2534/FCX 1021/SAXF 1021
cleveland   *american epic issue*
orchestra   lp: LC 3853/BC 1253
fleisher,   *other lp issue:* american columbia Y-32222
piano   cd: sony MH2K 63225

33CX 1891/schubert string quartet no 15 d887/american epic
recorded in columbia studios new york between 3 and 12 december 1962/published in 1964/ lp matrix numbers LC 3860A-3860B
juilliard   lp: SAX 2535
string quartet   *american epic issues*
                 lp: LC 3860/BC 1260
                 cd: sony SMK 62707

33CX 1892/concerti by mozart and strauss/american epic
recorded in severance hall cleveland on 27 and 12 october 1961 respectively/producer thomas frost/published in june 1964/lp matrix numbers LC 3841A-3841B

szell	**mozart clarinet concerto**
cleveland	lp: SAX 2536/QCX 10493
orchestra	*american epic issues*
marcellus,	lp: LC 3841/BC 1241
clarinet	*other lp issues:* american columbia ML 6368/MS 6968/ D3M 33261/cbs 61195
	cd: sony MYK 42598/SBK 62424

szell	**strauss horn concerto no 1**
cleveland	lp: SAX 2536/QCX 10493
orchestra	*american epic issues*
bloom, horn	lp: LC 3841/BC 1241
	other lp issue: cbs 61355

33CX 1893/see 33CX 1094-1095

33CX 1894/mozart mass in c minor k427
recorded in johanneskirche kornwestheim in may 1963/producers gerd berg and christfried bickenbach/published in september 1964/lp matrix numbers XRX 1117-1118

gönnenwein	lp: SAX 2544/FCX 1014/SAXF 1014/C 91295/STC 91295
south-west	cd: emi CDZ 767 0192
german chamber	
orchestra	
and chorus	
mathis	
donath	
altmeyer	
crass	

33CX 1895/handel dettingen te deum
recorded in johanneskirche kornwestheim in may 1963/producers gerd berg and christfried bickenbach/published in april 1964/lp matrix numbers XRX 1115-1116

gönnenwein	lp: SAX 2538/FCX 1005/SAXF 1005/C 91294/STC 91294
south-west	
german chamber	
orchestra	
and chorus	
pütz	
lisken	
altmeyer	
crass	

33CX 1896/orchestral works by debussy and ravel/american epic
recorded in severance hall cleveland on 11-12 january 1963/producer paul myers/published in july 1964/lp matrix numbers LC 3863A-3863B

szell **la mer**
cleveland lp: SAX 2532
orchestra *american epic issues*
lp: LC 3863/BC 1263
other lp issues: american columbia Y-31298/cbs 61075
cd: sony MBK 44804
daphnis et chloé second suite
lp: SAX 2532
american epic issues
lp: LC 3863/BC 1263
other lp issues: american columbia Y-31298/cbs 61075
cd: sony MBK 44804/SBK 47664
pavane pour une infante défunte
lp: SAX 2532
american epic issues:
lp: LC 3863/LC 3891/BC 1263/BC 1291/BC 24146
other lp issues: american columbia M2X 787/Y-31298/
   cbs 61075
cd: sony MBK 44805

33CX 1897/see 33CX 1226

33CX 1898/berlioz symphonie fantastique
recorded in kingsway hall london on 23-26 april 1963/producer walter legge/published in august 1964/lp matrix numbers XAX 2589-2590
klemperer lp: SAX 2537/FCX 1013/SAXF 1013/SAXQ 7375/
philharmonia STC 91352
other lp issues: angel 36196/emi SLS 5003/EMX 2030/
   1C191 52130-52134
cd: emi CDM 764 1432
recording completed on 17-18 september 1963

33CX 1899/orchestral music by dvorak and smetana/american epic origin
recorded in severance hall cleveland on 4-5 january 1963/producer thomas frost/published in august 1964/lp matrix numbers LC 3868A-3868B

szell
cleveland
orchestra

carnival overture
lp: SAX 2539
american epic issues
lp: LC 3868/BC 1268
other lp issues: american columbia M2L 326/M2S 726/Y-30049/Y2-33524/cbs 78299
cd: sony MBK 44958/M2HK 63151

slavonic dances nos 1, 3, 10 and 15
lp: SAX 2539/33SX 6053/SCX 6053
american epic issues
lp: LC 3868/BC 1268
other lp issues: american columbia M2L 326/M2S 726/MS 7208/MS 7524/Y-30049/Y2-33524
cd: sony MBK 44802/SBK 48161

the moldau/ma vlast
lp: SAX 2539/33SX 6053/SCX 6053
american epic issues
lp: LC 3868/BC 1269
other lp issues: american columbia MS 7435/M2X 787/Y-30049
cd: sony MBK 44958/MYK 42530/SBK 48264

polka, furiant and dance of the comedians/the bartered bride
lp: SAX 2539/33SX 6053/SCX 6053
american epic issues
lp: LC 3868/LC 3891/BC 1268/BC 1291/BC 24146
other lp issues: american columbia M2X 787/Y-30049
cd: sony MBK 44958/SBK 48279

33CX 1900/arias by mozart, beethoven and weber
recorded in salle wagram paris in december 1963 and january 1964/producer michel glotz/published in august 1964/lp matrix numbers XLX 1098-1099

rescigno
conservatoire
orchestra
callas

porgi amor/le nozze di figaro
lp: SAX 2540/FCX 1004/SAXF 1004/QCX 10497/C 91359/STC 91359
other lp issues: angel 36200/3743/world records T 690/ST 690/emi 1C053 01360/2C069 01360/3C065 01360/2C165 54178-54188
cd: emi CDC 749 0052/CDM 565 7472/CDS 749 4532/CMS 565 9522/CMS 557 0622/566 6182

33CX 1900/arias by mozart, beethoven and weber/concluded
rescigno   **or sai chi l'onore; non mi dir; mi tradi/don giovanni**
conservaroire   lp: SAX 2540/FCX 1004/SAXF 1004/QCX 10497/
orchestra   C 91359/STC 91359
callas   *other lp issues:* angel 36200/world records T 690/ST 690/
                      emi 1C053 01360/2C069 01360/3C065 01360/
                      2C165 54178-54188
                      cd: emi CDC 749 0052/CDS 749 4532/566 6182
                      ah perfido! concert aria
                      lp: SAX 2540/FCX 1004/SAXF 1004/QCX 10497/
                      C 91359/STC 91359
                      other lp issues: angel 36200/world records T 690/ST 690/
                      emi 1C053 01360/2C069 01360/3C065 01360/
                      2C165 54178-54188
                      cd: emi CDC 754 4372/CDS 749 4532/CMS 763 6252/
                      CMS 565 5342/CZS 252 6142/566 6182
                      ozean du ungeheuer!/oberon *sung in english*
                      lp: SAX 2540/FCX 1004/SAXF 1004/QCX 10497/
                      C 91359/STC 91359
                      other lp issues: angel 36200/world records T 690/ST 690/
                      emi 1C053 01360/2C069 01360/3C065 01360/
                      2C165 54178-54188
                      cd: emi CDC 749 0052/CDC 754 4372/CDS 749 4532/
                      566 6182

33CX 1901/brahms piano quintet op 34/american epic
recorded in columbia studios new york on 11-12 march 1963/published in september 1964/
lp matrix numbers LC 3865A-3865B
juilliard   lp: SAX 2541/FCX 1011/SAXF 1011
string quartet   *american epic issues*
fleisher,   lp: LC 3865/BC 1265
piano

33CX 1902/beethoven overtures
recorded in kingsway hall london on 4-7 november 1963 (leonore I, II and III)/producer
walter legge/published in 1964/lp matrix numbers XAX 2585-2586
klemperer   **fidelio** see 33CX 1804-1806
philharmonia   **leonore no 1**
                  lp: SAX 2542/SMC 80898
                  other lp issues: angel 36209/34441/angel seraphim 60261/
                      emi SLS 788/ASD 2565/SXDW 3032/ED 29 04011/
                      1C177 00794-00802/1C151 00801-00802/1C063 00583/
                      1C197 03103-03104/1C147 53400-53419/2C069 00795/
                      2C147 50298-50318/1A 137 53562-53563
                      cd: emi CDC 747 1902/CDM 763 6112/CDZ 568 0572/
                      CZS 479 5622/CZS 573 8952

33CX 1902/beethoven overtures/concluded
klemperer   **leonore no 2**
philharmonia   lp: SAX 2542/SMC 80898
              other lp issues: angel 36209/34441/angel seraphim 60261/
                  emi SLS 788/ASD 2561/SXDW 3032/ED 29 04011/
                  1C177 00794-00802/1C151 00801-00802.1C063 00583/
                  1C197 03103-03104/1C147 53400-53419/2C069 00795/
                  2C147 50298-50318/1A137 53562-53563
              cd: emi CDC 747 1902/CDM 763 6112/CDZ 568 0572/
                  CZS 479 5622/CZS 573 8952
            leonore no 3
            lp: SAX 2542/SMC 80898/SMC 80944
            other lp issues: angel 36209/34441/angel seraphim 60261/
                  emi SLS 788/SLS 790/SXDW 3032/ED 29 04011/
                  1C177 07794-07802/1C151 00801-00802/1C063 00583/
                  1C197 03103-03104/1C147 53400-53419/
                  2C147 50298-50318/1A137 53562-53563
              cd: emi CDC 747 1902/CDM 763 6112/CDZ 568 0572/
                  CZS 479 5622/CZS 573 8952

33CX 1903/beethoven piano concerto no 3
recorded in abbey road studios london on 20 april 1963/producer walter legge/published in september 1964/lp matrix numbers XAX 2541-2542
giulini   lp: SAX 2543
philharmonia
richter-haaser,
piano

33CX 1904/strauss sinfonia domestica/american columbia
recorded in severance hall cleveland on 10 january 1964/producer paul myers/published in october 1964
szell   lp: SAX 2545
cleveland   *american columbia issues*
orchestra   lp: ML 6027/MS 6627
              other lp issue: cbs 61355
              cd: sony SBK 53511

239

33CX 1905/beethoven symphony no 6 "pastoral"/american epic
recorded in severance hall cleveland on 19-21 january 1962/producer thomas frost/published in november 1964/lp matrix numbers LC 3849A-3849B
szell lp: SAX 2547
cleveland *american epic issues*
orchestra lp: LC 3849/BC 1249/SC 6050/SC 6063/BSC 150/BSC 163
 other lp issues: american columbia M7X 30281/cbs 61153/
  4163/77704
 cd: sony SB5K 48396/SBK 46532/MBK 44810

33CX 1906/symphonies by mozart
recorded in abbey road studios london on 16-19 october 1963/producer walter legge/ published in 1964/lp matrix numbers XAX 2567-2568
klemperer **symphony no 31 "paris"**
philharmonia lp: SAX 2546/FCX 1015/SAXF 1015/STC 91332
 other lp issues: angel 36216/34470/emi SLS 5048/EX 29 04823/
  1C147 01842-01847/1C197 53714-53738
 cd: emi CMS 763 2722/CMS 763 5852/CDM 567 3312
 symphony no 34
 lp: SAX 2546/FCX 1015/SAXF 1015/STC 91332
 other lp issues: angel 36216/34470/emi SLS 5048/EX 29 04823/
  1C147 01842-01847/1C197 53714-53738
 cd: emi CMS 763 2722/CDM 567 3322

33CX 1907/catalogue number appears not to have been allocated

33CX 1908/orchestral works by debussy
recorded in salle wagram paris on 10-14 september 1963/producer rené challan/published in november 1964/lp matrix numbers XLX 1075-1076
cluytens **jeux**
conservatoire lp: SAX 2548/FCX 993/SAXF 993
orchestra *other lp issues:* angel 36212/world records T 910/ST 910
 cd: emi CZS 568 2202
 images pour orchestre
 lp: SAX 2548/FCX 993/SAXF 993
 other lp issues: angel 36212/world records T 910/ST 910
 cd: emi CZS 575 1062

33CX 1909/piano music by liszt and bartok/american epic
recorded in columbia studios new york/lp matrix numbers LC 3878A-3878B
rosen, piano *american epic issues*
 lp: LC 3878/BC 1278

33CX 1910/verdi arias from otello, aroldo and don carlo
recorded in salle wagram paris between 16 and 27 december 1963, on 6 january 1964 and on 20-21 february 1964/producer michel glotz/published in august 1964/lp matrix numbers XLX 1100-1101

rescigno   lp: SAX 2550/FCX 1008/SAXF 1008/SMC 91385
conservatoire   *other lp issues:* angel 36221/emi 1C053 01020/2C069 01020/
orchestra   3C065 01020/2C181 53452-43453/2C165 54178-54188
callas   cd: emi CDC 747 9432/CDS 749 4532/566 6182
     selections from the recital
     lp: angel 36930/3696/emi 1C187 01398-01399/SHZE 101
     cd: emi CDC 555 0162/CDC 252 9382/CMS 565 7462/
     CDS 754 1032/CMS 565 9522/CMS 557 0622/557 7600

33CX 1911/beethoven diabelli variations
recorded in abbey road studios london in 1964/producer walter jellinek/published in january 1965/lp matrix numbers XAX 2579-2580

richter-haaser,   lp: SAX 2557/FCX 1018/SAXF 1018
piano

33CX 1912/symphonies by beethoven and mozart /american epic
recorded in severance hall cleveland on 11 october 1963/producer paul myers/published in december 1964/lp matrix numbers LC 3882A-3882B

szell   **symphony no 5**
cleveland   lp: SAX 2552
orchestra   *american epic issue*
     lp: LC 3882/BC 1282/SC 6050/SC 6063/BSC 150/BSC 163
     other lp issues: american columbia M7X 30281/MG 30371/
     Y-34600/cbs 61152/4455/5455
     cd: sony SB5K 48396/SBK 47651/SB3K 62773
     symphony no 41 "jupiter"
     lp: SAX 2552
     american epic issues
     lp: LC 3882/BC 1282
     other lp issues: american columbia ML 6369/MS 6969/
     MG 30368/MG 30841/cbs 61228
     cd: sony MYK 42538/SBK 46333/SB3K 62773/SM3K 46515
     recordings completed on 25 october 1963

33CX 1913/orchestral works by mozart/american epic
recorded in severance hall cleveland on 26 october 1962 and 20 april 1963 respectively/ producer paul myers/published in november 1964/lp matrix numbers LC 3873A-3873B

szell	**symphony no 33**
cleveland	lp: SAX 2553
orchestra	*american epic issues*
	lp: LC 3873/BC 1273
	other lp issues: american columbia ML 6258/MS 6858/ cbs 61197
	cd: sony SBK 46515
	divertimento no 2 k131
	lp: SAX 2553
	american epic issues
	lp: LC 3873/BC 1273
	other lp issues: american columbia ML 6368/MS 6968/ D3M 33261

33CX 1914/dvorak symphony no 9 "from the new world"
recorded in kingsway hall london on 30 october-2 november 1963/producer walter legge/ published in november 1964/lp matrix numbers XAX 2577-2578

klemperer	lp: SAX 2554/FCX 1017/SAXF 1017
philharmonia	*other lp issues:* angel 36246/emi SLS 5003/1C063 00587/ 1C197 52130-52134
	cd: emi CDM 763 8962

33CX 1915/britten 4 sea interludes from peter grimes; variations and fugue on a theme of purcell
recorded in kingsway hall london on 2-9 october 1962/producer walter legge/published in november 1964/lp matrix numbers XAX 2563-2564

giulini	lp: SAX 2555
philharmonia	*other lp issues:* angel 36215/emi SXLP 30240/1C053 00588
	cd: emi CZS 767 7232

33CX 1916/works by mussorgsky-ravel and stravinsky/american epic
recorded in severance hall cleveland on 30 october 1963 and 22-23 january 1961 respectively/producer paul myers/published in january 1965

szell
cleveland orchestra

pictures from an exhibition
lp: SAX 2556
american epic issues
lp: LC 3872/LC 3890/BC 1272/BC 1290
other lp issues: american columbia Y-32223/cbs 4462/5462
cd: sony MBK 44805/SBK 48162
firebird 1919 suite
lp: SAX 2556
american epic issues
lp: LC 3812/LC 3890/BC 1149/BC 1290
other lp issues: cbs 4462/5462
cd: sony SBK 47664
recording of firebird suite completed on 3 march 1961

33CX 1917/mendelssohn string quartets nos 2 and 3/american epic
recorded in columbia studios new york on 10-12 december 1963/published in january 1965/lp matrix numbers LC 3887A-3887B

juilliard string quartet

lp: SAX 2558
american epic issues
lp: LC 3887/BC 1287

33CX 1918/see 33CX 1717-1720

33CX 1919/rossini overtures
recorded in kingsway hall london on 13 april 1962 (la cenerentola), 13-14 december 1962 (semiramide and guillaume tell), 2-3 april 1964 (gazza ladra) and 3 june 1964 (tancredi)/ producers walter legge and walter jellinek/published in february 1965/lp matrix numbers XAX 2705-2706

giulini
philharmonia

tancredi
lp: SAX 2560
other lp issues: angel seraphim 60048/emi SXLP 30143/
1C037 00814/1C053 00814/2C053 00814/3C047 00079/
2C181 52567-52568
cd: emi CZS 575 4622/562 8022

33CX 1919/overtures by rossini/concluded
giulini **la cenerentola**
philharmonia lp: SAX 2560
other lp issues: angel seraphim 60048/emi SXLP 30143/
1C037 00814/1C053 00814/2C053 00814/3C033 00590/
3C047 00079/2C181 52567-52568
cd: emi CDM 769 0422/562 8022
recording completed on 1 april 1964
la gazza ladra; semiramide
lp: SAX 2560
other lp issues: angel seraphim 60048/emi SXLP 30143/
CFP 40379/1C037 00814/1C053 00814/2C053 00814/
3C033 00590/2C181 52567-52568
cd: emi CDM 769 0422/562 8022
guillaume tell
lp: SAX 2560
other lp issues: angel seraphim 60048/emi SXLP 30143/
SLS 5073/CFP 40379/1C037 00814/1C053 00814/
2C053 00814/3C033 00590/2C181 52567-52568
cd: emi CDM 769 0422/562 8022

33CX 1920/beethoven piano sonatas nos 3, 22 and 26 "les adieux"
recorded in abbey road studios london on 24-26 may 1963/producers walter legge and walter jellinek/published in march 1965/lp matrix numbers XAX 2671-2672
richter-haaser, lp: SAX 2561
piano

33CX 1921/orchestral works by roussel
recorded in salle wagram paris on 5-13 november 1963/producer rené challan/published in may 1965/lp matrix numbers XLX 1086-1087
cluytens **bacchus et ariane suite no 2; sinfonietta**
conservatoire lp: SAX 2562/FCX 1001/SAXF 1001
orchestra *other lp issue:* angel 36225
cd: emi CZS 568 2202/testament SBT 1239/SBT 7247
le festin de l'araignée
lp: SAX 2562/FCX 1001/SAXF 1001
other lp issue: angel 36225
cd: emi CZS 568 2202/testament SBT 1238/SBT 7247

244

33CX 1922/arrangements for violin and orchestra of works by rachmaninov, mussorgsky, glazunov and rimsky-korsakov/
american angel
recorded in manhatten centre new york on 28-31 march 1962/published in 1965/
lp matrix numbers 36002-1 and 36002-2

irving	lp: SAX 2563/QCX 10488
orchestra	*other lp issue:* angel 36002
milstein, violin	cd: emi CDM 764 8302

33CX 1923/operatic arias by rossini and donizetti
recorded in salle wagram paris in december 1963, january 1964, february 1964 and april 1964/producer michel glotz/published in march 1965/ lp matrix numbers XLX 1119-1120

rescigno **nacqui all' affano/la cenerentola**
conservatoire lp: SAX 2564/FCX 1012/SAXF 1012/STC 91410
orchesrea *other lp issues:* angel 36239/36933/3743/emi 2C069 00592/
callas 3C065 00592/2C165 54178-54188
  cd: emi CDC 749 0052/CDS 749 4532/CDS 754 1032/
  566 6182
  sombre foret/guillaume tell *sung in italian*
  lp: SAX 2564/FCX 1012/SAXF 1012/STC 91410
  other lp issues: angel 36239/2C069 00592/3C065 00592/
  1C187 01398-01399/2C165 54178-54188
  cd: emi CDC 749 0052/CDS 749 4532/566 6182
  bel raggio lusinghier/semiramide
  lp: SAX 2564/FCX 1012/SAXF 1012/STC 91410
  other lp issues: angel 36239/emi 2C069 00592/3C065 00592/
  2C165 54178-54188
  cd: emi CDC 749 0052/CDS 749 4532/566 6182
  com' e bello/lucrezia borgia
  lp: SAX 2564/FCX 1012/SAXF 1012/STC 91410
  other lp issues: angel 36239/2C069 00592/3C065 00592/
  1C187 01398-01399/2C165 54178-54188
  cd: emi CDC 747 2832/CDS 749 4532/566 6182
  prendi per me/l'elisir d'amore
  lp: SAX 2564/FCX 1012/SAXF 1012/STC 91410
  other lp issues: angel 36239/2C069 00592/3C065 00592/
  2C165 54178-54188
  cd: emi CDC 747 2832/CDS 749 4532/CDM 565 7472/
  566 6182
  il faut partir/la fille du régiment *sung in italian*
  lp: SAX 2564/FCX 1012/SAXF 1012/STC 91410
  other lp issues: angel 36239/3743/2C069 00592/3C065 00592/
  2C165 54178-54188
  cd: emi CDC 747 2832/CDS 749 4532/566 6182

33CX 1924/symphonies by beethoven/american epic
recorded in severance hall cleveland on 2 and 23 october 1964 respectively/producer paul myers/ published in may 1965/lp matrix numbers LC 3892A-3892B

szell	**symphony no 1**
cleveland	lp: SAX 2565
orchestra	*american epic issues*
	lp: LC 3892/BC 1292/SC 6050/BSC 150
	other lp issues: american columbia M7X 30281/cbs 61150
	cd: sony SB5K 48396/SBK 46532
	symphony no 2
	lp: SAX 2565
	american epic issues
	lp: LC 3892/BC 1292/SC 6050/BSC 150
	other lp issues: american columbia M7X 30281/cbs 61150
	cd: sony SB5K 48396/SBK 47651/SB3K 62773

33CX 1925/bizet l'arlésienne suites 1 and 2; carmen suite
recorded in salle wagram paris on 13-15 january 1964/producer rené challan/published in april 1965/lp matrix numbers XLX 1102-1103

cluytens	lp: SAX 2566/FCX 1000/SAXF 1000/SMC 80918
conservatoire	*other lp issue:* angel seraphim 60064
orchestra	*excerpts from the suites*
	cd: emi 252 5782
	recordings completed on 21 january 1964

33CX 1926/jewish religious music and bible stories
kossoff

33CX 1927/lieder by schumann
recorded in 1964/published in 1965/lp matrix numbers XRX 1599-1600

prey	**dichterliebe song cycle**
engel, piano	lp: SAX 2567/FC 25506/SBOF 125506/SMC 91420
	other lp issues: emi 1C063 29074/1C187 52243-52244
	kerner-lieder
	lp: SAX 2567/C 70493/STC 70793
	selections from the recital
	lp: SMC 80941/SCXW 7679

33CX 1928/bruckner symphony no 4 "romantic"
recorded in kingsway hall london on 19-26 september 1963/producer walter legge/published in may 1965/lp matrix numbers XAX 2543-2544

klemperer	lp: SAX 2569/SMC 91356
philharmonia	*other lp issues:* angel 36245/32059/34456/emi SXLP 30167/ CCA 1039/1C047 00593/1C063 00593
	cd: emi CDM 769 1272/CZS 479 8852/562 8152

33CX 1929/catalogue number appears not to have been allocated

33CX 1930/overtures by beethoven
taken from the previous lps 33CX 1575, 33CX 1615, 33CX 1702 and 33CX 1721

33CX 1931/haydn symphonies nos 88 and 104 "london"
recorded in abbey road studios london on 12-16 october 1964/producer peter andry/published in may 1965/lp matrix numbers XAX 2780-2781

klemperer	lp: SAX 2571/FCX 1040/SAXF 1040/SMC 91409
new	*other lp issues:* angel 36346/34464/1C063 01196
philharmonia	cd: emi CMS 763 6672

33CX 1932/see 33CX 1318-1320

33CX 1933/orchestral works by brahms/american columbia
recorded in severance hall cleveland on 16-17 october 1964 and on 24 october 1964 respectively/producer paul myers/published in 1965

szell	**symphony no 3**
cleveland	lp: SAX 2572
orchestra	*american columbia issues*
	lp: ML 6085/MS 6685/D3L 358/D3S 758
	other lp issue: cbs 77356
	cd: sony SB3K 48398/SBK 47652/MYK 42531
	haydn variations
	lp: SAX 2572
	american columbia issues
	lp: ML 6085/ML 6365/MS 6685/MS 6965
	cd: sony MK 42531/SB3K 48398/SBK 46534

33CX 1934/see 33CX 1732-1735

33CX 1935/orchestral works by hindemith and walton/american columbia
recorded in severance hall cleveland on 9-10 october 1964/producer paul myers/published in 1965

szell	**hindemith symphonic metamorphoses on themes of weber**
cleveland	lp: SAX 2576
orchestra	*american columbia issue*
	lp: MS 7166
	other lp issue: cbs 61367
	cd: sony SBK 53258
	variations on a theme of hindemith
	lp: SAX 2576
	american columbia issues
	lp: ML 6136/MS 6736/Y-33519
	other lp issue: cbs 61087
	cd: sony MPK 46732/SBK 53258/SBK 62753

33CX 1936/beethoven piano sonatas nos 1 and 2
recorded in abbey road studios london in 1964/producer walter jellinek/published in 1965/ lp matrix numbers XAX 2673-2674

richter-haaser,   lp: SAX 2574
piano

33CX 1937/works by barber and william schuman/american columbia
recorded in severance hall cleveland on 3 january 1964 and 11 january 1964 respectively/ published in 1965

szell	**barber piano concerto**
cleveland	lp: SAX 2575
orchestra	*american columbia issues*
browning,	lp: ML 6038/MS 6638
piano	
szell	**schuman song of orpheus**
cleveland	lp: SAX 2575
orchestra	*american columbia issues*
	lp: ML 6038/MS 6638

248

33CX 1938/beethoven symphony no 3 "eroica"/american epic
recorded in severance hall cleveland on 22-23 february 1957/producer howard scott/ published in 1965/lp matrix numbers LC 3385A-3385B

szell	lp: SAX 2577
cleveland	*american epic issues*
orchestra	lp: LC 3385/BC 1001/SC 6050/BSC 150
	other lp issues: philips fontana EFL 2512/CFL 1001/SCFL 100/ 697 300EL/699 500CL/876 500CY/american columbia M7X 30281/cbs 61151/77704
	cd: sony SB5K 48396/SBK 46328/MBK 45639

33CX 1939/see 33CX 1410-1412

33CX 1940/works by bach and vivaldi/american angel
recorded in capitol studios hollywood on 26-28 march 1964/published in 1965/lp matrix numbers 36006-1 and 36006-2

milstein	**bach concerto for 2 violins bwv 1043**
orchestra	lp: SAX 2579/SME 91683
milstein and	*other lp issue:* angel 36006
morini, violins	

milstein	**vivaldi concerto for 2 violins op 3 no 11**
orchestra	lp: SAX 2579/SME 91683
milstein and	*other lp issue:* angel 36006
morini, violins	

milstein and	**bach sonata for 2 violins bwv 1037**
morini, violins	lp: SAX 2579/SME 91683
b.fischer, piano	*other lp issue:* angel 36006

33CX 1941/gounod roméo et juliette scenes
recorded in salle wagram paris in 1964/published in 1965/lp matrix numbers XLX 1187-1188

lombard	lp: SAX 2580/FCX 1026/SAXF 1026
paris opéra	*other lp issues:* angel 36287/2C061 11688/CVT 1026/ CCA 1026
orchestra	
carteri	
gedda	
dens	
rouleau	

33CX 1942/catalogue number appears not to have been allocated

33CX 1943/bruckner symphony no 6
recorded in kingsway hall london between 6 and 19 november 1964/producer peter andry/ published in 1965/lp matrix numbers XAX 2794-2795
klemperer   lp: SAX 2582/FCX 1051/SAXF 1051/SMC 91437
new   *other lp issues:* angel 36271/emi SXLP 30448/1C053 00599
philharmonia   cd: emi CDM 763 3512/562 3512

33CX 1944/schumann kinderszenen; kreisleriana
recorded in abbey road studios london in 1964/published in 1965/lp matrix numbers XAX 2826-2827
a.fischer,   lp: SAX 2583/SMC 91463
piano   cd: emi CZS 569 2172

33CX 1945/schütz historia von der freudenreichen geburt jesu christi
recorded in 1964/published in 1965/lp matrix numbers XRX 1119-1120
thamm   lp: SAX 2584/FCX 1003/SAXF 1003/SMC 91298
instrumentalists
mathis
jelden
ocker

33CX 1946/wolf songs from the romantic poets
recorded in abbey road studios london between 15 and 30 january 1961, 9 march 1962 and 3-7 december 1962/producer walter legge/published in 1965/lp matrix numbers XAX 707-708
schwarzkopf   lp: SAX 2589
moore, piano   *other lp issues:* angel 36308/emi SLS 5197
     selections from the recital
     cd: emi CMS 763 7902/CDM 763 6562/CHS 565 8602

33CX 1947/catalogue number appears not to have been allocated

33CX 1948/orchestral music by mozart
recorded in kingsway hall london between 24 march and 10 april 1964 (die zauberflöte) and in abbey road studios london between 16 october and 14 november 1964/producers walter legge and peter andry/published in november 1965/lp matrix numbers XAX 2816-2817

klemperer   **adagio and fugue in c minor** see 33CX 1438
philharmonia   **die entführung aus dem serail overture** see 33CX 1786
                die zauberflöte overture
                lp: SAX 2587/FCX 1007/SAXF 1007/SME 80933
                other lp issues: angel 36289/32099/34462/emi EX 29 04823/
                   2C069 00602/100 6024/CVA 1059/769 4081
                cd: emi CDM 763 6192
                this recording of zauberflöte overture taken from complete recording of the opera published simultaneously on the emi angel label

klemperer   **maurerische trauermusik; la clemenza di tito overture**
new   lp: SAX 2587/FCX 1007/SAXF 1007/SME 80933
philharmonia   *other lp issues:* angel 36289/32099/34462/emi SLS 5048/
                   EX 29 04823/1C147 01842-01847/2C069 00602/
                   1C147 30636-30637/1C197 53714-53738/100 6024/
                   CVA 1059/769 4081
                cd: emi CDM 763 6192
                cosi fan tutte; don giovanni; le nozze di figaro overtures
                lp: SAX 2587/FCX 1007/SAXF 1007/SME 80933
                other lp issues: angel 36289/32099/34462/emi SLS 5048/
                   EX 29 04823/1C147 01842-01847/2C069 00602/
                   100 6024/CVA 1059/769 4081

33CX 1949/orchestral works by stravinsky
recorded in kingsway hall london on 28-30 march 1962 and 18 february 1963 respectively/ producers walter legge and peter andry/published in november 1965/lp matrix numbers XAX 2595-2596

klemperer   **symphony in three movements**
philharmonia   lp: SAX 2588/FCX 1054/SAXF 1054/SMC 91436
                other lp issues: angel 36238/angel seraphim 60188
                cd: emi CDM 764 1422
                pulcinella suite
                lp: SAX 2588/FCX 1054/SAXF 1054/SMC 91436
                other lp issues: angel 36238/angel seraphim 60188
                cd: emi CDM 764 1422/testament SBT 1156

33C 1001/schumann piano concerto
recorded in abbey road studios london on 9-10 april 1948/producer walter legge/published in october 1952/lp matrix numbers XA 62-63

karajan
philharmonia
lipatti, piano

78: LX 1110-1113/LX 8624-8627/LCX 8012-8015/
GQX 11207-11210
lp: FCX 322/FCX 491/FCX 30096/FC 1016/FC 25078/
QCX 322/QC 1016/WC 1001/C 70082/VC 803
other lp issues: american columbia ML 2195/ML 4525/
3216 0141/toshiba EAC 37001-37018/emi XLP 30072/
HLM 7046/1C047 00770/1C061 00770/2C051 03713/
1C197 53780-53786M
cd: emi CDH 769 7922/CZS 767 1632/piano library PL 291

33C 1002/mozart symphony no 41 "jupiter"
recorded in kingsway hall london on 22 february 1950/producer lawrance collingwood/ published in october 1952/lp matrix numbers XA 98-99

beecham
royal
philharmonic

78: LX 1337-1340/GQX 11448-11451
other 78rpm issue: american columbia M 933
lp: FCX 235/QC 5006/VC 805
other lp issues: american columbia ML 4313/3216 0023/3236 0009/
philips fontana EFL 2518/697 209EL/philips classical
favourites GL 5747/GBR 6506/G03645L/G05668R/
cbs 54001
cd: sony SMK 89809

33C 1003/grieg piano concerto
recorded in kingsway hall london on 6-11 june 1951/producer walter legge/published in october 1952/lp matrix numbers XA 127-128

karajan
philharmonia
gieseking,
piano

78: LX 1503-1506/LX 8888-8891
lp: FCX 284/FC 1008/FC 25075/QC 1008/VC 80/
WC 1003/C 70083
other lp issues: american columbia ML 4331/ML 4885/toshiba
EAC 37001-37018/emi 1C047 00770M/1C047 01363M/
3C153 52425-52431M
cd: emi CDM 566 5972

33C 1004/falla el amor brujo ballet
recorded in paris/published in december 1952/lp matrix numbers XL 110-111

argenta
conservatoire
orchestra
iriarte

78: LFX 980-982
lp: FC 1010/QC 1010

33C 1005/chopin piano sonata no 3
recorded in abbey road studios london on 25-27 june 1951/published in december 1952/ lp matrix numbers XA 137-138
malcuzynski,   lp: QC 5001
piano

33C 1006/mendelssohn symphony no 4 "italian"
recorded in abbey road studios london on 19 december 1951/producer lawrance collingwood/ published in march 1953/lp matrix numbers XA 206-207

beecham   lp: FCX 236/QC 5002
royal   *other lp issues:* american columbia ML 4681/philips A01329L/
philharmonic   philips fontana CFL 1008/EFL 2507/EFR 2021/
   699 007CL/699 038CL/697 205EL/664 015ER/
   philips classical favourites GL 5745/G03642L
   cd: emi CDM 763 3982/sony SMK 87965
   recording completed in may and june 1952

33C 1007/beethoven piano concerto no 4
recorded in kingsway hall london on 9-11 june 1951/producer walter legge/published in april 1953/lp matrix numbers XA 129-130

karajan   78: LX 1443-1446/LX 8831-8834/GQX 11493-11496
philharmonia   lp: FC 1014/QCX 10499/QC 1012/VC 804/WCX 598/
gieseking,   WC 1007/C 91244/C 70085
piano   *other lp issues:* american columbia ML 4535/RL 3092/3216
   0371/toshiba EAC 37001-37019/emi 3C153 52425-52431M
   cd: emi CDM 566 6042/philips 456 8112

33C 1008/sibelius violin concerto
recorded in abbey road studios london on 7-8 november 1951/producer lawrance collingwood/published in february 1953

beecham   78: LX 8947-8950
royal   lp: FC 1022/QC 5003
philharmonic   *other lp issues:* american columbia ML 4550/Y-35200/philips
stern, violin   NBL 5030/N01250L/philips fontana 664 017ER/
   699 040CL/philips classical favourites GL 5718/G03630L
   cd: sony SMK 87799

33C 1009/mahler kindertotenlieder
recorded in kingsway hall london on 4 october 1949/producer walter legge/published in april 1953/lp matrix numbers XA 196-197
walter 78: LX 8939-8941
vienna lp: FC 1033/WC 1009/C 70086
philharmonic *other lp issues:* american columbia ML 2187/ML 4980/3226
ferrier 0016/cbs 60203/72317/emi HLM 7002/2C061 01209/
 1C147 01402-01403M
 cd: emi CDH 761 0032/CDM 566 9112/gala GL 307/
 naxos 811.0876

33C 1010/stravinsky l'oiseau de feu ballet suite/american columbia
recorded in carnegie hall new york on 28 january 1946/producer goddard lieberson/ lp matrix numbers LP 210-211
stravinsky 78: LOX 666-669
new york lp: QC 5004
philharmonic *american columbia issues*
 78: M 653
 lp: ML 4046/ML 4882
 other lp issue: philips A01307L
 cd: andante 1979-1981

33C 1011/operatic scenes by tchaikovsky and richard strauss/part american columbia
recorded in abbey road studios london on 22 may 1948 and in columbia studios new york on 14 march 1949 respectively/producers walter legge and goddard lieberson/published in april 1953/lp matrix numbers LP 1002-1003
susskind tatyana's letter scene/evgeny onegin *sung in german*
philharmonia 78: LX 1108-1109
welitsch *other 78rpm issue:* american columbia X 310
 lp: WC 1011/VC 806
 other lp issues: american columbia ML 2048/ML 4795/emi HLM
 7006/1C047 01267M/world records SH 289/angel seraphim
 60202
 cd: emi CDH 761 0072/CHS 764 8552

reiner **closing scene/salome**
metropolitan 78: LX 1241-1242
opera orchestra lp: WC 1011/VC 806
welitsch *american columbia issues*
 78: X 316
 lp: ML 2048/ML 4795/3216 0077
 45 rpm issue: philips ABE 10025
 other lp issue: cbs 61088
 cd: sony MH2K 62866/myto MCD 954 135

33C 1012/mozart piano concerto no 23 k488
recorded in kingsway hall london on 10 june 1951/producer walter legge/published in november 1953/lp matrix numbers XA 155-156

karajan	78: LX 1510-1513/LX 8894-8897
philharmonia	lp: FCX 30003/FC 1013/FC 25072/QC 5009/WC 1012/ C 70087
gieseking, piano	*other lp issues:* american columbia ML 4536/3216 0371/toshiba EAC 37001-37019/emi 3C153 52425-52431M
	cd: emi CHS 763 7092/philips 456 8112

33C 1013/wieniawski violin concerto no 2/american columbia
recorded in carnegie hall new york on 22 march 1946/published in april 1953/lp matrix numbers LP 338-339

kurtz	78: LOX 604-605
new york	*american columbia issues*
philharmonic	78: M 656
stern, violin	lp: ML 2012

33C 1014/piano music by schumann and debussy
recorded in abbey road studios london on 26-28 september 1951/producer walter legge/ published in june 1953/lp matrix numbers XA 148-149

gieseking, piano

kinderszenen
78: LX 8912-8913/GQX 8045-8046
lp: FCX 367/FC 1025/FC 25080/QC 5005/WC 1014/C 70088
other lp issues: american columbia ML 4540/angel 35321/ emi 1C047 01401/3C153 52434-52441M
excerpts
45: SEBQ 173
lp: 33CX 1761/QCX 10357
other lp excerpts: angel 35488

children's corner
78: LC 4000-4002
lp: FCX 306/FCX 30075/FC 1025/FC 25080/QC 5005/ WC 1014/C 70088
other lp issues: american columbia ML 4539/3236 0021/angel 36067/emi 2C061 01029/3C153 52331-52440M/ F667 473-478/RLS 143 6203
cd: emi 562 7982
excerpts
45: SEL 1540/SEBQ 140
lp: 33CX 1761/FCX 844/QCX 10357/QCX 10400
other lp excerpts: angel 35488

33C 1015/stravinsky orchestral works/american columbia
recorded in liederkranz hall new york on 4 april 1940 and in carnegie hall new york on 5 february 1945 respectively/published in november 1953/lp matrix numbers LP 212 and 282

stravinsky	**petrouchka ballet suite**
new york	lp: QC 5008
philharmonic	*american columbia issues*
	78: X 177
	lp: ML 4047
	cd issue: andante 1979-1981
	scenes de ballet
	lp: QC 5008
	american columbia issues
	78: X 245
	lp: ML 4047
	other 78rpm issue: canadian columbia J 87

33C 1016/orchestral works by walton
recorded in kingsway hall london on 18-21 march 1953/producers walter legge and g.pugh/ published in june 1953/lp matrix numbers XA 291-292

walton	**orb and sceptre march**
philharmonia	78: LX 1853/LOX 822
	45: SEL 1506/SEG 8217
	lp issues: angel 30000/35639/emi HQM 1006/SLS 5246
	cd: emi CHS 565 0032
	crown imperial march
	45: SEL 1504
	lp issues: angel 30000/35639/emi HQM 1006/SLS 5246
	cd: emi CHS 565 0032
	portsmouth point overture
	45: SEL 1506/SEG 8217
	lp issues: angel 30000/35639/emi HQM 1006/SLS 5246
	cd: emi CHS 565 0032
	sheep may safely graze/the wise virgins
	45: SEL 1504
	lp issue: angel 30000
	cd: emi CHS 565 0032
	crown imperial and sheep may safely graze also issued by angel in usa on a 45rpm disc

33C 1017/orchestral works by delius
recorded in abbey road studios london on 7 february 1950 and 27 october 1951 respectively/ producer lawrance collingwood/published in december 1953/lp matrix numbers XA 348-349

beecham royal philharmonic	**over the hills and far away** *other lp issues:* american columbia ML 2133/ML 5268/philips SBR 6242/S06665R/philips classical favourites GL 5713/ G03625L cd: sony SMK 89430/SX5K 87342 **in a summer garden** *other lp issues:* philips SBR 6242/S06665R/philips classical favourites GL 5713/G03625L/cbs 30056 cd: sony SMK 89429/SX5K 87342

33C 1018/sibelius scenes historiques
recorded in kingsway hall london on 28 september 1950/producer lawrance collingwood/ published in november 1953/lp matrix numbers XA 346-347

beecham royal philharmonic	lp: QC 5014 *other lp issues:* american columbia ML 4550/Y3-35200/ philips NBL 5030/N02150L/philips classical favourites GL 5718/G03630L cd: emi CDM 763 3972/sony SMK 87798 *excerpts* 45: SEB 3504/SEBQ 115 *other 45rpm excerpts:* philips SBF 269/S313 499F *recording completed in abbey road studios london in june and august 1952*

33C 1019/smetana the moldau and from bohemia's woods and fields/ ma vlast/american columbia
recorded in new york in january 1951/published in december 1954/lp matrix numbers LP 4878-4879

szell new york philharmonic	lp: QC 5019 *american columbia issues* 78: M 1004 lp: ML 2177/ML 4785/Y3-35231 *other lp issue:* cbs 4170

33C 1020/schumann dichterliebe/american columbia
recorded in columbia studios new york on 13 august 1941/published in december 1953
lehmann
walter, piano
    lp: FC 1034
    american columbia issues
    78: M 486
    lp: ML 2183/ML 4788/3216 0315
    other lp issue: cbs 61501
    cd: sony MPK 44840/vocal archives VA 1158

33C 1021/piano works by bach and mozart
recorded in radio geneva studios on 9 july 1950/producer walter legge/published in november 1953/lp matrix numbers XZ 14-15
lipatti, piano   **partita no 1 bwv 825**
    78: LX 8744-8745/LFX 954-955/GQX 11241-11242/
      M 15145-15146
    lp: FCX 494/FC 1023/FC 25009/QC 5013/WC 1021/C 60600
    other lp issues: american columbia ML 4633/3216 0320/emi
      HQM 1210/RLS 749/1C047 01406M/2C061 01963/
      1C197 53780-53786M
    cd: emi CDC 747 5172/CDH 769 8002/CZS 767 1632/
      566 9882
  mozart piano sonata no 8 k310
    78: LX 8788-8789/LFX 1005-1006/GQX 8031-8032
    lp: FCX 494/FC 1023/QC 5013/WC 1021/C 60600
    other lp issues: american columbia ML 4633/3216 0320/emi
      RLS 749/HQM 1210/1C047 01406M/2C061 01963/
      1C197 53780-53786M
    cd: emi CDC 747 5172/CDH 769 8002/CZS 767 1632/
      566 9882

33C 1022/tchaikovsky violin concerto/american columbia
recorded in philadelphia on 10 april 1949/published in 1953
hilsberg
philadelphia
orchestra
stern, violin
    78: LX 1316-1319
    lp: FCX 167/VC 807
    american columbia issues
    78: M 863
    45: A 1087
    lp: ML 4232
    other lp issue: philips S06672R

258

33C 1023/works by ravel/american columbia
recorded in academy of music philadelphia on 22 january 1947 and 24 december 1946 respectively/published in november 1953/lp matrix numbers LP 483 and 2797

ormandy	**piano concerto for the left hand**
philadelphia	78: LX 1088-1089/GQX 11461-11462
orchestra	lp: FC 1032/QC 5011
casadesus,	*american columbia issues*
piano	78: M 288
	lp: ML 4075
ormandy	**rapsodie espagnole**
philadelphia	lp: FC 1032/QC 5011
orchestra	*american columbia issues*
	78: M 342
	lp: ML 4306

33C 1024/mozart piano concerto no 21 k467/american columbia
recorded in new york on 20 december 1948/published in december 1953/lp matrix numbers LP 1512-1513

munch	78: LX 1412-1415
new york	lp: FC 1009/QC 5016/WC 1024
philharmonic	*american columbia issues*
casadesus,	78: M 866
piano	lp: ML 2067/ML 4791
	other lp issue: philips A01291L

33C 1025/orchestral works by prokofiev and rimsky-korsakov/
american columbia
recorded in academy of music philadelphia on 13 october 1946/published in february 1954/lp matrix numbers LP 593-594

ormandy	**symphony no 1 "classical"**
philadelphia	lp: FC 1007/QC 5015
orchestra	*american columbia issues*
	78: M 287
	lp: ML 2035
	russian easter festival overture
	78: LOX 670-671
	lp: FC 1007/QC 5015
	american columbia issues
	78: X 276
	lp: ML 2035

33C 1026/orchestral music by wagner/american columbia
recorded in carnegie hall new york on 17 november 1947 and in columbia studios new york on 4 april 1949 respectively/producer goddard lieberson/published in january 1954/ lp matrix numbers LP 2368 and 3114

stokowski	**wotan's farewell and magic fire music/die walküre**
new york	lp: FC 1027/QC 1027
philharmonic	*american columbia issues*
	78: M 301
	lp: ML 2153
	cd issue: cala/stokowski society CACD 0533
	rienzi overture
	lp: FC 1027/QC 1027
	american columbia issue
	lp: ML 2153
	cd issue: cala/stokowski society CACD 0534

33C 1027/french orchestral music/american columbia
recorded in carnegie hall new york on 2 january 1946 and on 27 february 1945 respectively/ published in january 1954/lp matrix numbers LP 1845 and 1855

milhaud	**milhaud suite francaise**
new york	78: LFX 860-861
philharmonic	lp: FC 1003
	american columbia issue
	lp: ML 2093
	other lp issue: philips A01256L

rodzinski	**ibert escales**
new york	lp: FC 1003
philharmonic	*american columbia issues*
	78: X 263
	lp: ML 2093/RL 6629
	other 78rpm issue: canadian columbia J 90
	also published as an american v-disc

33C 1028/mozart piano concerto no 27 k595/american columbia
recorded in carnegie hall new york on 3 november 1941/published in february 1954/ lp matrix numbers LP 2745-2746

barbirolli	*american columbia issues*
new york	78: M 490
philharmonic	lp: ML 2186/ML 4791
casdadesus,	*other lp issue:* philips A01291L
piano	cd: dante HPC 100/dutton awaiting publication/ archipel ARPCD 0194

33C 1029/works for violin and orchestra/american columbia
recorded in academy of music philadelphia on 5 november 1950/published in january 1954
ormandy philadelphia orchestra francescatti, violin

chausson poeme pour violon et orchestre
lp: FC 1017
american columbia issues
lp: ML 2194/ML 5253
other lp issue: philips A01275L
cd: sony M2HK 62339
saint-saens introduction and rondo capriccioso
lp: FC 1017
american columbia issues
lp: ML 2194/ML 5253
other lp issues: philips SBL 5234/S04643L

33C 1030/berg violin concerto
recorded in kingsway hall london on 17-19 august 1953/producer lawrance collingwood/ published in february 1954/lp matrix numbers XA 361-362
kletzki philharmonia gertler, violin

lp: FCX 297/WC 1030/C 70090
other lp issue: angel 35091
cd: hungaroton HCD 31635

33C 1031/piano music by franck and liszt
recorded in abbey road studios london on 26-29 october 1949 and 21 june 1951 respectively/published in november 1954/lp matrix numbers XA 97-98
malcuzynski, piano

prélude choral et fugue
78: LX 1269-1270
lp: FC 1028/QC 1028/WC 1031
rapsodie espagnole
78: LX 8922-8923
lp: FC 1028/QC 1028/WC 1031

33C 1032/viennese songs
recorded in brahmssaal vienna on 30 november 1948/producer walter legge/published in november 1954/lp matrix numbers XHA 1001-1002
faltl-kemmeter schrammel- orchester kunz

lp: VP 801
other lp issue: angel seraphim 65034/world records SH 284
selections from the recital
78: LB 83/LB 90/LB 115/LB 129/DV 1460/DV 1471/ DV 1538/DW 5081
lp: emi 1C147 03580-03581M
recordings completed in january, october and november 1949

33C 1033/schumann piano concerto
recorded in kingsway hall london on 24-25 august 1953/producer walter jellinek/published in november 1954/lp matrix numbers XA 436-437

karajan	lp: FCX 284/FCX 322/QCX 10239/QC 5022/QC 10222/
philharmonia	WC 1033/C 70091/C 91234
gieseking,	*other lp issues:* angel 35321/toshiba EAC 37001-37019/
piano	emi 1C047 01401M/3C153 52425-52431M
	cd: emi CDM 566 5972

33C 1034/orchestral works by ravel
recorded in théatre des champs-elysées paris on 31 march 1953 and 30 april 1953 respectively/producer rené challan/published in october 1954/lp matrix numbers XA 536-537

cluytens	**le tombeau de couperin**
orchestre	lp: FCX 214/QCX 10107/QC 5022
national	*other lp issue:* angel 35102
	cd: testament SBT 1236/SBT 7247
	recording completed on 12 april 1953
	boléro
	lp: FCX 214/QCX 10107/QC 5022
	other lp issue: angel 35102

33C 1035/wagner der fliegende holländer scenes
recorded in kingsway hall london on 18-21 april 1952/producer walter legge/published in november 1954/lp matrix numbers XA 549-550

schüchter	**die frist ist um**
philharmonia	78: LX 1562
s.björling	lp: FC 1039/QC 5023

schüchter	**jo-ho-hoe!**
philharmonia	78: LX 1573/LOX 820
covent garden	lp: FC 1039/QC 5023
chorus	*other lp issue:* emi 1C147 29150-29151M
rysanek	cd: emi CDH 565 2012

schüchter	**wie aus der ferne**
philharmonia	lp: FC 1039/QC 5023
rysanek	*other lp issue:* emi 1C147 29150-29151M
s.björling	cd: emi CDH 565 2012

33C 1036/sibelius violin concerto
recorded in stockholm on 10-11 june 1954/producer edward fowler/published in may 1955/lp matrix numbers XCS 105-106

ehrling	lp: FCX 245/FC 1035/QC 5025/WC 1036/C 70094/
stockholm	C 91395
festival	*other lp issues:* angel 35315/hmv LBLP 1031/emi
orchestra	SLS 5004/HC 102
oistrakh, violin	cd: testament SBT 1032

262

33C 1037-1039/catalogue numbers appear not to have been allocated

33C 1040/grieg piano concerto
recorded in abbey road studios london on 18 september 1947/producer walter legge/ published in september 1955/lp matrix numbers XA 244-245

galliera	78: LX 1029-1032/LX 8579-8582/LFX 810-813/
philharmonia	GQX 11163-11166
lipatti, piano	lp: FCX 322/FCX 491/FCX 30096/QCX 322/QCX 10213/
	QC 5026/WC 1040/C 70095
	other lp issues: american columbia ML 4525/3216 0141/emi XLP 30072/HLM 7046/1C047 00770M/2C061 00770/ 2C051 43321/1C197 53580-53586M/100 7701
	cd: emi CDM 763 4972/CZS 767 1632

33C 1041/khachaturian gayaneh ballet suite
recorded in kingsway hall london on 24-27 november 1954/producer walter legge/ published in october 1955/lp matrix numbers XA 707-708

khachaturian	lp: QC 5027
philharmonia	*other lp issues:* angel 35277/angel seraphim 60226

33C 1042/orchestral music by smetana
recorded in abbey road studios london on 10 september 1953 and in kingsway hall london on 25 september 1954 respectively/producer walter jellinek/published in november 1955/ lp matrix numbers XA 705-706

ackermann	**the moldau/ma vlast**
philharmonia	45: SEL 1619/SEBQ 199
	lp: QC 5042
	from bohemia's woods and fields/ma vlast
	lp: QC 5042

33C 1043/orchestral music by khachaturian
recorded in kingsway hall london on 3-4 december 1954/producer walter legge/published in november 1955/lp matrix numbers XA 709-710

khachaturian	**in memoriam**
philharmonia	lp: QC 5028
	waltz, nocturne and mazurka/masquerade
	lp: QC 5028
	other lp issues: angel 35277/angel seraphim 60226

33C 1044/rawsthorne practical cats
recorded in kingsway hall london between 24 and 29 september 1954/producer walter legge/ published in december 1957/lp matrix numbers XA 758-759
rawsthorne   *other lp issues:* angel 30002/angel seraphim 60042
philharmonia   *narration superimposed at a later date*
donat, narrator

33C 1045/mussorgsky pictures from an exhibition
recorded in abbey road studios london on 14-18 november 1955/published in may 1956/ lp matrix numbers XA 888-889
malinin, piano

33C 1046/bartok sonata for unaccompanied violin
recorded in abbey road studios london on 13-15 october 1953/producer lawrance collingwood/ published in december 1956/lp matrix numbers XA 556-557
gertler, violin

33C 1047/beethoven violin sonata no 9 "kreutzer"
recorded in paris in june 1953/published in september 1956/lp matrix numbers XL 326-327
oistrakh, violin   lp: WC 1047/C 70100
oborin, piano   *other lp issues:* melodiya D 03894-03895/colosseum CRLP 153/
                          hmv LBLP 1050/musical appreciation society 572/
                          monitor MC 2042/chant du monde LDA 8077/
                          vanguard VRS 6024
                      cd: vanguard OVC 4080-4082/testament SBT 1115

33C 1048/luigi infantino sings romantic songs from italy
recorded in 1954/published in september 1956/lp matrix numbers XB 151-152
guarino and   lp: QC 5017
f. patané
orchestra
infantino

33C 1049-1050/soviet army ensemble sing folksongs
recorded in abbey road studios london in 1955/producer walter legge/published in december 1956/lp matrix numbers XA 1021-1024
alexandrov
soviet army
ensemble

33C 1051/beethoven symphony no 5
recorded in kingsway hall london on 6-7 october 1955/producer walter legge/published in december 1956/lp matrix numbers XA 1025-1026
klemperer lp: FC 25037/QC 5037/WC 1051/C 70101/C 90157
philharmonia *other lp issues:* 35329/emi SLS 873/EX 29 04573/
　　　　　　　　1C191 01526-01528
　　　　　　cd: emi CDM 763 8682/567 8512

33C 1052/operatic arias by leoncavallo, verdi, rossini and giordano
recorded in kingsway hall london on 1-6 october 1953/producer walter legge/published in march 1957/lp matrix numbers XA 933-934
galliera lp: QC 5038
philharmonia
panerai

33C 1053/orchestral music by handel and mozart
recorded in abbey road studios london on 25-28 march 1956/producer walter legge/ published in march 1957
klemperer **concerto grosso op 6 no 4**
philharmonia 45: SEL 1594/ESL 6254/ESLQ 1001/ESLW 6254
　　　　　　lp: SBO 2751/33CX 5252/SAX 5252/SBOF 1001/
　　　　　　　　WC 1053/WC 544/SBOW 8504/C 70102/
　　　　　　　　C 70461/STC 70102/STC 70461
　　　　　　cd: emi CDM 764 1462/testament SBT 2131
　　　　　　recording completed on 26 july 1956
　　　　　　eine kleine nachtmusik
　　　　　　45: SEBQ 194/C 50517/STC 50517
　　　　　　lp: SBO 2751/SBOF 1001/WC 1053/WC 544/SBOW 2751/
　　　　　　　　SBOW 8504/C 70102/C 70461/STC 70102/STC 70461
　　　　　　cd: testament SBT 1093

33C 1054/orchestral works by walton
recorded in kingsway hall london on 26 march 1957 and 20 april 1955 respectively/ producer walter legge/published in march 1958/lp matrix numbers XA 1190-1191
walton **johannesburg festival overture**
philharmonia *other lp issues:* angel 35639/emi SLS 5246/HQM 1006
　　　　　　cd: emi CHS 565 6032
　　　　　　two suites for orchestra from facade
　　　　　　other lp issues: angel 35639/emi SLS 5246/HQM 1006
　　　　　　cd: emi CHS 565 6032
　　　　　　excerpts from the suites
　　　　　　45: SED 5556
　　　　　　recording of the suites completed on 26 march 1957

33C 1055/beethoven piano concerto no 4
recorded in abbey road studios london on 27 april-1 may 1957/producers walter legge and walter jellinek/published in march 1958/lp matrix numbers XA 1320-1321
ludwig   lp: SBO 2752/FCX 673/FCX 30254/SBOF 1005
philharmonia   *other lp issues:* angel 35511/emi XLP 30086/SXLP 30086/
gilels, piano   cd: emi 483 4182/testament SBT 1095

33C 1056/schumann symphony no 4
recorded in grünewaldkirche berlin on 25-26 april 1957/producer fritz ganss/published in may 1958/lp matrix numbers XR 31-32
karajan   lp: FC 1070/QC 5043/WC 504/C 70080
berlin   *other lp issues:* emi RLS 768/F669 711-715/1C047 01441M/
philharmonic   1C137 54095-54097
    cd: emi CDF 3000 122/CMS 763 3212

33C 1057/chopin piano concerto no 1
recorded in abbey road studios london on 30-31 july 1956/producer walter jellinek/published in 1957/lp matrix numbers XA 1381-1382
galliera   lp: WC 1057/C 70388
philharmonia   *other lp issues:* angel 35631/emi TRI 33199
anda, piano   cd: testament SBT 1066

33C 1058/beethoven piano concerto no 4
recorded in abbey road studios london on 6-7 september 1955/producer walter jellinek/lp matrix numbers XA 1397-1398
galliera   lp: FCX 1037/SAXF 1037/SMC 91481
philharmonia   cd: emi CDZ 762 6072
gieseking,
piano

33C 1059/lalo symphonie espagnole
recorded in maison de la mutualité paris on 21-22 february 1955/producer rené challan/published in 1957/lp matrix numbers XL 78-79
bruck   lp: FCX 403/QCX 10307
conservatoire   cd: testament SBT 1226/SBT6 1248
orchestra
kogan, violin

33C 1060/wagner siegfried idyll; strauss don juan
recorded in kingsway hall london on 28-29 january 1957/producer walter legge/published in 1958/lp matrix numbers XA 1208-1209
galliera   lp: QC 5044
philharmonia   *other lp issue:* angel 35784

33C 1061/mozart arias from exsultate jubilate, mass in c minor, die entführung aus dem serail, il re pastore and die zauberflöte; misera dove son, concert aria
recorded in abbey road studios london on 17-18 may 1958/producers walter legge and walter jellinek/published in 1959/lp matrix numbers XA 1555-1556
galliera cd: testament SBT 1193
philharmonia *selections from the recital*
moffo lp: QCX 10349
    other lp selections: angel 35716/RL 3080/angel seraphim 60110

33C 1062/beethoven triple concerto
recorded in abbey road studios London on 10 may 1958/producer walter legge/published in 1957/lp matrix numbers XA 1457-1458
sargent lp: SBO 2753/SBOF 1004/QCX 10351/SAXQ 7312/
philharmonia WC 525/C 70387
oborin, piano *other lp issues:* angel 35697/36727/34400/emi XLP 20081/
oistrakh, violin SXLP 20081/SXLP 30378/SREG 1098/EMX 2035/
knushevitsky, 1C037 01974/1C053 01974/SHZE 706/melodiya
cello D22551-22552
    cd: emi CDZ 762 8542/CDM 769 3312/483 4182/ 826 6542

33C 1063/mozart arias from cosi fan tutte, don giovanni and le nozze di figaro
recorded in abbey road studios london on 17-18 may 1958/producer walter legge/published in 1959/lp matrix numbers XA 1557-1558
galliera lp: SBO 2754/QCX 10349
philharmonia *other lp issues:* angel 35716/RL 3080/angel seraphim 60110
moffo cd: testament SBT 1193
    selections from the recital
    45: SEL 1661/SEL 1667/SEL 1690/ESL 6275/ ESL 6279/ESL 6292

33C 1064/mozart piano concerto no 21 k467
recorded at a concert in kunsthaus lucerne on 23 august 1950/published in january 1961/ lp matrix numbers XZ 9003-9004
karajan lp: QC 5046/WC 1064/WS 545/C 60714/C 80964
lucerne *other lp issues:* angel 35931/emi RLS 749/1C047 01469M/
festival 2C051 03713/155 0963/1C197 53780-53786M
orchestra cd: emi CDH 769 7922/CZS 767 1632
lipatti, piano

33C 1065/see 33CX 1752-1753

33SX 1001/sullivan-mackerras/pineapple poll
recorded in abbey road studios london on 7-8 june 1951/producers leonard smith and p.de jongh/published in october 1952/lp matrix numbers XAX 157-158

mackerras	78: DX 1765-1770
sadlers wells	*also published in australia under the lp number 33OSX 1002;*
orchestra	*also published on cd by regis*

33SX 1002/non-classical repertoire

33SX 1003/works by lambert and walton
recorded in abbey road studios on 13-14 january 1949 and on 27 september 1950 (walton)/ producer walter legge/published in february 1953/lp matrix numbers XAX 163 and 180

lambert	**the rio grande**
philharmonia	78: DX 1591-1592
bbc chorus	*other lp issues:* american columbia ML 2145/emi HQM 1078
ripley	cd: emi CDH 763 9112
greenbaum,	
piano	

lambert	**horoscope ballet suite**
philharmonia	78: DX 1567-1568
	other lp issues: american columbia ML 2083/emi HQM 1078
	excerpts
	cd: emi CDH 763 9112

lambert	**facade suites 1 and 2**
philharmonia	78: DX 1734-1736/DX 8374-8376
	other lp issue: american columbia ML 4793
	cd: somm SOMMCD 023

33SX 1004-1005/non-classical repertoire

33SX 1006/overtures by rossini
recorded in kingsway hall london on 19-21 january 1953/producer walter jellinek/published in september 1953/lp matrix numbers XAX 255-256

galliera	**semiramide; guillaume tell; il signor bruschino;**
philharmonia	**la cenerentola**
	lp: FCX 208/QCX 208
	other lp issues: angel 35011/emi MFP 2031
	l'italiana in algeri
	78: DX 1910
	45: SED 5502/SEBQ 104
	lp: FCX 208/QCX 208
	other lp issues: angel 35011/emi MFP 2031

268
33SX 1006/overures by rossini/concluded
galliera　　　la scala di seta
philharmonia　　45: SEBQ 104
　　　　　　　　lp: FCX 208/QCX 208
　　　　　　　　other lp issues: angel 35011/emi MFP 2031

33SX 1007/rimsky-korsakov scheherazade
recorded in abbey road studios london on 17-18 december 1952/producers walter legge and p.de jongh/published in september 1953/lp matrix numbers XAX 268-269
dobrowen　　 lp: FCX 268/FCX 30207/QCX 10021/VSX 501
philharmonia　　*other lp issue:* angel 35009/hmv LALP 234
　　　　　　　　recording completed on 5 january 1953

33SX 1008/don cossacks on parade/american columbia
published in november 1953/lp matrix numbers XLP 4479-4480
jaroff
don cossack
choir

33SX 1009/overtures by verdi
recorded in kingsway hall london on 22-23 january 1953/producers walter legge and published in october 1953/lp matrix numbers XAX 257-258
galliera　　　**aida; i vespri siciliani**
philharmonia　　lp: FCX 209/QCX 10094
　　　　　　　　other lp issue: angel 35012
　　　　　　　　la traviata acts 1 and 3
　　　　　　　　78: DX 1890
　　　　　　　　45: SED 5517/SCD 2126
　　　　　　　　la forza del destino
　　　　　　　　45: SED 5505/ESBF 5119/SEBQ 109
　　　　　　　　lp: FCX 209/QCX 10094
　　　　　　　　other lp issue: angel 35012
　　　　　　　　nabucco
　　　　　　　　78: DX 1904/GQX 11547
　　　　　　　　45: SED 5505/ESBF 5119/SEBQ 109
　　　　　　　　lp: FCX 209/QCX 10094
　　　　　　　　other lp issue: angel 35012

33SX 1010/rimsky-korsakov suites from tsar sultan and le coq d'or
recorded in kingsway hall london on 4-6 december 1952/producer walter legge/published in october 1953/lp matrix numbers XAX 297-298
dobrowen　　 lp: FCX 207/QCX 207
philharmonia　　*other lp issues:* angel 35010/emi XLP 30003/QIMX 7016
　　　　　　　　excerpts from the suites
　　　　　　　　45: SED 5551

33SX 1011/chopin-gretchaninov les sylphides; villa-lobos uirapuru/
american columbia
published in november 1953/lp matrix numbers XLP 1756-1757
kurtz   *american columbia issue*
new york   lp: ML 4255
philharmonic

33SX 1012/khachaturian ballet suites from gayaneh/american columbia
published in november 1953/lp matrix numbers XLP 253 and 292
kurtz   **suite no 1**
new york   78: DX 1499-1501/GFX 163-165
philharmonic   *american columbia issues*
                78: M 664
                lp: ML 4030
                suite no 2
                78: DX 1641-1642
                american columbia issues
                78: M 292
                lp: ML 4030

33SX 1013/orchestral works by liszt and tchaikovsky
recorded in kingsway hall london on 23-24 january 1953/producers walter legge and nicholas boyle/published in february 1954/lp matrix numbers XAX 324 and 327
galliera   **les préludes**
philharmonia   lp: FCX 239/QCX 10074
                other lp issues: angel 35047/emi MFP 2087
                capriccio italien
                45: SEL 1612
                lp: FCX 239/FC 25092/QCX 10074
                other lp issues: angel 35047/emi MFP 2087

33SX 1014/liszt hungarian rhapsodies nos 2, 6, 12 and 15
recorded in abbey road studios london in 1953/published in march 1954/lp matrix numbers XAX 295-296
kentner, piano

33SX 1015-1016/non-classical repertoire

33SX 1017/bruch violin concerto no 1; mozart violin concerto no 1
recorded in abbey road studios london on 2-3 january 1953/producer lawrance collingwood/published in march 1954/lp matrix numbers XAX 438-439
susskind
philharmonia
varga, violin

33SX 1018/works by dohnanyi and mozart
recorded in abbey road studios london on 14 january 1953 and 11 december 1952 respectively/producer lawrance collingwood/published in march 1954/lp matrix numbers XAX 431-432

sargent philharmonia smith, piano	variations on a nursery song lp: 33SX 1579
smith and sellick, pianos	mozart sonata for 2 pianos k448

33SX 1019/orchestral works by vaughan williams, bax and holst
recorded in abbey road studios london on 24 july 1953 and 29-30 october 1953 (tintagel)/ producer brian culverhouse/published in april 1954/lp matrix numbers XAX 441-442

weldon london symphony	the wasps aristophanic suite cd: dutton CDCLP 4002 *excerpts* 45: SED 5522/SCD 2039 *recording completed on 29 october 1953* the perfect fool ballet music *other lp issue:* emi XLP 30049 cd: dutton CDCLP 4002 tintagel cd: dutton CDCLP 4002

33SX 1020/non-classical repertoire

33SX 1021/beethoven piano sonatas 15 "pastoral" and 21 "waldstein"
recorded in abbey road studios london on 7-8 january, 25-27 march and 5-8 may 1953/ producer walter legge (january sessions only)/published in may 1954/lp matrix numbers XAX 399 and 401
matthews,
piano

33SX 1022/non-classical repertoire

33SX 1023/beethoven piano sonatas 10 and 23 "appassionata"
recorded in abbey road studios london on 20 february 1953 and 5 march 1953 respectively/published in july 1954/lp matrix numbers XAX 400 and 435
matthews,
piano

271

33SX 1024/orchestral works by elgar
recorded in kingsway hall london on 30 june, 8-9 october and 6 november 1953/producers walter legge and brian culverhouse/published in december 1954/lp matrix numbers XAX 489-490

weldon **enigma variations**
philharmonia *excerpts*
  45: SED 5520/SCD 2139
  recording completed on 8-9 october 1953
  cockaigne overture; pomp and circumstance march no 4
  other lp issue: emi MFP 2093
  pomp and circumstance march no 1
  45: SED 5520
  other lp issue: emi MFP 2093

33SX 1025/dvorak symphony no 9 "from the new world"
recorded in kingsway hall london on 7-8 october 1953/producer walter legge/published in september 1954/lp matrix numbers XAX 429-430
galliera lp: FCX 124/QCX 10128
philharmonia *other lp issue:* angel 35085

33SX 1026/catalogue number appears not to have been allocated

33SX 1027/non-classical repertoire

33SX 1028/works by elgar
recorded in abbey road studios london on 26 february 1954 and 19 february 1954 respectively/producer brian culverhouse/published in july 1954/lp matrix numbers XAX 526-527
weldon **sea pictures**
london *other lp issue:* emi MFP 2093/capitol P 18017
symphony
ripley

weldon **in the south overture**
london
symphony

33SX 1029/catalogue number appears not to have been allocated

33SX 1030/orchestral works by elgar
recorded in abbey road studios london on 11 november 1953/producer brian culverhouse/ published in september 1954/lp matrix numbers XAX 499-500

collingwood	nursery suite
london	45: SED 5527
symphony	**serenade for strings**
	excerpts
	45: SED 5523
	three bavarian dances
	excerpts
	45: SED 5523/SCD 2036

33SX 1031/mozart piano concerti nos 12 k414 and 14 k449
recorded in kingsway hall london on 22-23 march 1954/producer walter legge/published in october 1954/lp matrix numbers XAX 542-543
schwarz
philharmonia
matthews, piano

33SX 1032/popular concert no 1
recorded in kingsway hall london on 3 july 1951 (bach and ippolotov-ivanov), in kingsway hall london on 8-9 november 1951 (mascagni, tchaikovsky and offenbach) and in abbey road studios london on 7 march 1953 (liszt and suppé)/producers walter legge and brian culverhouse/published in january 1955/lp matrix numbers XAX 562-563

weldon	**suppé light cavalry overture**
philharmonia	78: DX 1873
	45: SED 5501/SCD 2108
	liszt hungarian rhapsody no 2
	78: DX 1886
	45: SCD 2131
	bach-walton sheep may safely graze
	78: DB 3164
	45: SED 5509
	ippolitov-ivanov procession of the sardar/caucasian sketches
	78: DX 1792
	45: SED 5552/SCD 2024

33SX 1032/popular concert no 1/concluded
weldon   **mascagni cavalleria rusticana intermezzo**
philharmonia   78: DX 1807/DWX 5073
jones, organ   45: SED 5518/SEDQ 543

weldon   **tchaikovsky sleeping beauty waltz**
philharmonia   78: DX 1807/DWX 5073
                  45: SED 5518/SCD 2024/SEDQ 543
                  offenbach orfée aux enfers overture
                  78: DX 1823/DWX 5077/GQX 16654
                  45: SED 5522
                  other lp issue: american columbia RL 3072

33SX 1033/chopin the 4 scherzi
recorded in abbey road studios london on 7-12 may 1952/published in november 1954/ lp matrix numbers XAX 501-502
kentner, piano

33SX 1034/dvorak symphony no 8; scherzo capriccioso
recorded in kingsway hall london on 12-15 june 1954/producer geraint jones/published in january 1955/lp matrix numbers XAX 594-595
sawallisch
philharmonia

33SX 1035-1041/numbers appear not to have been allocated

33SX 1042/non-classical repertoire

33SX 1043/the unashamed accompanist
recorded in abbey road studios london on 11-12 april 1955/producer walter legge/ published in november 1955/lp matrix numbers XAX 754-755
moore, piano   *other lp issues:* angel 35262/emi XLP 30069
and narrator

33SX 1044/mozart piano concerti nos 17 k453 and 25 k503
recorded in abbey road studios on 15 january 1953 and 29 june 1955 respectively/published in may 1956/lp matrix numbers XAX 815 and 836
blech   *recording of concerto no 17 completed on 23 february 1953 and on*
london mozart   *28 june 1955; however it has been reissued on cd by dutton, where it*
players   *is described as an unpublished performance by the same artists*
matthews,   *recorded on 9 january 1953*
piano

33SX 1045/popular concert no 2
recorded in abbey road studios london on 13 april 1953 (sullivan), 23 july 1953 (tchaikovsky, bach and handel march), 29 october 1953 (handel queen of sheba), 11 december 1953 (elgar) and 19 february 1954 (handel-elgar)/producer brian culverhouse/published in february 1956/ lp matrix numbers XAX 816-817

weldon	**elgar chanson de matin**
london	78: DX 1908
symphony	45: SCD 2035
	handel arrival of the queen of sheba/solomon
	78: DB 3388
	45: SED 5516
	handel march from the occasional oratorio
	78: DB 3399
	45: SED 5516
	tchaikovsky marche slave
	78: DX 1894
	bach gavotte from third violin partita, arranged by wood; air from the third orchestral suite, arranged by wilhelmi
	78: DX 1896
	45: SCD 2030
	handel-elgar overture in d
	45: SED 5516
	sullivan di ballo overture

33SX 1046/non-classical repertoire

33SX 1047/beethoven piano sonatas nos 4 and 17 "tempest"
recorded in abbey road studios london on 1-2 june 1954 and on 10 and 31 may 1954 respectively/producer alec robertson/published in june 1956/lp matrix numbers XAX 824-825

matthews, *both recordings completed on 2-3 june 1955*
piano

33SX 1048/waltzes by waldteufel
recorded in kingsway hall london on 5-6 january 1956/producer walter legge/published in october 1956/lp matrix numbers XAX 927-928

h.krips
philharmonia

mon reve
lp: SCX 3251/SGXF 104/QSX 12023
other lp issues: angel 35426/emi XLP 30035/SXLP 30035/
CFP 40305/QIM 6364/SQIM 6364/1C037 01496

les grenadiers; pomona
45: SED 5535
lp: SCX 3251/SGXF 104/QSX 12023
other lp issues: angel 35426/emi XLP 30035/SXLP 30035/
CFP 40305/ESD 7251/QIM 6364/SQIM 6364/
1C037 01496

les patineurs
45: SED 5544/SEDQ 668/ESDQ 2002
lp: SCX 3251/FC 25088/SGXF 104/QSX 12023
other lp issues: angel 35426/emi XLP 30055/SXLP 30055/
CFP 40305/QIM 6364/SQIM 6364/1C037 01496

espana
45: SED 5544/SCD 2198/SEDQ 668/ESDQ 2002
lp: SCX 3251/FC 25088/SGXF 104/QSX 12023
other lp issues: angel 35426/emi XLP 30055/SXLP 30035/
CFP 40305/QIM 6364/SQIM 6364/1C037 01496

estudiantina
45: SCD 2198
lp: SCX 3251/SGXF 104/QSX 12023
other lp issues: angel 35426/emi XLP 30055/SXLP 30055/
CFP 40305/QIM 6364/SQIM 6364/1C037 01496
orchestra described for these recordings as philharmonia promenade orchestra

33SX 1049/waltzes by johann strauss
published in september 1956/lp matrix numbers XAX 923-924

schönherr
and hofman
orchestra of
wiener volksoper

these are abbreviated versions of the waltzes

33SX 1050-1052/non-classical repertoire

33SX 1053/overtures by suppé
recorded in kingsway hall london on 9-10 january 1956/producers walter legge and walter jellinek/published in october 1957/lp matrix numbers XAX 929-930

h.krips light cavalry
philharmonia 45: SED 5562
lp: SCX 3256/FC 25088/QSX 12030/SMC 83951
other lp issues: angel 35427/emi XLP 30037/SXLP 30037/ ESD 7253/QIM 6366/SQIM 6366/1C037 01034
cd: emi CDZ 252 3582
poet and peasant
lp: SCX 3256/FC 25088/QSX 12030/SMC 83951
other lp issues: angel 35427/emi XLP 30037/SXLP 30037/ QIM 6366/SQIM 6366/1C037 01034
cd: emi CDZ 252 3582
pique dame
45: SED 5562
lp: SCX 3256/QSX 12030/SMC 83951
other lp issues: angel 35427/emi XLP 30037/SXLP 30037/ ESD 7253/QIM 6366/SQIM 6366/1C037 01034
cd: emi CDZ 252 3582
morning noon and night in vienna; tantalusqualen; die irrfahrt ins glück
lp: SCX 3256/QSX 12030/SMC 83951
other lp issues: angel 35427/emi XLP 30037/SXLP 30037/ QIM 6366/SQIM 6366/1C037 01034
cd: emi CDZ 252 3582
orchestra described for this recording as philharmonia promenade orchestra

33SX 1054/popular concert no 3
recorded in kingsway hall london on 12-14 march 1956/producer brian culverhouse/ published in march 1957/lp matrix numbers XAX 1001-1002

weldon mendelssohn hebrides overture
philharmonia *other lp issue:* emi MFP 2037
nicolai die lustigen weiber von windsor overture
45: SED 5550
other lp issue: emi MFP 2037
ponchielli dance of the hours/la gioconda
other lp issue: emi MFP 2037
sibelius finlandia
other lp issue: emi MFP 2037
saint-saens danse macabre; bacchanale/samson et dalila
45: SED 5543
other lp issue: emi MFP 2037

33SX 1055-1056/non-classical repertoire

33SX 1057/orchestral music by grieg
recorded in kingsway hall london on 13 march 1956 and in abbey road studios london on 26 may 1956 respectively/producer walter jellinek/published in september 1957/lp matrix numbers XAX 939-940
susskind   peer gynt suites nos 1 and 2
philharmonia   lp: QCX 10294
                other lp issues: emi XLP 30105/SXLP 30105
                excerpts
                45: SED 5555/ESD 7256/SEDQ 674
                4 norwegian dances
                lp: QCX 10294
                other lp issues: emi XLP 30105/SXLP 30105/CFP 40214

33SX 1058-1094/non-classical repertoire

33SX 1095-1096/tchaikovsky the sleeping beauty
recorded in kingsway hall london on 14 march 1956/producers brian culverhouse and walter jellinek/published in september 1958/lp matrix numbers XAX 1167-1170
weldon   *other lp issues:* emi CFPD 4458
philharmonia   cd: emi CDCFPD 4458
                excerpts
                lp: emi XLP 30012/SXLP 30012
                recording completed on 18-19 april and 10 may 1956

33SX 1097-1156/non-classical repertoire

33SX 1157/viennese dances by nussio and schönherr
recorded in kingsway hall london on 3-6 january 1958/producer walter jellinek/published in june 1959/lp matrix numbers XAX 1508-1509
h.krips   lp: SCX 3269
philharmonia   *orchestra described for this recording as philharmonia promenade orchestra*

33SX 1158-1166/non-classical repertoire

33SX 1167/waltzes by ziehrer, gungl, ivanovici, lanner and lehar
recorded in kingsway hall london on 6-7 january 1958/producer walter jellinek/published in september 1959/lp matrix numbers XAX 1510-1511
h.krips   lp: SCX 3279/SMC 83960
philharmonia   *other lp issues:* emi XLP 30027/SXLP 30027/CFP 40213
                orchestra described for this recording as philharmonia promenade orchestra

33SX 1168-1206/non-classical repertoire

33SX 1207/ballet music by chopin, ponchielli and meyerbeer
recorded in kingsway hall london on 12 november 1958 (meyerbeer and ponchielli) and on 29 may 1959/producer walter jellinek/published in february 1960/lp matrix numbers XAX 1877-1878

mackerras	**les sylphides, arranged by jacob**
philharmonia	45: SED 5570-5571/ESD 7262-7263
	lp: SCX 3291
	other lp issue: angel 35833
	dance of the hours/la gioconda
	lp: SCX 3291
	other lp issues: angel 35833/ emi ESD 7115
	cd: testament SBT 1326
	les patineurs, arranged by lambert
	45: SED 5563/ESD 7254
	lp: SCX 3291
	other lp issue: angel 35833

33SX 1208-1299/non-classical repertoire

33SX 1300/waltzes by tchaikovsky, gounod, délibes, berlioz and chabrier
recorded in kingsway hall london on 25-29 february 1960/producer walter jellinek/ published in may 1961/lp matrix numbers XAX 1903-1904

h.krips	**sleeping beauty; swan lake; nutcracker; serenade;**
philharmonia	**evgeny onegin; faust; naila; symphonie fantastique;**
	fete polonaise/le roi malgré lui
	lp: SCX 3362
	orchestra described for this recording as philharmonia promenade orchestra

33SX 1301-1377/non-classical repertoire

33SX 1378/orchestral music by grieg
recorded in abbey road studios london between 11 and 24 may 1961/producer brian culverhouse/published in march 1962/lp matrix numbers XAX 2187-2188

weldon philharmonia **holberg suite; sigurd jorsalfar; 2 norwegian melodies; 2 elegiac melodies**
lp: SCX 3416
other lp issue: emi CFP 40225

33SX 1379-1388/non-classical repertoire

33SX 1389/dances by dvorak, smetana, brahms, bartok and enesco
recorded in kingsway hall london on 25 may 1959 (brahms) and on 28 october 1960 (slavonic dances nos 1, 3 and 10) and in abbey road studios london on 30-31 october 1960/ producers walter legge and walter jellinek/published in february 1962/lp matrix numbers XAX 2051-2052

mackerras philharmonia **brahms hungarian dances nos 5 and 6; dvorak slavonic dances nos 1, 2, 3 and 10; smetana 2 dances from the bartered bride**
lp: SCX 3427
other lp issues: capitol P 8680/SP 8680/emi CFP 40214
bartok rumanian folkdances
lp: SCX 3427
other lp issues: capitol P 8680/SP 8680/angel seraphim 6061
enesco rumanian rhapsody no 2
lp: SCX 3427
other lp issues: capitol P 8680/SP 8680

33SX 1390-1393/non-classical repertoire

33SX 1394/famous tunes from the classics
extracts drawn from a variety of previous columbia and hmv recordings/lp matrix numbers XAX 2242-2243

33SX 1395-1435/non-classical repertoire

33SX 1436/popular pieces by glinka, bach, smetana, vaughan williams, falla, mozart, delius, prokofiev, grainger and holst
recorded in abbey road studios london on 30-31 may 1961/producer brian culverhouse/ published in november 1962

weldon philharmonia	russlan and lyudmila overture; dance of the comedians/ the bartered bride; le nozze di figaro overture; ritual fire dance/el amor brujo; march/the love of 3 oranges lp: SCX 3446 **air/orchestral suite no 3** lp: SCX 3446/33SX 1394 **greensleeves; mock morris** lp: SCX 3446 *other lp issues:* emi XLP 30123/SXLP 30123/CFP 4510 **la calinda/koanga** lp: SCX 3446 *other lp issues:* emi XLP 30123/SXLP 30123/CFP 4510 cd: emi CDEMX 2198 **jupiter/the planets** lp: SCX 3446 *other lp issue:* emi XLP 30049

33SX 1437-1523/non-classical repertoire

33SX 1524/a tribute to sir henry wood
lp transfers of columbia recordings from 1929 (dvorak and mendelssohn), 1932 (bach), 1934 (mozart), 1939 (sea songs) and 1940 (berlioz)/producers joe batten and walter legge (1939-1940)/published in july 1963/lp matrix numbers XAX 2475-2476

wood london symphony	mozart don giovanni overture 78: DX 587 *other lp issue:* melodiya M10 43701-43702 **wood fantasia on british sea songs** 78: DX 954-955 *other lp issue:* emi STAMP 1 cd: dutton CDAX 8008
wood london philharmonic	berlioz carnaval romain overture 78: DX 982 cd: dutton CDAX 8008

33SX 1524/a tribute to sir henry wood/concluded

wood	**bach brandenburg concerto no 3**
british	78: LX 173
symphony	cd: dutton 2CDAX 2002
orchestra	

wood	**dvorak slavonic dance op 46 no 8**
new queen's	78: L 2313
hall orchestra	**mendelssohn spring song; the bees wedding/lieder ohne worte**
	78: 9844

33SX 1525-1569/non-classical repertoire

33SX 1570/orchestral works by tchaikovsky, mendelssohn, dvorak, verdi and smetana

recorded in kingsway hall london on 11 april 1963 and 18-21 may 1963 (1812 overture)/ producer brian culverhouse/published in january 1964/lp matrix numbers XAX 2508-2509

weldon	**1812 ouverture solennelle**
philharmonia	lp: SCX 3499
royal marines	*other lp issues:* emi XLP 30123/SXLP 30123
band	

weldon	**waltz from serenade for strings**
philharmonia	lp: SCX 3499
	other lp issues: emi XLP 30123/SXLP 30123
	carnival overture; scherzo from a midsummer night's dream; act one prelude/la traviata; polka/the bartered bride
	lp: SCX 3499

33SX 1571-1578/non-classical repertoire

33SX 1579/works for piano and orchestra by dohnanyi and rachmaninov

recorded in abbey road studios london on 1 october 1948 (rachmaninov)/producer lawrance collingwood/published in january 1964/lp matrix numbers 431 and 2522

           variations on a nursery song see 33SX 1018

sargent	**rhapsody on a theme of paganini**
philharmonia	78: DX 1608-1610/DX 8334-8336
smith, piano	

33CX 1843

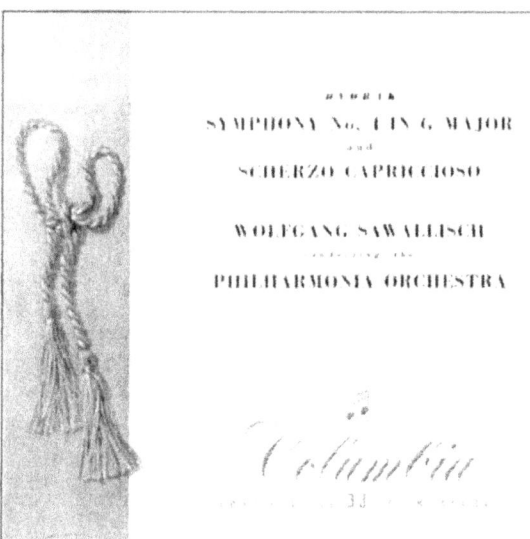

33SX 1034

33S 1001/dohnanyi suite in f sharp minor
recorded in abbey road studios on 14 december 1948/producer lawrance collingwood/ published in october 1952/lp matrix numbers XA 73-74
sargent   78: DX 1742-1745/DX 8377-8380
london
symphony

33S 1002/debussy trois nocturnes
recorded in kingsway hall london on 11-12 october 1950/producer walter legge/published in october 1952/lp matrix numbers XA 123-124
galliera   lp: QS 6003/WS 1002
philharmonia   *fetes and sirenes only*
glyndebourne   45: SED 5510/SEBQ 111
festival chorus

33S 1003/works by gershwin/american columbia
recorded in new york on 11 december 1944 and in philadelphia on 20 may 1945 respectively/published in july 1953/lp matrix numbers LP 373-374
rodzinski   **an american in paris**
new york   78: GQX 11161-11162
philharmonic   lp: QS 1002/FA 1001/VS 801
                american columbia issues
                78: X 246
                lp: ML 4026/ML 4879/CL 700/CS 8641/XSM 55976
                other 78 issue: afrs music library C 329
                other 45 issue: philips NBE 11125

ormandy   **rhapsody in blue**
philadelphia   78: DX 1212-1213
orchestra   *american columbia issues*
levant, piano   78: X 251
                lp: ML 4026

33S 1004/bach italian concerto; chromatic fantasia and fugue
recorded in abbey road studios london on 21-23 february 1952/producer walter legge (italian concerto)/published in june 1953/lp matrix numbers XA 214-215
matthews,
piano

33S 1005/non-classical repertoire

33S 1006/waltzes by waldteufel
recorded in kingsway hall london on 22 march 1950 and 14 september 1950 (pomona and sur la plage)/producer walter legge/published in october 1953/lp matrix numbers XA 118-119

lambert	**les patineurs**
philharmonia	78: DX 1674
	45: SCD 2097
	lp: QS 6007
	other lp issue: american columbia RL 3054
	cd: somm SOMMCD 023
	estudiantina
	78: DX 1693
	45: SED 5506/SEBQ 113
	lp: QS 6007
	other lp issue: american columbia RL 3054
	cd: somm SOMMCD 023
	pomona
	78: DX 1713
	lp: QS 6007
	other lp issue: american columbia RL 3054
	cd: somm SOMMCD 023
	sur la plage
	78: DX 1755
	45: SED 5504/SEBQ 512
	lp: QS 6007
	cd: somm SOMMCD 023

33S 1007-1008/non-classical repertoire

33S 1009/rossini-respighi la boutique fantasque
recorded in kingsway hall london on 15 april 1953/producer walter legge/published in november 1953/lp matrix numbers XA 340-341

galliera	lp: FC 1031/QC 5010
philharmonia	*other lp issues:* angel 30001/35324

33S 1010-1021/non-classical repertoire

33S 1022/dances by edward german
recorded in abbey road studios on 17 october 1952 (henry VIII), 13 april 1953 (merrie england and nell gwyn) and 11 december 1953 (tom jones)/producer brian culverhouse/published in may 1954/lp matrix numbers XA 468-469

weldon	**henry VIII**
london	78: DB 3217
symphony	**merrie england**
	78: DX 1877
	nell gwyn
	78: DB 3329-3330
	tom jones

33S 1023/works for harmonica and orchestra
recorded in abbey road studios london on 17 august 1953 and in october 1952 respectively/ producers john hughes, david bicknell and lawrance collingwood/published in may 1954/ lp matrix numbers XA 424-425

cameron	**benjamin harmonica concerto**
london	cd: emi CDM 764 1342
symphony	
adler, harmonica	

sargent	**vaughan williams romance**
orchestra	78: DX 1861
adler, harmonica	cd: emi CDM 565 4662

33S 1024-1031/non-classical repertoire

33S 1032/mozart piano concerto no 27 k595
recorded in kingsway hall london on 1 april 1954/producer walter legge/published in september 1954/lp matrix numbers XA 538-539
schwarz
philharmonia
matthews,
piano

33S 1033-1038/non-classical repertoire

33S 1039/mozart piano concerto no 23 k488
recorded in kingsway hall london on 1 april 1954/producer walter legge/published in september 1954/lp matrix numbers XA 540-541

schwarz	lp: QC 5021
philharmonia	
matthews,	
piano	

33S 1040-1081/non-classical repertoire

33S 1082/kalman scenes from gräfin maritza and czardasfürstin
recorded in esplanade berlin on 4 february 1953/producer helmut klare/published in january 1956/lp matrix numbers XR 201-202

schüchter	lp: WS 504/C 60127
berliner	*selections from the recording*
symphoniker	cd: emi CZS 767 1832/CDZ 585 2852
barabas	
schock	
glawitsch	

33S 1083-1090/non-classical repertoire

33S 1091/grieg peer gynt suites nos 1 and 2
recorded in abbey road studios london on 17 october 1952 and on 12 september 1955 respectively/producers lawrance collingwood and brian culverhouse/published in september 1956/ lp matrix numbers XA 866-867
weldon
london
symphony

33S 1092/music by eric coates
recorded in abbey road studios london on 23-34 may 1956/producer brian culverhouse/ published in december 1956/lp matrix numbers XA 937-938

mackerras	**the three bears; the man from the sea; merrymakers**
london	**overture; at the dance; by the sleepy lagoon**
symphony	cd: emi CDB 762 5572
	oxford street march; queen elizabeth march

33S 1093-1099/non-classical repertoire

33S 1100/orchestral music by holst
recorded in kingsway hall london on 14 september 1953 (st paul's suite) and in abbey road studios london on 12 september 1955/producer brian culverhouse/published in november 1956/ lp matrix numbers XA 864-865

weldon	**st pauls' suite**
philharmonia	cd: dutton CDCLP 4002
parikian, violin	
weldon	**somerset rhapsody; marching song**
london	cd: dutton CDCLP 4002
symphony	

33S 1101-1131/non-classical repertoire

33S 1132/kodaly dances from galanta; dances of marosszek
recorded in abbey road studios london on 1-2 may 1957/producers walter legge and walter jellinek/published in 1958/lp matrix numbers XA 1246-1247
ludwig
philharmonia

columbia artists roster and index: conductors

numbers refer to the lp catalogue numbers and not to page numbers; numbers in the main CX series are followed by those in the subsidiary C, SX and S series; artists under contract to american columbia or epic are marked with an asterisk

ackermann otto
1051-1052	1107	1114-1115	1186-1187
1224-1225	1329-1330	1366	1369
1373	1395	1568	1570
1688-1689	C 1042		

amis john
1617

argenta ataulfo
C 1004

arnold malcolm
1406

*barbirolli sir john
C 1028

beecham sir thomas
1019	1037	1038	1039
1062	1067	1078-1079	1085
1086	1087	1104	1105
1112	1363	1397-1398	1429
1450	1462-1463	C 1002	C 1006
C 1008	C 1017	C 1018	

*bernstein leonard
1029

blech harry
SX 1044

bliss sir arthur
1205

boult sir adrian
1538	1597	1671	1686

braithwaite warwick
1651

bruck charles
1506	1562	C 1059

cameron basil
1395	S 1023

caracciolo franco
1171	1276-1277	1354	1378
1414	1475		

*casals pablo
1088-1092	1108	1109	1113

cluytens andré

1016-1018	1064	1076	1134
1135	1145	1150-1152	1153
1173	1188	1190	1217
1218	1232-1233	1282	1299-1301
1323	1353	1413	1437
1505	1524	1528	1544
1604-1605	1672	1673	1699
1747	1832-1835	1884	1908
1921	1925	C 1034	

collingwood lawrance

SX 1030

davis colin

1728

del mar norman

1406	1617	1785

dervaux pierre

1795-1796

dobrowen issay

SX 1007	SX 1010

ehrling sixten

1194	C 1036

fistoulari anatole

1678

fourestier louis

1158

froment louis de

1503	1520-1521

galliera alceo

1130	1143	1156	1302
1305	1328	1333	1339
1356	1403	1422	1487
1507-1509	1531	1545	1597
1616	1625	1653	1660
1663	1696	1731	1776
C 1040	C 1052	C 1057	C 1061
C 1063	SX 1006	SX 1009	SX 1013
SX 1025	S 1002	S 1009	

gavazzeni gianandrea

1289-1291

giulini carlo maria
1075	1215-1216	1340	1365
1518	1523	1539	1579
1589	1662	1665	1694
1716	1717-1720	1726	1732-1735
1739	1759	1773	1778
1815	1818	1822	1840
1855	1872	1903	1915
1919			

gönnenwein wolfgang
1894   1895

goossens sir eugene
1141

gorzinski zdzislaw
1563

halffter ernesto
1221

*hilsberg alexander
C 1022

hindemith paul
1512   1533   1676

hoffnung gerard
1617

hofmann karl
SX 1049

inghelbrecht désiré-émile
1229

irving robert
1922

iturbi josé
1525   1578

karajan herbert von

1001	1002	1004	1005-1006
1007-1009	1010	1013-1015	1021-1025
1026	1033	1035	1046
1047	1053	1054	1065
1096-1097	1099	1121-1123	1124
1125	1133	1136	1139
1140	1159	1178	1206
1227	1262-1264	1265	1266
1278	1292-1294	1296-1298	1309-1310
1327	1335	1341	1349
1355	1361	1362	1377
1391-1392	1393	1410-1412	1421
1483-1485	1492-1495	1496	1511
1526	1548	1559	1571
1586-1587	1588	1608	1634-1635
1642	1680	1703	1704
1729	1730	1741	1750
1758	1774	1783	1791
C 1001	C 1003	C 1007	C 1012
C 1033	C 1056	C 1064	

kertesz istvan

1757	1775	1780

khachaturian aram

1303	C 1041	C 1043

klemperer otto

1239-1240	1241	1257	1270
1346	1379	1438	1457
1486	1504	1517	1532
1536	1554	1574-1575	1591
1615	1697-1698	1702	1710
1715	1721	1736	1746
1748	1751	1754	1760
1763-1764	1765	1769	1770
1781-1782	1786	1789	1793
1799-1803	1804-1806	1808-1809	1812
1814	1817	1820	1824
1829-1830	1842	1843	1851
1854	1870	1898	1902
1906	1914	1928	1931
1943	1948	1949	C 1051
C 1053			

kletzki paul
1003	1066	1129	1157
1161	1164	1165	1167
1174	1189	1207	1218
1250-1251	1311	1332	1419
1449	1475	1497	1541
1565	1573	C 1030	

kondrashin kyrill
1683   1692

krips henry
SX 1048	SX 1054	SX 1157	SX 1167
SX 1300			

*kurtz efrem
C 1013   SX 1011   SX 1012

lambert constant
SX 1003   S 1006

leinsdorf erich
1400-1401   1863

leonard lawrence
1406

lombard alain
1941

ludwig leopold
1490	1522	1542	1637
C 1055	S 1132		

maazel lorin
1823   1841

mackerras charles
1482	SX 1001	SX 1207	SX 1389
S 1092			

malko nicolai
1390   1481

markevitch igor
1049	1175	1197-1199	1208
1228	1273	1353	1394
1440	1458	1560	1590
1691			

martinon jean
1246

matacic lovro von
1226	1268	1274-1275	1280
1281	1420	1631-1633	1636
1654	1752-1753	1772	

milhaud darius
C 1027
milstein nathan
1874   1940
*mitropoulos dimitri
1068
*munch charles
1116   1118   C 1024
nobel felix de
1567   1641
oistrakh david
1660
orff carl
1549-1550
*ormandy eugene
1011   1027   1028   1070
1071   1080   C 1023   C 1025
C 1029   S 1003
pretre georges
1771   1798   1837   1838
1858
pritchard john
1069
rawsthorne alan
C 1044
*reiner fritz
C 1011
rescigno nicola
1628   1645   1900   1910
1923
rieger fritz
1048
*rodzinski artur
C 1027   S 1003
rosbaud hans
1235
rowicki witold
1871   1889
sabata victor de
1094-1095   1195-1196
sanzogno nino
1166   1434-1436

sawallisch wolfgang
1446-1447	1480	1491	1534-1535
1600-1602	1623	1630	1647
1652	1655	1677	1766-1768
SX 1034			

sargent sir malcolm
1146-1148	1247-1248	1347-1348	1407
1431-1433	1668-1670	C 1062	SX 1018
SX 1579	S 1001	S 1023	

schippers thomas
1451	1543	1561	1596
1609			

schönherr max
SX 1049

schüchter wilhelm
1514	1594	C 1035	S 1082

schwarz rudolf
SX 1031	S 1032	S 1039

serafin tullio
1058-1060	1131-1132	1179-1181	1182-1183
1204	1211-1212	1231	1258-1260
1318-1320	1324-1326	1370-1371	1376
1540	1555-1557	1583-1585	1618-1620
1649-1650	1684	1723-1724	1766-1768

sherman alec
1020

silvestri constantin
1711	1738	1744

stein horst
1846

***stern** isaac
1071

***stokowski** leopold
1030	C 1026

***stravinsky** igor
1083	1100	C 1010	C 1015

susskind walter
1106	1425	1477	1595
1651	1658	1695	C 1011
SX 1017	SX 1057		

*szell george
1028	1816	1831	1845
1847	1850	1852	1853
1856	1861	1867-1868	1869
1873	1880	1882	1885
1890	1892	1896	1899
1904	1905	1912	1913
1916	1924	1933	1935
1937	1938	C 1019	

thamm hans
1945

toldra edoardo
1551

tonini antonio
1598

tzipine georges
1238	1252-1253	1577

vandernoot andré
1546	1622	1667	1671

villa-lobos heitor
1648

votto antonino
1464-1465	1469-1471	1472-1474	1706-1708

wallberg heinz
1629	1658	1674

*****walter** bruno
1034	1036	1045	1077
1082	1117	1120	C 1009

walton sir william
1313	1679	1883	C 1016
C 1054			

weldon george
1118	SX 1019	SX 1024	SX 1028
SX 1032	SX 1045	SX 1055	SX 1095-1096
SX 1378	SX 1436	SX 1570	S 1022
S 1091	S 1100		

wolf-ferrari manno
1638

wood sir henry
SX 1524

columbia artists roster and index: orchestras

numbers refer to the lp catalogue numbers and not to page numbers; numbers in the main CX series are followed by those in the subsidiary C, SX and S series; orchestras under contract to american columbia or epic are marked with an asterisk

alessandro scarlatti orchestra
1171	1276-1277	1354	1378
1414	1451	1475	

bayreuth festival orchestra
1005-1006   1021-1025

berlin philharmonic
1496	1586-1587	1642	1680
1703	1704	1741	1783
1791	C 1056		

berlin symphony orchestra
1846   S 1082

berlin staatskapelle
1637

british symphony orchestra
SX 1524

*cleveland orchestra
1816	1831	1845	1847
1850	1852	1853	1856
1861	1867-1868	1869	1873
1880	1882	1885	1890
1892	1896	1899	1904
1905	1912	1913	1916
1924	1933	1935	1937
1938			

colonne orchestra
1158   1525   1578

*columbia symphony orchestra
1029   1037   1071

de froment chamber orchestra
1503

feltl-kemmeter schrammelorchester
C 1032

hoffnung symphony orchestra
1617   1785

israel philharmonic
1207	1219	1250-1251	1419
1449	1475		

liverpool philharmonic
1146-1148	1247-1248	1347-1348	1431-1433
1668-1670			

london mozart players
SX 1044
london philharmonic
SX 1524
london symphony orchestra

1268	1395	1695	SX 1019
SX 1028	SX 1030	SX 1045	SX 1524
S 1001	S 1022	S 1023	S 1091
S 1092	S 1100		

lucerne festival orchestra
C 1064
*metropolitan opera orchestra
C 1011
milan symphony orchestra
1598
*minneapolis symphony orchestra
1068
morley college symphony orchestra
1406
new london orchestra
1020
new philharmonia

| 1943 | 1948 |

new queens hall orchestra
SX 1524
new york city ballet orchestra
1543
*new york philharmonic

1030	1034	1036	1045
1077	1082	1116	1117
1118	1120	C 1010	C 1013
C 1015	C 1019	C 1026	C 1027
C 1028	SX 1011	SX 1012	S 1003

orchestra of la scala milan
1058-1060	1094-1095	1166	1179-1181
1182-1183	1195-1196	1211-1212	1215-1216
1258-1260	1289-1291	1296-1298	1318-1320
1324-1326	1340	1370-1371	1376
1434-1436	1464-1465	1469-1471	1472-1474
1483-1485	1540	1555-1557	1583-1585
1618-1620	1631-1633	1649-1650	1706-1708
1752-1753	1772		

orchestra of maggio musicale fiorentino
1131-1132

orchestra of saint-eustache paris
1145

orchestre national de belgique
1884

orchestre national de france
1064	1134	1135	1153
1173	1208	1221	1228
1229	1238	1282	1394
1437	1439	1440	1458
1481	1551	1560	1590
1604-1605	1648	1765	1771
1798	1837	C 1034	

paris conservatoire orchestra
1173	1188	1190	1217
1252-1253	1299-1301	1323	1413
1506	1520-1521	1528	1544
1546	1562	1622	1667
1711	1738	1744	1747
1832-1835	1858	1900	1908
1910	1921	1923	1925
C 1004	C 1059		

paris opéra orchestra
1505	1524	1544	1838
1941			

paris opéra-comique orchestra
1016-1018	1076	1150-1152	1232-1233
1577	1795-1796		

*perpignan festival orchestra
1088-1092

*philadelphia orchestra
1011	1027	1028	1070
1071	1080	1082	C 1022
C 1023	C 1025	C 1029	

philharmonia

1001	1002	1003	1010
1033	1035	1046	1047
1048	1049	1051-1052	1053
1054	1065	1066	1069
1096-1097	1099	1106	1107
1114-1115	1118	1121-1123	1124
1125	1129	1130	1133
1136	1139	1140	1141
1156	1157	1159	1161
1164	1165	1167	1174
1175	1178	1186-1187	1189
1197-1199	1204	1205	1206
1224-1225	1226	1227	1231
1235	1239-1240	1241	1246
1257	1262-1264	1265	1266
1270	1273	1274-1275	1278
1292-1294	1302	1303	1305
1309-1310	1311	1313	1327
1328	1329-1330	1332	1333
1335	1339	1341	1346
1349	1355	1356	1361
1362	1366	1369	1373
1377	1379	1390	1391-1392
1393	1395	1400-1401	1403
1407	1410-1412	1420	1421
1422	1425	1438	1446-1447
1477	1482	1486	1487
1490	1491	1492-1495	1497
1504	1507-1509	1511	1512
1517	1518	1522	1523
1526	1531	1532	1533
1534-1535	1536	1538	1539
1541	1542	1545	1548
1554	1559	1561	1568
1570	1571	1574-1575	1579
1588	1589	1591	1595
1596	1597	1608	1609
1615	1616	1623	1625
1628	1629	1630	1634-1635

philharmonia/concluded

1636	1645	1647	1651
1652	1653	1654	1655
1658	1660	1662	1663
1665	1671	1673	1674
1676	1677	1678	1679
1683	1684	1686	1688-1689
1691	1692	1694	1696
1697-1698	1699	1702	1703
1710	1715	1716	1717-1720
1721	1723-1724	1726	1728
1729	1730	1731	1732-1735
1736	1739	1741	1746
1748	1750	1751	1754
1757	1758	1759	1760
1763-1764	1769	1770	1773
1774	1775	1776	1778
1780	1781-1782	1786	1789
1793	1799-1803	1804-1806	1808-1809
1812	1814	1815	1817
1818	1820	1822	1823
1824	1829-1830	1840	1841
1842	1843	1851	1854
1855	1863	1870	1872
1883	1889	1898	1902
1903	1906	1914	1915
1919	1928	1931	1948
1949	C 1001	C 1003	C 1007
C 1011	C 1012	C 1016	C 1030
C 1033	C 1035	C 1040	C 1041
C 1042	C 1043	C 1051	C 1052
C 1053	C 1054	C 1055	C 1057
C 1060	C 1061	C 1062	C 1063
SX 1003	SX 1006	SX 1007	SX 1009
SX 1010	SX 1013	SX 1017	SX 1018
SX 1024	SX 1025	SX 1031	SX 1032
SX 1034	SX 1048	SX 1054	SX 1055
SX 1057	SX 1095-1096	SX 1157	SX 1167
SX 1207	SX 1300	SX 1378	SX 1389
SX 1436	SX 1570	SX 1579	S 1002
S 1006	S 1009	S 1032	S 1039
S 1100	S 1132		

*prades festival orchestra
1108	1109	1113	

pro arte orchestra
1514	1594

royal marines band
SX 1570

royal philharmonic
1019	1038	1039	1062
1067	1078-1079	1085	1086
1087	1104	1105	1112
1363	1397-1398	1429	1450
1462-1463	1565	1573	1684
C 1002	C 1006	C 1008	C 1017
C 1018			

sadlers wells orchestra
SX 1001

santa cecilia orchestra
1075	1353

south-west german chamber orchestra
1894	1895

stockholm festival orchestra
1194	C 1036

vienna philharmonic
1004	1007-1009	1013-1015	1026
C 1009			

vienna volksoper orchestra
SX 1049

warsaw philharmonic
1563	1871

wdr orchestra cologne
1480

*woody herman orchestra
1100

columbia artists roster and index: chamber ensembles

numbers refer to the lp catalogue numbers and not to page numbers; numbers in the main CX series are followed by those in the subsidiary C, SX and S series; ensembles under contract to american columbia or epic are marked with an asterisk

amadeus string quartet
1592

armenian state string quartet
1279	1284	1334

*budapest string quartet
1031	1050	1061

dennis brain chamber ensemble
1687

drolc string quartet
1859	1886

hungarian string quartet
1168	1172	1191	1203
1236	1254	1272	1405
1442	1460	1527	1566
1581	1599	1614	1749

i musici
1163	1170	1192	1306-1307
1357			

*juilliard string quartet
1826-1828	1891	1901	1917

kroll string quartet
1865	1875	1876

pascal string quartet
1353

quartetto italiano
1101	1102	1103	1155
1230	1244	1295	1367
1383	1396	1408	1430
1722	1727		

smetana string quartet
1424

vegh string quartet
1245	1267	1285

columbia artists roster and index: pianists

numbers refer to the lp catalogue numbers and not to page numbers; numbers in the main CX series are followed by those in the subsidiary C, SX and S series; pianists under contract to american columbia or epic are marked with an asterisk

anda geza
1072	1143	1156	1175
1176	1202	1283	1302
1316	1366	1403	1427
1459	1624	C 1057	

antonietti jean
1359	1372	1399

arrau claudio
1080	1333	1443-1444	1513
1531	1569	1610	1616
1625	1653	1696	1709
1731	1739	1742	1755
1822			

ashkenazy vladimir
1563	1621	1637	1813

*bernstein leonard
1029

*baumgartner paul
1110

*browning john
1937

casadesus jean
1622

*casadesus robert
1111	1118	C 1023	C 1024
C 1028			

ciccolini aldo
1190	1221	1884

*curzon clifford
1050

engel karl
1927

favaretto giorgio
1607

fischer annie
1593	1630	1664	1675
1686	1756	1807	1842
1944			

fischer betty
1940

fleisher leon
1839	1882	1890	1901

francois samson
1135	1238	1747	1825
1877	1889		

gieseking walter
1010	1055	1073	1098
1120	1137	1142	1149
1160	1220	1235	1242
1255-1256	1261	1271	1304
1315	1321	1322	1345
1350-1352	1358	1374	1417
1428	1453	1467-1468	1479
1488	1498	1519	1526
1537	1564	1603	1611-1612
1761	C 1003	C 1007	C 1012
C 1014	C 1033		

gilels emil
1188	1217	1323	1364
1490	1667	C 1055	

ginzburg anton
1740

greenbaum kyla
SX 1003

haskil clara
1109	1403

*****hess** dame myra
1091

*****horszowski** mieczyslaw
1113

iturbi josé
1368	1380	1525	1578
1701	1743	1788	

kentner louis
SX 1014	SX 1033

*****levant** oscar
S 1003

levin robert
1409

lipatti dinu
1032	1337	1386	1499-1500
C 1001	C 1021	C 1040	C 1064

malcolm george
1687

malcuzynski witold

1048	1066	1106	1138
1144	1161	1338	1344
1382	1481	1639	1690
1695	1797	1821	1864
1871	C 1005	C 1031	

malinin eugene

1343	1369	C 1045	

mälzer martin

1862

matthews denis

SX 1021	SX 1023	SX 1031	SX 1044
SX 1047	S 1004	S 1032	S 1039

moore gerald

1040	1044	1154	1162
1213	1222-1223	1243	1269
1331	1404	1448	1552
1606	1626	1644	1657
1661	1693	1705	1714
1860	1946	SX 1043	

mytnik andrei

1381	1546	1562

oborin lev

1627	1643	C 1062

poulenc francis

1119

richter-haaser hans

1666	1680	1737	1757
1762	1775	1780	1879
1903	1911	1920	1936

***rosen** charles

1836	1849	1857	1878
1888			

sellick phyllis
SX 1018

***serkin** rudolf

1012	1027	1043	1070
1092	1093	1110	

siki bela

1175	1185	1416	1445

smith cyril
SX 1018   SX 1579

solchany george
1547

***stravinsky** igor
1100

trovillo giorgio
1553

***walter** bruno
C 1020

weissenborn günther
1866

yampolsky vladimir

1201	1342	1415	1466
1580	C 1047		

columbia artists roster and index: violinists

numbers refer to the lp catalogue numbers and not to page numbers; numbers in the main CX series are followed by those in the subsidiary C, SX and S series; violinists under contract to american columbia or epic are marked with an asterisk

busch adolf
1012 1043
***francescatti** zino
1011 1111 C 1029
gertler andré
C 1030 C 1046
gilels elisaveta
1373 1887
kogan leonid
1373 1381 1395 1506
1546 1562 1683 1692
1711 1738 1744 1887
C 1059
martzy johanna
1165 1286-1288 1359 1372
1399 1497
milstein nathan
1863 1874 1922 1940
morini erica
1940
oistrakh david
1194 1201 1246 1268
1303 1342 1390 1415
1423 1466 1487 1580
1627 1643 1660 1672
1765 C 1036 C 1047 C 1062
oistrakh igor
1141 1514 1594 1740
parikian manoug
1265 1365 S 1100
rabin michael
1422 1538 1597
***schneider** alexander
1113
***stern** isaac
1071 1089 1090 1109
C 1008 C 1013 C 1022
***szigeti** joseph
1100 1113
varga tibor
SX 1017

columbia artists roster and index: cellists

numbers refer to the lp catalogue numbers and not to page numbers; numbers in the main CX series are followed by those in the subsidiary C, SX and S series; cellists under contract to american columbia or epic are marked with an asterisk

busch hermann
1012   1043
*casals pablo
1093   1110
fournier pierre
1407   1487   1606   1644
1852
knushevitzky sviatoslav
1423   1627   1643   C 1062
starker janos
1425   1477   1515   1579
1595   1656   1665   1700
1745
tortelier paul
1090

columbia artists roster and index: other instrumentalists

numbers refer to the lp catalogue numbers and not to page numbers; numbers in the main CX seies are followed by those in the subsidiary C, SX and S series; instrumentalists under contract to american columbia or epic are marked with an asterisk

adler larry/*harmonica*
S 1023
*bloom myron/*horn*
1892
brain dennis/*horn*
1140   1178   1322   1406
1491   1676
brain dennis/*organ*
1265
cahuzac louis/*clarinet*
1533
civil alan/*horn*
1760
commette edouard/*organ*
1478
duruflé maurice/*organ*
1145   1798
gottesmann hans/*viola*
1012
james cecil/*bassoon*
1178   1322
jones geraint/*organ*
SX 1032
*marcellus robert/*clarinet*
1892
*nies-berger/*organ*
1116
*primrose william/*viola*
1019   1089   1090
roget henriette/*organ*
1413
*schweitzer albert/*organ*
1074   1081   1084   1249
segovia andres/*guitar*
1020
sutcliffe sidney/*oboe*
1178   1322
*tabuteau marcel/*oboe*
1090
*trampler walter/*viola*
1031
walton bernard/*clarinet*
1178   1322   1361
*wummer john/*flute*
1113

columbia artists roster and index: choirs
numbers refer to the lp catalogue nunbers and not to page numbers; numbers in the main CX series are followed by those in the subsidiary C, SX and S series; artists under contract to american columbia or epic are marked with an asterisk

aix festival chorus
1520-1521
anonymous chorus *used for recordings with philharmonia prior to formation of philharmonia chorus*
1186-1187	1224-1225	1262-1264	1309-1310
1329-1330	1400-1401	1410-1412	1482
1492-1495	1507-1509	1522	1534-1535
1570			

bayreuth festival chorus
1021-1025
bbc chorus
1051-1052	1114-1115	1174	SX 1003

beecham choral society
1397-1398	1429	1462-1463

briclot choir
1134
cambridge university madrigal society
1063
capilla clasica polifonica
1308
chorus of saint-eustache paris
1145
chorus of orchestre national paris
1208	1437	1798

chorus of la scala milan
1058-1060	1094-1095	1166	1179-1181
1182-1183	1195-1196	1211-1212	1215-1216
1258-1260	1289-1291	1296-1298	1318-1320
1324-1326	1370-1371	1376	1434-1436
1464-1465	1469-1471	1472-1474	1483-1485
1583-1585	1618-1620	1631-1633	1649-1650
1706-1708	1752-1753		

chorus of the paris opéra
1838
chorus of the paris opéra-comique
1016-1018	1150-1152	1232-1233	1795-1796

chorus of the maggio musicale fiorentino
1131-1132
chorus of the royal opera house covent garden
C 1035

cleveland orchestra chorus
1867-1868
elisabeth brasseur choir
1252
glyndebourne festival chorus
S 1002
hampstead church choir
1799-1803
hoffnung festival chorus
1617   1785
huddersfield choral society
1146-1148   1247-1248   1347-1348   1431-1433
1668-1670
london philharmonic choir
1078-1079
netherlands chamber choir
1567   1641
philharmonia chorus
1574-1575   1645   1679   1688-1689
1717-1720   1734-1724   1732-1735   1746
1781-1782   1799-1803   1804-1806   1817
1818   1829-1830
rené duclos choir
1832
royal philharmonic chorus
1112
saint pauls cathedral choir
1193   1237
saltire music group
1317
santa cecilia chorus
1075   1353
south-west german chamber choir
1894-1895
soviet army ensemble
1844   C 1049-1050
vienna singverein der gesellschaft der musikfreunde
1013-1015   1121-1123   1391-1392   1634-1635
1741
vienna state opera chorus
1007-1009
wdr chorus cologne
1480

columbia artists roster and index: sopranos
numbers refer to the lp catalogue numbers and not to page numbers; numbers in the main CX series are followed by those in the subsidiary C, SX and S series; singers under contract to american columbia or epic are marked with an asterisk

*addison adele
1867-1868
amara lucine
1752-1753
angelici marthe
1016-1018   1145   1232-1233
barabas sari
S 1082
berton liliane
1520-1521
boué géori
1150-1152
bovy vina
1150-1152
callas maria
1058-1060   1094-1095   1131-1132   1179-1181
1182-1183   1204   1231   1258-1260
1289-1291   1296-1298   1318-1320   1324-1326
1464-1465   1469-1471   1472-1474   1483-1485
1507-1509   1540   1555-1557   1583-1585
1618-1620   1628   1645   1706-1708
1723-1724   1766-1768   1771   1858
1900   1910   1923
carosio margherita
1166
carteri rosanna
1340   1598   1649-1650   1798
1941
cole adrienne
1174
dobbs mattiwilda
1154   1305
donath helen
1894
doria renée
1150-1152
duval denise
1076   1218   1252
esposito andrée
1838
farrell eileen
1553   1596

felbermayer anny
1007-1009   1096-1097   1226
fisher sylvia
1078-1079
fusco elisabetta
1732-1735
gatta dora
1732-1735
giebel agnes
1480
grümmer elisabeth
1096-1097
***halban** desi
1034
hallstein ingeborg
1804-1806
harper heather
1746
hollweg ilse
1462-1463
jurinac sena
1007-1009   1013-1015
köth erika
1186-1187   1329-1330
***lehmann** lotte
C 1020
lipp wilma
1013-1015   1688-1689
loose emmy
1013-1015   1051-1052   1114-1115   1186-1187
1224-1225   1541
marshall lois
1397-1398   1462-1463
mathis edith
1894   1945
mcloughlin eileen
1174
micheau janine
1437   1503   1520-1521   1795-1796
moffo anna
1410-1412   1464-1465   1600-1602   1728
1732-1735   C 1061   C 1063
morison elsie
1146-1148   1347-1348   1397-1398   1431-1433
1668-1669

nilsson birgit
1522   1542   1574-1575   1629
1631-1633
nordmo-lövberg aase
1409   1574-1575   1651
otto lisa
1262-1264
pütz ruth-margret
1895
raisbeck rosina
1078-1079
rysanek leonie
1005-1006   C 1035
scheyrer gerda
1688-1689
schwarzkopf elisabeth
1007-1009   1021-1025   1040   1044
1051-1052   1069   1096-1097   1107
1114-1115   1121-1123   1186-1187   1195-1196
1224-1225   1226   1262-1264   1266
1278   1292-1294   1309-1310   1313
1321   1329-1330   1331   1391-1392
1400-1401   1404   1410-1412   1446-1447
1482   1492-1495   1555-1557   1570
1600-1602   1634-1635   1657   1658
1714   1717-1720   1732-1735   1781-1782
1799-1803   1829-1830   1946
sciutti graziella
1215-1216   1434-1436   1717-1720
scotto renata
1618-1620   1638
seefried irmgard
1007-1009   1013-1015   1292-1294   1331
stella antonietta
1370-1371
stich-randall teresa
1492-1495
streich rita
1292-1294
sutherland joan
1717-1720
*tourel jennie
1029
varnay astrid
1005-1006
vivalda janette
1299-1301
welitsch ljuba
1492-1495   C 1011
zareska eugenia
1607

columbia artists roster and index: mezzo-sopranos and contraltos

numbers refer to the lp catalogue numbers and not to page numbers; numbers in the main CX series are followed by those in the subsidiary C, SX and S series; singers under contract to american columbia or epic are marked with an asterisk

baker janet
1746
barbieri fedora
1318-1320   1410-1412   1472-1474   1483-1485
canali anna maria
1131-1132   1182-1183
carturan gabriella
1507-1509   1631-1633
cattelani aurora
1058-1060
cossotto fiorenza
1469-1471   1583-1585   1706-1708   1732-1735
danieli luisa
1296-1298
dominguez oralia
1195-1196
elkins margareta
1723-1724
ferrier kathleen
C 1009
gorr rita
1838
*hobson jane
1867-1868
höffgen marga
1121-1123   1391-1392
hoffman grace
1400-1401
höngen elisabeth
1007-1009
iriarte ana-maria
C 1004
lazzarini adriana
1324-1326
lisken emmy
1895

ludwig christa
1492-1495   1552   1574-1575   1600-1602
1634-1635   1658   1671   1688-1689
1693   1705   1766-1768   1799-1803
1804-1806   1817
malaniuk ira
1021-1025
merriman nan
1213   1243   1262-1264   1410-1412
michel solange
1016-1018
moizan genevieve
1437
nicolai elena
1258-1260
pirazzini miriam
1618-1620
ratti eugenia
1434-1436   1469-1471   1472-1474
revoil fanély
1150-1152
riegler friedl
1013-1015
ripley gladys
SX 1003   SX 1028
rössl-majdan hilde
1829-1830
rubio consuelo
1551
schürhoff else
1013-1015   1096-1097
simionato giulietta
1215-1216
sinclair monica
1078-1079   1313   1329-1330   1347-1348
1645   1651
stignani ebe
1179-1181   1434-1436
thomas marjorie
1146-1148   1247-1248   1431-1433   1668-1670

columbia artists roster and index: tenors

numbers refer to the lp catalogue numbers and not to page numbers; numbers in the main CX seroes are followed by those in the subsidiary C, SX and S series; singers under contract to american columbia or epic are marked with an asterisk

altmeyer theo
1894   1895
alva luigi
1410-1412   1434-1436   1507-1509   1649-1650
1717-1720
casellato renzo
1723-1724
chauvet guy
1838
christ rudolf
1309-1310   1446-1447   1534-1535
corelli franco
1752-1753   1766-1768
craig charles
1078-1079
dermota anton
1013-1015   1688-1689
ercolani renato
1631-1633   1732-1735
fernandi eugenio
1555-1557
ferraro pier miranda
1706-1708
filippeschi mario
1179-1181
gedda nicolai
1051-1052   1114-1115   1121-1123   1130
1186-1187   1224-1225   1226   1289-1291
1296-1298   1299-1301   1309-1310   1329-1330
1400-1401   1492-1495   1503   1520-1521
1528   1600-1602   1634-1635   1795-1796
1799-1803   1837   1941
gibin joao
1631-1633
giraudeau jean
1076   1218   1437
glawitsch rupert
S 1082

haefliger ernst
1391-1392
hopf hans
1021-1025
infantino luigi
C 1048
jelden georg
1945
jobin raoul
1016-1018 1150-1152
kmentt waldemar
1574-1575
krebs helmut
1309-1310
kuen paul
1446-1447 1480 1534-1535
lanigan john
1645
legay henri
1232-1233
lewis richard
1146-1148 1247-1248 1313 1347-1348
1431-1433 1668-1670 1867-1868
mercuriali angelo
1058-1060 1752-1753
midgley walter
1429
monti nicola
1469-1471
natali valiano
1131-1132
pears peter
1799-1803
picchi mirto
1618-1620
prandelli giacinto
1166
robertson duncan
1645

schock rudolf
1292-1294   S 1082
simoneau léopold
1262-1264   1462-1463
stefano giuseppe di
1058-1060   1094-1095   1131-1132   1182-1183
1195-1196   1324-1326   1370-1371   1464-1465
1472-1474   1483-1485   1583-1585   1598
tagliavini ferruccio
1723-1724
terkal karl
1688-1689
troy dermot
1600-1602
tucker richard
1258-1260   1318-1320
unger gerhard
1021-1025   1400-1401   1462-1463   1804-1806
valletti cesare
1215-1216
vickers jon
1804-1806
young alexander
1397-1398

columbia artists roster and index: baritones and basses
numbers refer to the lp catalogue numbers and not to page numbers; numbers in the main CX series are followed by those in the subsidiary C, SX and S series; singers under contract to americam columbia or epic are marked with an asterisk

arié raffaele
1131-1132
badioli carlo
1434-1436
bell donald
1679   1867-1868
bernac pierre
1119
berry walter
1688-1689   1799-1803   1804-1806
bianco rené
1838
björling sigurd
1005-1006   C 1035
blanc ernest
1795-1796
borriello mario
1296-1298
bourdin roger
1150-1152
boyce bruce
1078-1079
bruscantini sesto
1262-1264
calabrese franco
1289-1291   1434-1436   1583-1585
cameron john
1247-1248   1397-1398   1431-1432
campi enrico
1166   1215-1216
capecchi renato
1258-1260
cappuccilli piero
1706-1708   1717-1720   1723-1724
cordes marcel
1446-1447   1480
crass franz
1804-1806   1894   1895
dalberg friedrich
1021-1025

dens michel
1016-1018   1232-1233   1299-1301   1941
dönch karl
1186-1187   1224-1225   1292-1294
edelmann otto
1021-1025   1391-1392   1492-1495   1568
fioravanti giulio
1583-1585
fischer-dieskau dietrich
1600-1602   1781-1782   1799-1803
forti carlo
1058-1060
frick gottlob
1446-1447   1462-1463   1717-1720   1804-1806
gobbi tito
1094-1095   1131-1132   1318-1320   1324-1326
1370-1371   1410-1412   1472-1474   1507-1509
1752-1753
hotter hans
1162   1222-1223   1269   1448
1534-1535   1542   1574-1575   1600-1602
1626   1661
kraus otakar
1051-1052   1114-1115
kunz erich
1007-1009   1013-1015   1021-1025   1051-1052
1114-1115   1186-1187   1224-1225   1309-1310
1688-1689   C 1032
kusche benno
1446-1447
ladysz bernard
1678   1723-1724
london george
1007-1009   1013-1015
mars jacques
1795-1796
metternich josef
1096-1097   1226
milligan james
1668-1670
modesti giuseppe
1318-1320   1376   1618-1620

1150-1152
neidlinger gustav
1446-1447
nessi giuseppe
1555-1557
niessner anton
1051-1052
noguéra louis
1145   1232-1233
ocker klaus
1945
panerai rolando
1058-1060   1166   1182-1183   1262-1264
1305   1410-1412   1464-1465   1483-1485
1649-1650
pernet andré
1150-1152
petri mario
1215-1216
prey hermann
1292-1294   1329-1330   1400-1401   1446-1447
1846   1860   1862   1866
1927
rehfuss heinz
1121-1123
rossi-lemeni nicola
1058-1060   1179-1181   1258-1260   1289-1291
1340
rouleau joseph
1645   1941
roux michel
1437   1503
schlott theodor
1226
schmidinger josef
1051-1052
schmitt-walter karl
1534-1535   1600-1602
siepi cesare
1195-1196
sordello enzo
1631-1633

stabile mariano
1289-1291
taddei giuseppe
1649-1650   1717-1720   1732-1735
tagliabue carlo
1258-1260
vinco ivo
1706-1708   1732-1735
wächter eberhard
1400-1401   1492-1495   1600-1602   1688-1689
1717-1720   1732-1735
walker norman
1146-1148
weber ludwig
1013-1015
zaccaria nicola
1318-1320   1324-1326   1370-1371   1410-1412
1464-1465   1469-1471   1483-1485   1766-1768
1631-1633   1634-1635   1507-1509   1555-1557
zanasi mario
1752-1753

Discographies by Travis & Emery:
Discographies by John Hunt.

1987: 978-1-906857-14-1: From Adam to Webern: the Recordings of von Karajan.
1991: 978-0-951026-83-0: 3 Italian Conductors and 7 Viennese Sopranos: 10 Discographies: Arturo Toscanini, Guido Cantelli, Carlo Maria Giulini, Elisabeth Schwarzkopf, Irmgard Seefried, Elisabeth Gruemmer, Sena Jurinac, Hilde Gueden, Lisa Della Casa, Rita Streich.
1992: 978-0-951026-85-4: Mid-Century Conductors and More Viennese Singers: 10 Discographies: Karl Boehm, Victor De Sabata, Hans Knappertsbusch, Tullio Serafin, Clemens Krauss, Anton Dermota, Leonie Rysanek, Eberhard Waechter, Maria Reining, Erich Kunz.
1993: 978-0-951026-87-8: More 20th Century Conductors: 7 Discographies: Eugen Jochum, Ferenc Fricsay, Carl Schuricht, Felix Weingartner, Josef Krips, Otto Klemperer, Erich Kleiber.
1994: 978-0-951026-88-5: Giants of the Keyboard: 6 Discographies: Wilhelm Kempff, Walter Gieseking, Edwin Fischer, Clara Haskil, Wilhelm Backhaus, Artur Schnabel.
1994: 978-0-951026-89-2: Six Wagnerian Sopranos: 6 Discographies: Frieda Leider, Kirsten Flagstad, Astrid Varnay, Martha Moedl, Birgit Nilsson, Gwyneth Jones.
1995: 978-0-952582-70-0: Musical Knights: 6 Discographies: Henry Wood, Thomas Beecham, Adrian Boult, John Barbirolli, Reginald Goodall, Malcolm Sargent.
1995: 978-0-952582-71-7: A Notable Quartet: 4 Discographies: Gundula Janowitz, Christa Ludwig, Nicolai Gedda, Dietrich Fischer-Dieskau.
1996: 978-0-952582-72-4: The Post-War German Tradition: 5 Discographies: Rudolf Kempe, Joseph Keilberth, Wolfgang Sawallisch, Rafael Kubelik, Andre Cluytens.
1996: 978-0-952582-73-1: Teachers and Pupils: 7 Discographies: Elisabeth Schwarzkopf, Maria Ivoguen, Maria Cebotari, Meta Seinemeyer, Ljuba Welitsch, Rita Streich, Erna Berger.
1996: 978-0-952582-77-9: Tenors in a Lyric Tradition: 3 Discographies: Peter Anders, Walther Ludwig, Fritz Wunderlich.
1997: 978-0-952582-78-6: The Lyric Baritone: 5 Discographies: Hans Reinmar, Gerhard Huesch, Josef Metternich, Hermann Uhde, Eberhard Waechter.
1997: 978-0-952582-79-3: Hungarians in Exile: 3 Discographies: Fritz Reiner, Antal Dorati, George Szell.
1997: 978-1-901395-00-6: The Art of the Diva: 3 Discographies: Claudia Muzio, Maria Callas, Magda Olivero.
1997: 978-1-901395-01-3: Metropolitan Sopranos: 4 Discographies: Rosa Ponselle, Eleanor Steber, Zinka Milanov, Leontyne Price.
1997: 978-1-901395-02-0: Back From The Shadows: 4 Discographies: Willem Mengelberg, Dimitri Mitropoulos, Hermann Abendroth, Eduard Van Beinum.
1997: 978-1-901395-03-7: More Musical Knights: 4 Discographies: Hamilton Harty, Charles Mackerras, Simon Rattle, John Pritchard.
1998: 978-1-901395-94-5: Conductors On The Yellow Label: 8 Discographies: Fritz Lehmann, Ferdinand Leitner, Ferenc Fricsay, Eugen Jochum, Leopold Ludwig, Artur Rother, Franz Konwitschny, Igor Markevitch.
1998: 978-1-901395-95-2: More Giants of the Keyboard: 5 Discographies: Claudio Arrau, Gyorgy Cziffra, Vladimir Horowitz, Dinu Lipatti, Artur Rubinstein.
1998: 978-1-901395-96-9: Mezzo and Contraltos: 5 Discographies: Janet Baker, Margarete Klose, Kathleen Ferrier, Giulietta Simionato, Elisabeth Hoengen.

1999: 978-1-901395-97-6: The Furtwaengler Sound Sixth Edition: Discography and Concert Listing.
1999: 978-1-901395-98-3: The Great Dictators: 3 Discographies: Evgeny Mravinsky, Artur Rodzinski, Sergiu Celibidache.
1999: 978-1-901395-99-0: Sviatoslav Richter: Pianist of the Century: Discography.
2000: 978-1-901395-04-4: Philharmonic Autocrat 1: Discography of: Herbert Von Karajan [Third Edition].
2000: 978-1-901395-05-1: Wiener Philharmoniker 1 - Vienna Philharmonic and Vienna State Opera Orchestras: Discography Part 1 1905-1954.
2000: 978-1-901395-06-8: Wiener Philharmoniker 2 - Vienna Philharmonic and Vienna State Opera Orchestras: Discography Part 2 1954-1989.
2001: 978-1-901395-07-5: Gramophone Stalwarts: 3 Separate Discographies: Bruno Walter, Erich Leinsdorf, Georg Solti.
2001: 978-1-901395-08-2: Singers of the Third Reich: 5 Discographies: Helge Roswaenge, Tiana Lemnitz, Franz Voelker, Maria Mueller, Max Lorenz.
2001: 978-1-901395-09-9: Philharmonic Autocrat 2: Concert Register of Herbert Von Karajan Second Edition.
2002: 978-1-901395-10-5: Sächsische Staatskapelle Dresden: Complete Discography.
2002: 978-1-901395-11-2: Carlo Maria Giulini: Discography and Concert Register.
2002: 978-1-901395-12-9: Pianists For The Connoisseur: 6 Discographies: Arturo Benedetti Michelangeli, Alfred Cortot, Alexis Weissenberg, Clifford Curzon, Solomon, Elly Ney.
2003: 978-1-901395-14-3: Singers on the Yellow Label: 7 Discographies: Maria Stader, Elfriede Troetschel, Annelies Kupper, Wolfgang Windgassen, Ernst Haefliger, Josef Greindl, Kim Borg.
2003: 978-1-901395-15-0: A Gallic Trio: 3 Discographies: Charles Muench, Paul Paray, Pierre Monteux.
2004: 978-1-901395-16-7: Antal Dorati 1906-1988: Discography and Concert Register.
2004: 978-1-901395-17-4: Columbia 33CX Label Discography.
2004: 978-1-901395-18-1: Great Violinists: 3 Discographies: David Oistrakh, Wolfgang Schneiderhan, Arthur Grumiaux.
2006: 978-1-901395-19-8: Leopold Stokowski: Second Edition of the Discography.
2006: 978-1-901395-20-4: Wagner Im Festspielhaus: Discography of the Bayreuth Festival.
2006: 978-1-901395-21-1: Her Master's Voice: Concert Register and Discography of Dame Elisabeth Schwarzkopf [Third Edition].
2007: 978-1-901395-22-8: Hans Knappertsbusch: Kna: Concert Register and Discography of Hans Knappertsbusch, 1888-1965. Second Edition.
2008: 978-1-901395-23-5: Philips Minigroove: Second Extended Version of the European Discography.
2009: 978-1-901395--24-2: American Classics: The Discographies of Leonard Bernstein and Eugene Ormandy.

Discography by Stephen J. Pettitt, edited by John Hunt:
1987: 978-1-906857-16-5: Philharmonia Orchestra: Complete Discography 1945-1987

Available from: Travis & Emery at 17 Cecil Court, London, UK. (+44) 20 7 240 2129. email on sales@travis-and-emery.com .

© Travis & Emery 2009

Music and Books published by Travis & Emery Music Bookshop:
Anon.: Hymnarium Sarisburiense, cum Rubricis et Notis Musicis.
Agricola, Johann Friedrich from Tosi: Anleitung zur Singkunst.
Bach, C.P.E.: edited W. Emery: Nekrolog or Obituary Notice of J.S. Bach.
Bateson, Naomi Judith: Alcock of Salisbury
Bathe, William: A Briefe Introduction to the Skill of Song
Bax, Arnold: Symphony #5, Arranged for Piano Four Hands by Walter Emery
Burney, Charles: The Present State of Music in France and Italy
Burney, Charles: The Present State of Music in Germany, The Netherlands …
Burney, Charles: An Account of the Musical Performances … Handel
Burney, Karl: Nachricht von Georg Friedrich Handel's Lebensumstanden.
Cobbett, W.W.: Cobbett's Cyclopedic Survey of Chamber Music. (2 vols.)
Corrette, Michel: Le Maitre de Clavecin
Crimp, Bryan: Dear Mr. Rosenthal … Dear Mr. Gaisberg …
Crimp, Bryan: Solo: The Biography of Solomon
d'Indy, Vincent: Beethoven: Biographie Critique
d'Indy, Vincent: Beethoven: A Critical Biography
d'Indy, Vincent: César Franck (in French)
Frescobaldi, Girolamo: D'Arie Musicali per Cantarsi. Primo & Secondo Libro.
Geminiani, Francesco: The Art of Playing the Violin.
Handel; Purcell; Boyce; Geene et al: Calliope or English Harmony: Volume First.
Häuser: Musikalisches Lexikon. 2 vols in one.
Hawkins, John: A General History of the Science and Practice of Music (5 vols.)
Herbert-Caesari, Edgar: The Science and Sensations of Vocal Tone
Herbert-Caesari, Edgar: Vocal Truth
Hopkins and Rimboult: The Organ. Its History and Construction.
Hunt, John: Adam to Webern: the recordings of von Karajan
Isaacs, Lewis: Hänsel and Gretel. A Guide to Humperdinck's Opera.
Isaacs, Lewis: Königskinder (Royal Children) A Guide to Humperdinck's Opera.
Kastner: Manuel Général de Musique Militaire
Lacassagne, M. l'Abbé Joseph : Traité Général des élémens du Chant.
Lascelles (née Catley), Anne: The Life of Miss Anne Catley.
Mainwaring, John: Memoirs of the Life of the Late George Frederic Handel
Malcolm, Alexander: A Treaty of Music: Speculative, Practical and Historical
Marx, Adolph Bernhard: Die Kunst des Gesanges, Theoretisch-Practisch
May, Florence: The Life of Brahms
May, Florence: The Girlhood Of Clara Schumann: Clara Wieck And Her Time.
Mellers, Wilfrid: Angels of the Night: Popular Female Singers of Our Time
Mellers, Wilfrid: Bach and the Dance of God
Mellers, Wilfrid: Beethoven and the Voice of God
Mellers, Wilfrid: Caliban Reborn - Renewal in Twentieth Century Music

Music and Books published by Travis & Emery Music Bookshop:
Mellers, Wilfrid: François Couperin and the French Classical Tradition
Mellers, Wilfrid: Harmonious Meeting
Mellers, Wilfrid: Le Jardin Retrouvé, The Music of Frederic Mompou
Mellers, Wilfrid: Music and Society, England and the European Tradition
Mellers, Wilfrid: Music in a New Found Land: ... ... American Music
Mellers, Wilfrid: Romanticism and the Twentieth Century (from 1800)
Mellers, Wilfrid: The Masks of Orpheus: ...... the Story of European Music.
Mellers, Wilfrid: The Sonata Principle (from c. 1750)
Mellers, Wilfrid: Vaughan Williams and the Vision of Albion
Panchianio, Cattuffio: Rutzvanscad Il Giovine
Pearce, Charles: Sims Reeves, Fifty Years of Music in England.
Playford, John: An Introduction to the Skill of Musick.
Purcell, Henry et al: Harmonia Sacra ... The First Book, (1726)
Purcell, Henry et al: Harmonia Sacra ... Book II (1726)
Quantz, Johann: Versuch einer Anweisung die Flöte traversiere zu spielen.
Rameau, Jean-Philippe: Code de Musique Pratique, ou Methodes.
Rastall, Richard: The Notation of Western Music.
Rimbault, Edward: The Pianoforte, Its Origins, Progress, and Construction.
Rousseau, Jean Jacques: Dictionnaire de Musique
Rubinstein, Anton : Guide to the proper use of the Pianoforte Pedals.
Sainsbury, John S.: Dictionary of Musicians. Vol. 1. (1825). 2 vols.
Serré de Rieux, Jean de : Les dons des Enfans de Latone
Simpson, Christopher: A Compendium of Practical Musick in Five Parts
Spohr, Louis: Autobiography
Spohr, Louis: Grand Violin School
Tans'ur, William: A New Musical Grammar; or The Harmonical Spectator
Terry, Charles Sanford: J.S. Bach's Original Hymn-Tunes for Congregational Use.
Terry, Charles Sanford: Four-Part Chorals of J.S. Bach. (German & English)
Terry, Charles Sanford: Joh. Seb. Bach, Cantata Texts, Sacred and Secular.
Terry, Charles Sanford: The Origins of the Family of Bach Musicians.
Tosi, Pierfrancesco: Opinioni de' Cantori Antichi, e Moderni
Van der Straeten, Edmund: History of the Violoncello, The Viol da Gamba ...
Van der Straeten, Edmund: History of the Violin, Its Ancestors... (2 vols.)
Waltern: Musikalisches Lexicon
Walther, J. G.: Musicalisches Lexikon ober Musicalische Bibliothec

Travis & Emery Music Bookshop
17 Cecil Court, London, WC2N 4EZ, United Kingdom.
Tel. (+44) 20 7240 2129

© Travis & Emery 2009

www.ingramcontent.com/pod-product-compliance
Lightning Source LLC
Chambersburg PA
CBHW052052230426
43671CB00011B/1879